The Greatest Fly Fishing Around the World

TROUT, SALMON, AND SALTWATER FISHING
ON THE WORLD'S MOST BEAUTIFUL WATERS

PHOTOGRAPHY BY

R. Valentine Atkinson

FOREWORD BY NICK LYONS

The Greatest Fly Fishing
Around the World

TROUT, SALMON, AND SALTWATER FISHING
ON THE WORLD'S MOST BEAUTIFUL WATERS

PHOTOGRAPHY BY

R. Valentine Atkinson

FOREWORD BY NICK LYONS

THE LYONS PRESS
Guilford, Connecticut
An imprint of The Globe Pequot Press

First Lyons Press Edition 2003
Copyright © 1997, 1999, 2003 by Duncan Baird Publishers

Copyright of photographs © R. Valentine Atkinson
Copyright information for individual articles, artwork and photographs available on pages 319–320.
Commissioned illustrations, maps, and studio photography
copyright © Duncan Baird Publishers 1997, 1999, 2003

The Lyons Press is an imprint of The Globe Pequot Press.

2 4 6 8 10 9 7 5 3 1

ISBN: 1-59228-086-2

Conceived, created and designed by
Duncan Baird Publishers Ltd
Sixth Floor
Castle House
75–76 Wells Street
London W1T 3QH
Britain

Typeset in 10.5 pt Ehrhardt MT

Color reproduction by Colourscan, Singapore
Printed and bound in Singapore by Imago Limited.

The Library of Congress Cataloging-in-Publication Data is available upon request.

PUBLISHER'S NOTE

The captions in this book are by R. Valentine Atkinson. The publishers and the photographer would like to voice their support for the principles of "catch and release" and all other forms of fishery enhancement and conservation.

Contents

Foreword

What a visual and verbal feast, this collection of superb photographs and wonderful essays!

The essays seek to capture the physical qualities of the places depicted in this rich book – from the United States to Russia, with sections on Canada, Iceland, Scotland, Ireland, England, Norway, New Zealand, Chile, Argentina, Mexico and Christmas Island. But the prose goes further. In the various voices of the writer-anglers, and through their differing eyes, we meet unforgettable local characters, eat some memorable meals, and experience the suspense and drama of a hundred fishing occasions, from the common to the fully uncommon. Big fish are hooked and caught – or perhaps they are lost; but you can also travel with John Gierach, always the best of company, up a western canyon to its headwaters, where the "fish are eager, slightly stupid, and not large," where you get a strike nearly every time you put a good cast over a rising trout. And from there we're off to big fish again, Tom McGuane's "hard-running ocean-bright fish," a salmon that ends in the net, "a big deep hanging silver arc." Fish are caught because fishermen know not only how to fish but, first, where to find them. Throughout these essays there is the kind of knowledge that must always come before catching is possible. "Salmon hold in its first sixty meters of current," writes Ernest Schwiebert of a Norwegian river. "They lie under swirling currents of sapphire and spume, where the stream wells up silken and smooth, before the river grows shallow over a tail of fine cobble." And between the big fish and the small fish, the portraits of people and waters, the shrewd knowledge of where the fish are, there is the fishing itself,

as wonderfully real and even abrupt as one might want. "Running a fly down Rocky Cast one evening," writes David Profumo, "there was a flash of grey flank and my small Stoat just below the surface was cancelled like a typing error."

Surrounding the words, both illuminating them and forming a world and story – or, rather, many stories – all their own, are Val's photographs. They are the finest of his that I have ever seen. There is one photograph of a small headwaters stream, with a man cross-legged, nearly camouflaged, resting and watching. In another, two men peer down from an old stone bridge, as I have done a thousand times, as all fishermen have done and will always do – for a bridge uniquely puts you directly above a river, not to its side, and you can peer down into the mysterious, watery world of our quarry, even as Nick Adams did in the Hemingway story, and see resting or working trout, and marvel at their lithe movements, and learn just a bit more about a world that is not ours. I have learned volumes by staring down into that three-dimensional liquid from bridges: where trout rest, how they hold in the current, the nature of their rise, how they take a nymph, and so much more.

What I love most, I think, is that Val's eye catches the quintessential moments of fly-fishing, those elemental times when everyone who fishes with this kind of equipment becomes part of the same process. His photographs are especially remarkable in their ability to define for us what we all love so much about the sport.

Nick Lyons

A FEW WORDS FROM THE PHOTOGRAPHER

Fly-fishing, photography and travel work very well together – each one complements the others. I've grown up with an insatiable wanderlust – a love of visiting and fishing new places. When I'm not actually traveling I'm often daydreaming about some beautiful new destination with rivers full of trout or salmon. I also love running film through my camera, so that I might have some evidence of this beauty to share with others. My father is a photographer and he helped instill a love of photography in me at an early age. I feel extremely fortunate to have managed to combine these passions over the years into a profession. I love my job.

Friends often ask me how in the world I manage to find time to photograph when I'm out fishing. How can I really do two things at once? The secret is timing. It's simply a question of when you put down the rod and

pick up the camera. I always have both at the ready. When out on the stream, I'm looking for good light in a spectacular setting. I'll shoot *action* whenever and wherever it occurs. As I head out in the morning, I carry a backpack which holds my fly-rod as well as my tripod and an assortment of lenses. I can photograph until the sun rises too high for good pictures, warming the water as it climbs: there consequently may be a hatch, and I'll put away the camera and go fishing. The trick is knowing when to do what. I often follow friends and models around waiting for something to happen. When it does and I've taken some good shots, I'll put down the camera and fish awhile myself. Sometimes I'll even catch something!

It is my sincere desire that my images share with you my passion for wild, romantic places – and for cherishing what wilderness remains in our world.

R. Valentine Atkinson

6

Headwaters

Western U.S.A.

JOHN GIERACH

"Four ponds and a dozen fair-to-middling trout later, you hook a heavy fish back in some flooded brush – a heavy *fish. He fights well but stays in the open, where you play him carefully. You wish you'd brought a net, even though you'd have snagged it in the brush two hundred times by now. You play the fish out more than you'd like to, finally hand-landing him as gently as possible. As you hold him by the lower jaw to remove the barbless hook, he wiggles and his teeth cut into your thumb, starting a small stain of blood in the water."*

As you follow the stream up into the canyon, it seems to get smaller and colder all at once, an illusion caused by leaving behind the civilized water where the pools are named and where there are places to park. Going upstream here, where the cliff forces the road away from the stream, feels a little like going back in time, and the trout – still mostly browns – seem as liquid and transparent as the water. You're elated, still on your first wind.

This is pocket water and there's lots of it – miles and miles of it – so rather than fish it thoroughly, you keep moving, now and then casting a dry caddis (an obscure local pattern named for the stream you're on) over a good-looking spot. It seems appropriate and it works. Later there will be a hatch of caddis or maybe even mayflies and you'll stop and get down to business, but since you're more interested in distance now, you fish casually from the bank in hiking boots with the pack on your back.

You go carefully because you're walking with the rod strung, sometimes having to thread it through the brush and low limbs ahead. The cloth bag is stuffed in your pants pocket but, in the interest of lightness and mobility, you've left the aluminum case at home.

It's your favorite cane rod, a 7½-footer for a #5 line. You debated over the choice, weighing the risk to the rod against how perfectly it was suited to this little stream. Finally the honey-colored rod with its English reel won out. It's idiotic, you thought, to spend hundreds of dollars on a fine rig you're afraid to use. And now you're pleased: the wood rod casts beautifully, and through it you can almost feel the heartbeats of the small trout. When you stop for lunch you lean it very carefully against the springy branches of a short blue spruce.

You've been walking easily and haven't gone far, but already it feels good to have the pack off. It's not as light as it could be – they never are – but considering how long you'll be out, it's not bad. You're figuring three days, maybe four, and you were very careful not to say exactly when you'd be back.

You haven't had to rummage in the pack yet, so it still seems a model of efficiency, ever so slightly virginal, leaning in the shade of a lichen-covered ledge. Tied on the top are the rolled-up sleeping pad and the poncho which can be worn to cover you and all the gear or made into a serviceable free-form rain fly. The down sleeping bag is tied to the bottom and the old number 44 "Cold Handle" frying pan is strapped securely to the back. The pan always seems a little too big, but it will hold two butterfly-filleted, eight- to twelve-inch trout perfectly. You'll eat fish on this trip or come back early; your provisions are composed of just-add-water starches and soups with some coffee, one can of pork and beans (a treat), some oil,

RIGHT *An angler selects the first fly of the morning on Nelson's Spring Creek in Montana.*

ABOVE *A Grasshopper.*

salt, pepper, and lemon juice. Side dishes. The main courses are still in the water.

Beyond that, there isn't much: clothing you can wear all at once if necessary (wool shirt, sweater, down vest, wool hat), coffeepot, fork and spoon, spare socks, flyweight waders, wading shoes (low-cut tennis shoes actually, because they're smaller and lighter than the real thing), and your tin cup. It's in the side pocket now, but if you were farther north you'd tie it next to the frying pan as a bear bell. Packed in the coffee cup is a heavy plastic bag to put the tennis shoes in once they're wet.

There's a camera in there, too, and the pack is so pretty in the mottled shade you think about digging it out and taking a shot, but it's only a thought. At the moment you don't feel like looking at the world through a piece of glass, even an expensive piece.

The only luxuries you've allowed yourself are a full-sized coffeepot, a notebook, and a modest-sized bottle of good bourbon – but maybe they're not entirely luxuries, at that. The coffeepot doubles as a saucepan, and holds enough water to completely douse the campfire in three trips to the stream. Your life has been such that there's the normal background noise of guilt, but so far, you haven't burned down a forest and don't plan to; you are meticulously careful with your fires.

The bourbon is still in the glass bottle because it just doesn't taste right from the lighter plastic flask, and whether the whiskey itself is a luxury or a necessity isn't worth worrying about at the moment. The notebook might be considered nonessential except that you generally use more of its pages to start fires than to jot down lines of poetry and notes of cosmic significance.

After lunch – a deli ham-and-cheese sandwich in waxed paper – you put the rod in the bag and walk. The trail is gone now, and the country is more rugged. Dippers splash in the stream; you spook a doe mule deer coming around a bend; and you get very close to a marmot sunning on a rock before he wakes up and bolts, giving the warning whistle, even though he seems to be alone.

At one point you find yourself within five feet of a pair of typically innocent blue grouse. You consider the possibility of getting one with a rock and have a momentary olfactory hallucination: roasting grouse and frying trout. You decide against it, though, probably because it's illegal.

And then it's late afternoon, the canyon has begun to level out a little, and the stream has a distinct shady side. The pocket water has given way to a long run, the bank on one side of which is open and grassy. There are delicious-looking under-cuts. With several hours of daylight left, you find a level spot away from the stream (away from mosquitoes and morning dew or frost) and lean the pack against a tree,

ABOVE *Sun-up on Burney Creek in California. The trout here go for tiny stoneflies and terrestrials. What to choose from the Wheatley Box?*

unroll the sleeping bag to air out, clean out a fire pit, gather wood, and set out coffeepot, frying pan, and tin cup.

The spot you've chosen is a tiny meadow stretch only a few hundred yards long. The open sky is pleasant after the closed-in, forested canyon below, and ahead, for the first time today, you can see the snowcapped high country. The weather is still shirt-sleeve warm with a comfortable hint of evening chill. There is as much spruce and fir as pine now on the hillsides, and you can see patches of aspen. You think you hear the screech of a hawk but see nothing when you scan the sky.

You could probably fish the stream here without wading, but you dig out the waders and put them on because you carried them in and are gonna use them; it's important. There's no fly vest; instead you're wearing a four-pocketed canvas fishing shirt which you load now from the side pocket of the pack: three spools of leader material in the lower right-hand pocket, bug dope, fly floatant, and clippers in the lower left. Each breast pocket holds a fly box – one with nymphs and streamers, the other with dries. In the interest of razor-sharp efficiency, you wanted to have a single box, but the bigger ones didn't fit anywhere and you only toyed for a few minutes with the idea of rebuilding the fishing shirt. Anyhow, the bulges are more symmetrical this way.

You saw two small rises at the tail of the run when you first arrived, and now you notice what looks like a bigger fish working along the far grassy bank. There are a few tan-colored bugs that you assume are caddis flies fluttering over the surface, but without pondering the situation further, you tie on a #16 Tan-Bodied Adams. The trout in these mountain streams see few anglers and are seldom selective (though your two fly boxes are evidence of the occasional exceptions) and the Tan Adams is a favorite. The tails are of medium-dark moose body hair, the body of light raccoon fur; the grizzly hackle is mixed with ginger instead of brown and the wings are wide and darkly barred – from a hen neck. It's a personal variation you often think of as a "generic bug," an excellent high-country pattern.

You work the tail of the run first and, on the first cast, take a tiny rainbow that still has his parr marks, a wild fish. Then you take a slightly larger one that wasn't rising but came up to your fly anyway, and then you take the fish along the bank – a nine-inch brown.

The fish are eager, slightly stupid, and not large; you get a strike nearly every time you put a good cast over a rising trout. Then you land and release a fine, chubby, ten-inch brown and remember what a friend once said: "If you're gonna keep fish, go ahead and keep 'em. If you wait for the last two, you'll be eating beans." So the next good fish, a fat, bright rainbow of ten or eleven inches, is tapped on the head and tossed on the bank in the direction of camp. This is something you seldom do anymore, but it doesn't feel too bad. In fact, it feels pretty good.

After five or six more fish, you take a firm brown that reaches the full twelve inches from the butt of the reel seat to the first T in the name on the rod. It's a male with a slightly hooked jaw and colors that remind you of a Midwestern autumn. You clean him, along with the rainbow, wrap them both in the wet grass, and lay them in the shadows that have now swallowed the stream and half the eastern ridge. You're camped on the west bank to catch the first morning sunlight.

You think of going to a streamer then, of running it past the undercut to see if there's a big brown there, but the dry fly and the wood rod are too hypnotic. You take a few more small fish and quit with just enough light to get situated in camp. You clip the tattered and now one-winged fly from the leader and drop it in the stream, like you'd smash a glass after a toast.

Supper is trout fried in oil with pepper and lemon juice, rice, and whiskey cut lightly with stream water – eaten by firelight. Then, lying in the down bag, you let the fire die to coals, think of the trout, the hike, home, people, career, the past, and you are asleep.

The morning is gray and cold, but blue holes perforate the clouds to the west. You put on the wool shirt and vest, build a fire, and start water for coffee. After one cup you go to the stream, waderless, and without ceremony take one nine-inch rainbow for breakfast. You roast him over the fire on a stick so as not to dirty the pan, and on another stick you make Bisquick muffins – a bit dry, but just fine. As someone (probably French) once said, "Hunger is the best sauce."

With the fire well doused and the pack loaded, you take one careful look around to make sure nothing was dropped or forgotten, then head off upstream with only a single look back at the undercut bank where you never did try a streamer.

By midmorning the sun is out, and you stop to shed some clothes before you get too sweaty. While putting the stuff in the pack, you're struck with the sudden certainty that you forgot the roll of nylon cord with which you can turn your poncho into whatever-shaped rain fly the terrain and handy trees allow; you can clearly picture it lying on the kitchen table at home. But then a short, carefully unfrantic search turns up the cord, as well as an apple you'd forgotten about. At least one attack of backpacker's paranoia per trip is normal, but you don't mind because it has served you well. You've never forgotten anything important.

With the rhythm of the walk broken, you decide to fish, and with the Tan Adams you take the first brook trout. But since you've taken only two other small fish after fifteen minutes, you shoulder the pack and move on.

ABOVE *Craig Fellin releasing a brown on the Beaverhead in Montana. An afternoon storm has just passed and beautiful Rembrandt light paints the scene. This is the time to put down the rod and grab the camera.*

Shortly you come to a road and, although it breaks the spell a little, you're glad it's there. On the way out you'll climb the grade and hitch a ride to the nearest cafe for pancakes or maybe a big, greasy burger, and then on into town. But now you go under the bridge with the stream, listening for the whine of a car and being glad not to hear one.

Above the road you come into a high, marshy meadow. Here the trees stop as the land levels out, giving way to tangles of willow; the only way to walk through it is up the stream, in waders. Wading and casting with the pack on and the hiking shoes dangling in back is clumsy but not impossible. You work only the best-looking spots at first, slowing down and concentrating a little more after you've spooked some good fish from what looked like uninteresting water. The trout are brookies now, with the occasional rainbow.

By the time you hit the beaver ponds, your back aches from the pack; so you set up camp on the first level, dry spot you come to. After a short break, you switch to

ABOVE This old spring pond on the Hat Creek Ranch in northern California is loaded with big, fat, sassy rainbows.

a streamer and creep down to the nearest pond. The fly is a little brook trout bucktail, and your past success with it has convinced you that brookies do, in fact, eat their smaller relatives, even though more than one fisheries biologist has told you that's not so. You think, science. *Truth.* The fish take the fly, so it's true; or maybe it's largely false but still works, and so might as well be true – like politics or religion. It occurs to you that the Great Questions are probably a hell of a lot more fun than the answers, but by the time you've made your fifth cast, you've forgotten about the whole thing.

Four ponds and a dozen fair-to-middling trout later, you hook a heavy fish in some flooded brush – a *heavy* fish. He fights well but stays in the open, where you play him carefully. You wish you'd brought a net, even though you'd have snagged it in the brush two hundred times by now. You play the fish out more than you'd like to, finally hand-landing him as gently as possible. As you hold him by the lower jaw to remove the barbless hook, he wiggles and his teeth cut into your thumb, starting a small stain of blood in the water.

Laid against the rod, the trout's tail reaches past the twelve-inch mark, well past. Sixteen inches? Possibly, and fat, too, and deeply, richly colored; the orange

BELOW *A Royal Wulff.*

BELOW *A visit to the American West wouldn't be complete without a float trip down the Yellowstone River through Paradise Valley, Montana.*

flanks are like a neon beer sign shining through a rainy night. You sit there like an idiot until the trout's struggles indicate that he's recovered from the fight. You release him then, and he swims away, leaving you with a momentary sense of absolute blankness, as if the synapses in your brain marked "good" and "bad" had fired simultaneously, shorting each other out.

Then you're hungry, and cold. You backtrack down the channel below the pond and keep the first three small trout you hook, trying to picture the exact size of the frying pan. Supper is eaten in chilly twilight; the waders are hung to dry; the rod, in its cloth case, is hung out of reach of porcupines who would chew up the cork grip

ABOVE *Freshwater springs pour down from lava outcroppings through mint, moss, and watercress to mix with snow melt from Mount Shasta at Mossbrae Falls on the Sacramento River, northern California. This is a very special place. We need to look after and protect it.*

16

for the salt, given half a chance. The dishes are washed, by feel, in muddy gravel.

The next morning you wake before dawn, soaking wet, freezing, and covered with mosquito bites, having slept dreamlessly on the edge of a bog through a substantial rain, with the poncho lying uselessly under you as a ground cloth. The curses you utter – the foulest ones you can think of – are the first words you've spoken aloud in two days.

Luckily the sky is clear now, and the sun comes up warm over the eastern ridge, helping along the effects of the smoky fire that took fifteen minutes to start. You recover by degrees, aided by coffee, and drape your gear in the willows to dry, everything angled to face the sun like the heads of flowers. Even the notebook was damp, toward the back, so you started the fire with pages that were written on, pages you did not read before lighting.

Breakfast is big and starchy, mostly half-ruined rice mixed with pond-water chicken soup, a shapeless candy bar you found while emptying the pack, and the apple. The candy-bar wrapper is burned in the fire, but the apple core is tossed in the brush for a squirrel or maybe an elk. After fluffing and turning the sleeping bag, you slog the half-mile to the head of the ponds and fish the stream, where you hook the first cutthroat – small, bright, and confused-looking. You feel a little more in touch with the place, having been soaked and frozen with, apparently, no ill effects.

Back in gear – the pack tight, dry, and efficient again – you leave the stream and hike the dry ridge toward the lake. Most of the time you can't even see the stream in its tunnels of tangled willow. You're moving well, feeling free on the dry ground in the shady spruce and fir, sensing the curves and cups of the land now instead of the bottom of the trough where the water runs.

You angle up unconsciously (almost always better to gain altitude than lose it when walking in the mountains) and come on the lake a little high, from a vantage point of no more than fifty extra feet. You wouldn't have planned that just for the view, but the view is excellent, with the small lake hanging in its tight cirque, smooth and blue-gray, with snowfields on the western slope and a soft-looking lawn of tundra around it. The trees here are short and flagged, bare of branches on the windward side.

You set up camp on a perfect, level spot, rigging a clumsy rain fly (thinking of last night) though the sky is cloudless. It seems early, *is* early, in fact, but the looming Continental Divide means dusk will come before it seems right. You stroll down to the outlet, the logical place for fish to be since the inlet is only snow melt from a scree slope, and sure enough, you spot a few rising cutts. You've tied on a #16 Michigan Chocolate Spinner, based on previous experience, time of day, location,

ABOVE *An epic struggle with a big cutthroat before a storm, on the Snake River in Wyoming.*

and hunch. You've also put on the wool shirt and hat because it's cool away from the shelter of the trees.

You stalk up to the water too quickly, too erect, and the trout don't exactly spook but solemnly stop rising. They don't know what you are, but they don't like you – a thought that cuts through the magazine-feature-article glitter of wilderness fly-fishing for the ten minutes it takes for two of the smaller fish to start feeding again.

The first cast is a good one, straight and sure with a downstream hook on the admittedly easy, uniform current, and a thirteen-inch cutt takes the spinner with a casual, unsuspicious rise. The fight is good, but because the fish has nowhere to go, you land him easily. It's supper and the last fish of the day; the others have vanished in that supernatural way trout have – they don't run like deer or fly away like grouse; they're just gone.

In camp you fry the trout, sitting close to the fire that seems to give little heat in the thin air. Camping alone isn't something you normally do, but you've done it often enough that it's familiar; you no longer get the horrors at night. You've gone out alone before because you were sad or happy, or neither or both – for any reason at all, the way some people drink. The lake is black now, and for a long moment you can't remember why you're here this time.

ABOVE *The Cassel Forebay at Clearwater House, northern California, in autumn provides good hatches and some very large fish.*

RIGHT *An angler returns home after the evening hatch on the lower Fall River in the shadow of Mount Shasta, California.*

WESTERN USA: FACTFILE

BACKGROUND

To quantify all of the western USA's trout fishing would take a lifetime of exploring. Apart from the places we feature in this book, Wyoming, Utah and Colorado are among the best states for fishing – but we have concentrated on some of the better-known streams of Montana, Idaho and northern California. These states contain classic rivers such as the Madison, Firehole, Yellowstone, Big Hole, Big Horn, Henry's Fork, Silver Creek, Hat Creek and Fall River. All have prolific hatches during the summer, and produce free-rising, selective-feeding trout, mainly rainbows and browns up to 5 or 6 lb.

All these rivers are public waterways whose sole restrictions are on the type of tackle used; many are in better condition today than they were fifty years ago; and most of the fish are wild. Although angling pressure has increased, you can find solitude easily if you look in the right places at the right times.

WHEN TO GO

Many of the best areas lie in mountainous regions, meaning that harsh winters with lots of snow are the rule. Some of the rivers are spring creeks, and their temperatures remain constant throughout the season. Generally, as the warmer summer months approach, the hatches intensify and feeding activity increases. During the cool of the morning and the late evening in midsummer, hatches often defy the imagination. There are times on the famous Henry's Fork in Idaho when it is hard to see the water for the overlapping wings of insects. During early June on Fall River, California, there appears what is known as "the carpet" – a solid mass of Pale Morning Duns, all hatching at the same time.

Often these western rivers have overlying and masking hatches, where several types of insect are hatching at the same time. The trick is to figure out exactly what the fish are feeding on. These trout can be extremely selective and difficult, and thus the best part of the season in terms of fly life can be the most demanding for a fly-fisherman.

LEFT *A.J. Derosa and Jim Sulham with a beautiful, fine-spotted Snake River cutthroat.*

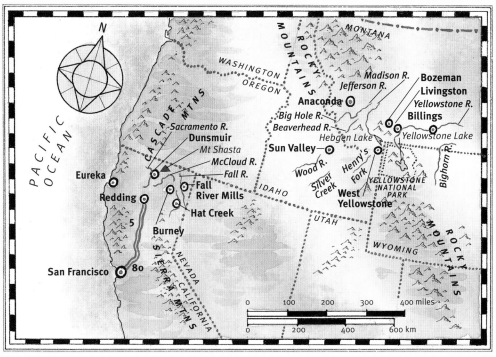

TACKLE

RODS: 9–10 ft for 4–8 wt lines, depending on the river system fished. Not all river systems will demand large rods and the wise fisherman will pack a 7 ft or 8 ft rod as well.

REELS: Direct-drive fly reels capable of holding at least 75 yards of backing.

LINES: A weight-forward floater will be very useful. However, a sink-tip and full sinking lines of different densities will have their moments, particularly early in the season.

LEADERS: Long and fine leaders are needed to approach selective feeders with the dry fly: 9–18 ft tapered to as light as 1.5 lb test. Shorter leaders for fishing wet flies: 8–12 ft tapered to 3 lb maximum.

FLIES: Dry flies – Parachute Adams, Tricos, Royal Wulff, Yellow Humpy, Pale Morning Dun and Goddard Caddis. Nymphs – Wooly Bugger, Zugbug, Muskrat and Pheasant Tail. Streamers – Renegade, Zonker, White and Black Marabou.

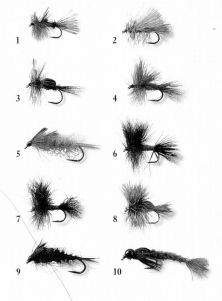

FLIES 1 *Royal Wulff* 2 *Stimulator* 3 *Humpy Adams* 4 *Gray Wulff* 5 *Perla Stone* 6 *Green Drake Wulff* 7 *Black Wulff* 8 *Yellow Humpy* 9 *Black Stone* 10 *Living Damsel*

Mornings
The Rocky Mountains

NICK LYONS

"Sometimes the crystalline water was slow and moody or flat; then there were the fifty or so great bends of the West Branch, some tight, some broad as avenues; there were riffles and chops and pools and tails and swampy runs and brisk runs and shallow flats a couple of hundred feet across, all in dozens of configurations, so that there were thousands of different fishing chances. Everywhere, the water was the clearest I'd ever seen, water in which the auburn, spotted forms of the trout and the wavering, hairlike masses of elodea and watercress were ghostlike."

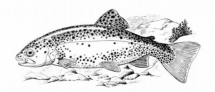

Every morning around ten, for 31 days, we'd stash our gear in the huge tan Suburban and head for the river. We'd head up the first hill, onto the highest bench, then rattle along the single rutted lane across the fields of wheatgrasses spotted with dark-green weed and sweet clover and pale-yellow prickly pear. There were always clusters of antelope in the fields. Often they would watch us – inert, wary, turning slightly so as always to be facing the car – until we came close enough to be a threat, though we were no threat. Often there were several spindly-legged fawns with them, born several weeks earlier; Herb had seen a doe drop one in the narrow road and he had stopped and watched and then gone around them. "Not enough meat to make a decent sandwich," he once said in his deep voice – the words always curt, final – watching a newborn antelope scamper away, already quick and lithe. Overhead, curlews with long curved beaks canted away, shrieking, and often we saw their chicks, which had no beaks yet, scuttling from us into the grasses.

Every morning, at the bluff that ended the last bench, we would stop the car and get out, and then look down into the valley, stretching off in front of us as far as we could see, with several braids of the river meandering through it like a blue ribbon stretched out casually upon a great green and tan rug. Except for the willows on the inner rim of the bench, near the headwaters of the East Branch, and the ragged line of cottonwoods in the distance, there were no trees: the river lay open and exposed and I knew at once that it would be hard to fish, with no cover, no breaks from the sun, with every movement of rod or line or person taken to be one of the trout's great predators here – pelican, osprey, kingfisher, merganser, heron, gull. An anthropologist who visited compared it to the Serengeti Plain, and it has that same broad fertile space.

We'd have the whole day, from then until dark, to fish the river. We could fish it anywhere we chose – miles and miles of it. We could fish it as hard or in as leisurely a manner as suited our fancy. We could go back to the ranch for lunch, or pack in a sandwich or some elk sticks, or fish straight through, hard, intently. Sometimes Pat, Herb's wife, and Mari would bring down lunch in the other Suburban.

I soon realized that Spring Creek was the most interesting river I had ever fished or could imagine; and I learned that it was loaded with secrets that would take exceptional skill to learn. At first I felt very privileged to be fishing the river, but soon my thoughts turned chiefly to where we'd fish and what the fishing would be like and when it would come and what fishing we'd already had. Within a week, the days blurred and I had to concentrate to separate them, keep them in sequence, though I have had no trouble finding in my brain the full and vivid picture of a

hundred moments, most of the fish I raised for the month I was there. Those were halcyon days and they changed my fly-fishing life forever.

From the top of the last bench the river looked blue, though up close it was green and blue and a dozen variants of amber, umber, coral, and beige; it was really colorless as water in a glass, pure spring water, but it took on the hues of its bottom and of the banks. Sometimes the crystalline water was slow and moody or flat; then there were the fifty or so great bends of the West Branch, some tight, some broad as avenues; there were riffles and chops and pools and tails and swampy runs and brisk runs and shallow flats a couple of hundred feet across, all in dozens of configurations, so that there were thousands of different fishing chances. Everywhere, the water was the clearest I'd ever seen, water in which the auburn, spotted forms of the trout and the wavering, hairlike masses of elodea and watercress were ghost-like. The river held trout large enough to make my eyes pop – mostly browns, all wild, with a scattering of rainbows – which would rise to flies the size of gnats.

ABOVE *The headwaters of Armstrong Spring Creek, Montana, with a first fresh snowfall on the mountain peaks. I once stood in this spot and caught four species of trout – rainbow, brook, brown, and cutthroat – on four consecutive casts.*

25

Nursed on the muddy, milky waters of the Croton watershed near New York City, where I had fished with worms and spinning lures, it all spooked me silly. The river seemed quite beyond the meager talents I thought I could bring to it.

When the wind did not ruffle the surface of the river too harshly – giving it a slate, opaque cover – the water was so translucent that you could see distinctly to the bottom of the deepest pools. What I could see in some of them, five to eight feet down, wavering like living shadows near the bottom, sent shock waves through me.

We would stop at the final bluff to look for the blue herons, which pecked holes in even very large trout and killed many smaller fish. They were astonishing hunters and several times I saw one result of their efforts: a beautiful, wild brown trout with a hole right on the top of its back, as if someone had shoved a pencil down an inch or so, very hard. Herb did not like them. "They can't even pick up some of the larger trout they stick," he said. After I'd seen three with that raw pencil hole in their backs, I felt the same, let the Audubon Society be damned. If there was a heron hunting, it would usually whirl into flight, its gigantic wings flapping heavily, merely at our appearance more than several hundred yards away. I never saw one until it was in flight, and at first mistook the six or seven pairs of sandhill cranes that nested in the valley for herons – though the sandhills traveled in pairs, the herons always alone.

We'd look for several minutes from the bluff, standing quite still and sometimes shivering from the early cold, and begin to think about the day and the weather and the flies and what had happened the day before and which section of Spring Creek we'd fish that day. Then we'd head down the last hill.

Now there was nothing to think about but the fishing. It was a truly remarkable river, but on a given day you could catch nothing; during the weeks I was there, three people – all fine fishermen – got skunked. Once I got none; Herb always got fish. Flies might hatch upriver but not down. The sun might be too bright, the wind too strong, relentless. The large pool on the East Branch might explode with feeding fish or remain perfectly placid, as if it did not contain a trout. The Two Islands Pool might go berserk. The Great Horseshoe Bend – as distinguished from many lesser Horseshoe Bends – might look barren, or might have one, three, or thirty fish rising. But once I had looked into several of the deepest pools I knew something of what the river contained, everywhere, and a shiver of expectation ran through me every time I looked at the water, anywhere, or pitched a fly into it, and still does even now, years later, whenever I think of Spring Creek.

In the deep pools, when the light was just right, you could see fifty or sixty wild browns, of all sizes – a few ten-inchers, a whole slew of fish between fifteen and

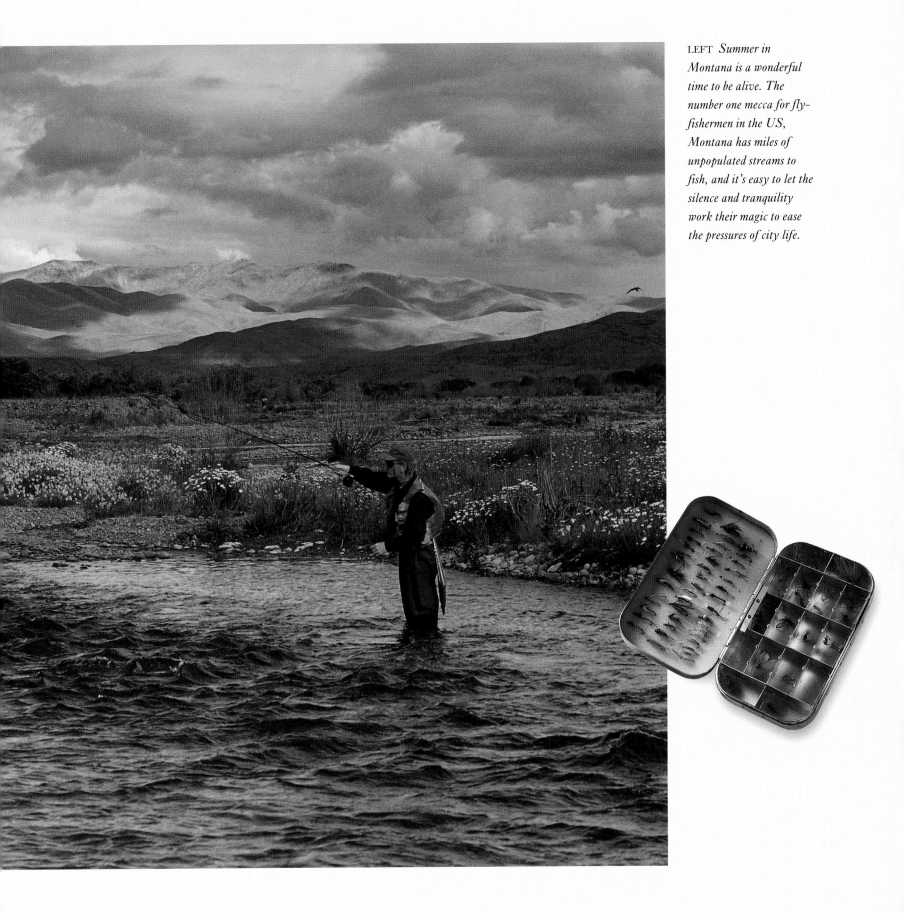

LEFT *Summer in Montana is a wonderful time to be alive. The number one mecca for fly-fishermen in the US, Montana has miles of unpopulated streams to fish, and it's easy to let the silence and tranquility work their magic to ease the pressures of city life.*

nineteen inches, and a few old alligators that would go 25 or more. Sometimes, concentrating on some deeply undercut bank, if you were lucky you could catch a glimpse of something dark and larger than anything your imagination could conjure. Was 32 or 34 inches an exaggeration? I don't think so. Several times, fishing carelessly up the West Branch, I'd spook one of those old fellows and it would bolt from a dark bank – black and too slow for a trout, as if it really wasn't afraid of me or anything else in the world, though prudence dictated it move: a fish the size of a muskrat or a dog, coming right past me, black and thick, scaring me half out of my boots.

But Spring Creek was also a place where solitude and quiet camaraderie were possible. It might be a river crammed with wild trout of great average size and great wariness, a place where I had more interesting fishing chances than I could imagine having anywhere else, but it was also a place where I made some great friends and learned more than I can tell.

At the bottom of the hill there was a shallow stretch of the river that the Suburban could ford easily. But usually before we crossed we made a short trip downstream to the right and the Suburban leaned down toward the river and I leaned over Herb's shoulder to see the water. On the way back to the crossing, with the vehicle dipping low on my side now, I had an unobstructed view of the river. The water was thin here – perhaps a foot to eighteen inches deep, over a sandy bottom, spotted with waterweed. Darting across the bottom, their shadows more palpable than their bodies, were a couple dozen trout. They were long and tan – some darker than others – and from the car we never saw them at rest. They were elusive, evanescent; they seemed born paranoids, afraid of every motion, every shadow. I hadn't the faintest idea how to approach them, or how to catch such fish, but they were beautiful to watch in their wildness, and they were very large – some 22 inches or more – and they gave to each morning a kind of benediction. And they always roused my metabolism. I

called this the Paranoid Pool and, from the beginning, I never expected to catch a fish in it, though Herb said there were times, when there was a slight chop on the water perhaps, when the fish could be caught, when you might gain entrance to the Castle. As day after day passed, I grew more and more determined to be skillful enough to catch one of these fish, fish as tough to catch as any I have ever seen. By the third week I had found half a dozen such spots on the river, many of them even more difficult to fish.

Below the Paranoid Pool there was a huge shallow flat, several hundred feet across and twice as long, and then the water narrowed, rushed against the far bank, split off into a back channel and disappeared, and the main current formed an

exquisite run of several hundred yards that emptied into a broad right-angled bend as the back channel joined the main flow below the island. This was a deep pool, braided with a farrago of currents; it held a great head of trout and you could usually take a fish or two here, whatever the circumstances, but it was very hard to fish consistently well and wisely.

After we'd looked at the Farrago Pool we'd head back, then ford the river and rumble slowly up the rutted and pitted dirt track that skirted the dozens of S curves of the West Branch, looking for flies or rises, flushing more curlew and their chicks, as well as little killdeer that hugged the road and then disappeared into the grasses, spotting a white-tailed deer or a cluster of sandhill cranes beyond the fence that kept the cattle from trampling the banks of the river. In places you could see

ABOVE *This is the "ring of the rise": the moment a rainbow trout has just lifted in the water to sip a tiny mayfly. In this case it's a trico.*

ABOVE *Yellowstone
Park's midway Geyser
Basin sets the backdrop for
this angler fishing the
Firehole River.*

where an oxbow had silted in, grown grass, and caused the river to adjust its path. The older routes were a delicate, lighter, fresher green than the other grasses. Herb had been advised to tinker with the river, to add structures that would help prevent the silting of bends, but his principle of conservation was abrupt and final: Leave it alone. He believed that the river would change, shift, adjust, suffer, flourish, and take quite good care of itself, thank you. Fencing out the cattle was an exception. And once he and I, on a scorching July afternoon, planted about a hundred willow shoots – none of which survived.

As we drove slowly down the West Branch, we'd hear the ice in the lemonade jug rattle, and we'd keep an eye peeled to the river. We'd always pass the decaying carcass of a calf struck by lightning that spring, and I'd always look to see if it was less of itself. The interior had collapsed and the skin kept getting tighter. At first there was an eager mass of insects everywhere on it, but as the season progressed the carcass kept shrinking, as if by itself, as if it was struggling to get gone from this place. The carcass always made me think of Richard Eberhart's poem "The Groundhog," where that little creature keeps decaying until, near the end, the poet sees merely the beautiful architecture of its bones and then, at the very end, when

ABOVE *An overview of
Silver Creek on the
Nature Conservatory
Section. The stream here
braids and twists to form
channels big and small.
It is one of the prettiest
Spring Creeks and is a
photographer's paradise.*

ABOVE RIGHT *A brown trout takes to the air as the angler backs away from the bank to keep a tight line. A thunderstorm has just passed.*

there is less than a spot, thinks of Alexander in his tent and Saint Theresa in her wild lament, and about mortality and such large matters. The calf carcass didn't vanish that summer; it was too tough. But it decreased. I tried to find some metaphor in it but decided to let it remain simply a decaying calf's carcass, several yards east of a run that led to one of the best back bends on the West Branch.

In fifteen minutes we'd be at the south end of the property, opposite a huge bend pool that pinched into a slick that you could watch comfortably from the warm car while the world warmed. We rarely saw fish move on our early trip upriver, though we often paused at several of the larger bends for a moment or two. At the south end we had an unobstructed view of a lovely run; its glassy surface and slight gradient let us see instantly the slight bulge on the surface.

Herb usually saw signs of fish first.

He'd point and I'd have to look closely and then I'd see a dorsal slightly breaking the surface, or bending reeds near the far point, or a wake, or the delicate spreading flower of a sipping rise, or a quick black head, up then down.

Herb and I had exchanged hundreds of letters – often several a week – in the years before I first fished Spring Creek with him. Though he did not tie, his observations on fly design, the attitude of flies on the water, knots, new gadgets, leaders, fly-rod length and design and action, technological improvements of various kinds, books old and new, and dozens of other fly-fishing subjects were acute and frank. He fished only with the dry fly and his observations were directed exclusively to matters connected to a fly that floats – but the word "purist" would sound silly if I used it to describe anything about him. He had more fun fishing the dry fly; he conceded the rest of the river to the trout; he enjoyed that visual connection to his quarry – the link that occurs where our world of air meets theirs, on the surface. He could be growly on the subject, claiming that he was a "fly" fisherman, not an "artificial bait" fisherman, but the heart of the matter was less philosophy than hedonism, I think: he enjoyed the one more than the other.

He had clearly read far more than I ever will about fly-fishing and he read with a shrewd and independent mind, guffawing at pretenders and second-handers and people who didn't give credit and "lightweights" (a favorite term of his), even if I had published or edited or introduced such people. An English friend – the author of half a dozen books on fly-fishing – said: "He has a wonderfully grumpy, bollocking exterior which hides a man of great kindness. He is also a remarkable fly-fisherman and makes me feel like a novice." I did not know when I flew out to be with him whether he was the superb fly-fisher the Englishman and others said he was, but his opinions were sharp, often raw, always telling, even when they made me smart. What he did he insisted upon doing deftly. He spoke abruptly, sometimes in half sentences, often with laconic wit, in low baritone. He scared the socks off at least one mutual friend. Thinking back, these many years later, I realize that mingled with the special expectation you feel when you sense you are about to begin the new and unknown was the nagging sense that we were from wildly different worlds, that up close the visit would prove a disaster.

I came full of expectation and some trepidation, and then, as early as that first morning, I forgot what I had expected and whatever it was I might have feared, and thought only of the water before us and the discrete possibilities of the day. The days were crammed with surprises anyway, of the kind that any great river provides, and I could not have imagined what happened any more than I have the imagination to invent a river like Spring Creek. For years it has so dominated my thoughts that I have been able to think and write of practically nothing else. Setting out to write this essay has become as much an exorcism as a report, a private rage for order, for clarity. I want very much to see that period clearly, from

LEFT *Ah, the camaraderie of the picnic table! These anglers are totally absorbed in their conversation about which flies to use.*

33

ABOVE *This license plate offers up a definitive statement on the world of fly-fishing. Do you think there's a 7X?*

LEFT *This old fishing hat now lies at the bottom of the Green River. Only the memories and the photograph remain.*

mornings to evenings, from knowing nothing to knowing something, in all its tension, intensity, challenge, and fun, from when I met the river in late June to when I left it in the bright sun of late July.

In the mornings, when the grasses were still wet with a bright silver sheen and the antelope fled and the curlew flew ahead of us as we rattled along the rutted and pitted track across the benches down to the river, we always felt the nervous tingling of expectation.

At first I wanted to fish all of the river at once, and I felt anxious when we chose one spot. The fishing might be better upriver or down, I thought. It made me uneasy. But after a few days I settled down, took matters one at a time and carefully, and felt content as we reconnoitered downstream, past Paranoid Pool and the big flat and Farrago Pool, then looked at the first few pools on the East Branch, and then drove slowly up the length of the West Branch, noting the carcass and the old oxbows, pausing at four or five bends.

Few flies would hatch until 10.15 am or a bit later, depending upon the temperature, and we'd sit and talk quietly in the big tan Suburban, about books or fishing or the condition of the water, or not talk, and then we'd see some flies on the front window. They might be small dark caddis or the first Pale Morning Duns, delicate and faint yellow. Herb would point and mumble and I'd give a little electric exclamation. Then a fish would show.

Was it a one-riser?

Yes, one rise, then gone.

"Not exactly a feeding frenzy," Herb might say.

But then there was another. And another. It was starting. We'd both make guttural sounds and not voice the obvious. One of us would point.

"Better get your rod down," Herb would say, and I'd say that he should get his down. In a few more moments one of us, usually me, would get out of the car ever so slowly, never taking eyes from the river, unsnap the rod from the carrier on the car roof, select and tie on a fly, and prepare to fish.

In the mornings we always looked and talked first. Then the sun grew warmer and before too long we would find some fish working. The river was merely what a river ought to be – varied, fecund, wild, with large trout, skittery as hummingbirds, that pretty-much liked a fly to look pretty-much like the thing it was eating – and as I looked from the Suburban and then went out to meet it I always felt that the world and I were moments from being born.

RIGHT *Evening on the Henry's Fork of the Snake, one of North America's most challenging blue-ribbon trout streams. Experiencing a heavy hatch on the Railroad Ranch section is something you'll never forget.*

THE ROCKY MOUNTAINS – FACTFILE

BACKGROUND

The Rocky Mountains run the length of the United States, from the border with Mexico in the south to the Yukon in northern Canada – a spectacular "spine" down the whole country, with a beauty that cannot be beaten. Runoff and meltwater from the snow-covered peaks provide household water for one quarter of the American population.

Fly-fishing for trout in the blue-ribbon rivers is a number one experience for fly-fishermen around the world. There's a certain magic in the names of rivers such as the Madison, Firehole, Yellowstone, Gallatin, Big Hole, Big Horn, Green, and Henry's Fork, to name but a few of the famous western waters. These rivers have been a part of angling tradition for a hundred years, and still fishermen make a pilgrimage to these hallowed waters.

The best fly-fishing to be found in the Rocky Mountain region encompasses huge areas of Montana, Wyoming, Idaho, Colorado, and Utah. However, probably the most concentrated area for great fishing is Yellowstone National Park and its immediate environs.

WHEN TO GO

The Rocky Mountains usually have long, harsh winters with lots of snow. Consequently, the fishing season does not really come into its own until the spring thaw has come and gone. Depending on the snow pack at the high elevations (some above 12,000 ft) this is usually, but not always, in June when the water levels go down and the water temperature warms up, encouraging insect life. The season continues until October when the snow often starts to fly again.

Some of the best fishing of the season happens late in the year when the big brown trout start to spawn. The visiting angler planning a trip to this area should come prepared for the possibility of rugged mountain weather. It can and does snow every month of the year here. The nights can reach

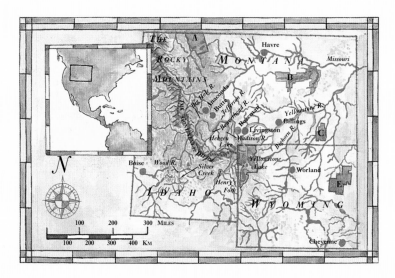

NATIONAL PARKS –
A GLACIER
B CHARLES M. RUSSELL
 NATIONAL WILDLIFE
C CUSTER
D YELLOWSTONE
E THUNDER BASIN
 NATIONAL GRASSLAND

STATE BOUNDARY

as low as freezing, but most of the summertime nights are mid-40's to mid-50's with daytime highs of 80's to 90's. Fishermen can start off a summer morning wearing a flannel shirt, sweater, and fishing jacket, and by noon shed almost everything but a tee-shirt.

THE FISHING

The wide variety of water in the Rocky Mountains presents the visiting angler with many different challenging fishing situations. An angler might find himself exercising small stream tactics in the morning on a tiny spring creek with a 4 wt rod, floating line, a 15 ft leader, 6X (2 lbs) tippet, and small size 18 dry flies for rainbows. That same afternoon he might find himself on a float trip down a major river such as the Yellowstone, and he might be throwing an 8 wt rod with a sinking-tip line, a short stout leader, and a Wooly Bugger for big browns. A serious visiting angler must be prepared for all fishing situations and all types of weather.

Brown, rainbow, brook, and cutthroat trout are the predominant species, with the cutthroat being the Rocky Mountains' only native species. All these fish grow quite well in the clean, pure waters of the Rockies. Fish of 4 and 5 lbs are caught regularly, and the average size is something like 12 to 15 inches, depending on location.

The philosophy of catch and release was conceived in this area when anglers realized that wild trout (as opposed to hatchery trout) were much too valuable a resource simply to be caught and killed. It was discovered that if fish were played gently and quickly on barbless hooks, they could be released back into the stream to continue living. Thus, other anglers would have an opportunity to catch the same fish (albeit, the fish becomes a wiser and more challenging quarry). If the angler wanted to eat fish, he could either catch and keep a hatchery fish, or buy trout in the grocery store.

TACKLE

RODS: Graphite rods of 8 to 9 ft for line weights of 4, 5, 6, and 8 will cover most situations. The 6 wt rod was once considered to be the standard trout rod for the Rocky Mountain area. However, these days rods are being made lighter, faster, and stronger, and both the fisherman and the fish expect smoother and more delicate presentations. Thus the 4 and 5 wt rods now predominate.

REELS: Single-action fly reels that are capable of holding at least 75 yards of 20 lb test backing in addition to the fly line will be sufficient. You can purchase spare spools and fill them with alternative lines for quick interchanging ability on the stream.

LINES: A full complement of different lines is recommended, from floating lines to sinking-tip lines, and slow-sinking to fast-sinking. However, the floating weight-forward line will possibly be the line most often used.

LEADERS: A good starting point for a leader would be 9 to 10 ft leader tapered to 4X (4 lbs), 5X (3 lbs), or 6X (2 lbs) depending on the selectivity of the fish and the type of water encountered. Finicky trout call for delicate leaders of 12 to 16 ft, tapered down to 6X (2 lbs) or 7X (1 lb) – it may even be necessary to use 8X (½ lb). It is a good idea to talk with a local tackle shop, of which there are quite a few located in the general Yellowstone area.

FLIES: One of the exciting challenges in these Rocky Mountain rivers is trying to "match the hatch." Many of the lush, green river meadows produce intense hatches of all sorts of insect life. The trick is figuring out which of several different types the fish are feeding on at a particular time. Take some of your favorite trout flies; but you might want to wait until you get to your destination and follow the advice of your guides before you buy the bulk of your flies.

Some tried-and-tested patterns for western US waters are: for dry flies, Parachute Adams, Royal Wulff, Yellow Humpy, Goddard Caddis, Elk Hair Caddis, Pale Morning Dun, Tricos, Green Drakes, and Stonefly patterns; for nymphs, Hare's Ear, Wooly Bugger, Stonefly, Pheasant Tail, Muskrat, Beadhead, Zugbug, and Prince Nymph; and for streamers, White and Black Marabou, Sculpins, Zonker, Renegade, and Spruceflies. Sizes for dry fly tend to vary between 12 and 20.

ESSENTIAL TRAVEL EQUIPMENT

Dress for Rocky Mountain fishing should be casual and comfortable. Chest waders are standard: either the lightweight nylon "bulletproof" waders or the new breathable Gore-tex waders work well for the summer months. Early and late in the season you might consider neoprenes.

The weather can change very abruptly in the mountain areas, and you should be prepared. It is best to dress in layers. Long johns and wool socks are often worn. On top, a flannel shirt, a warm sweater, a rain jacket, and a down vest are a good combination. Other important accessories not to forget are: polarized sunglasses, dry fly floatant, surgical forceps for releasing trout unharmed, a landing net, sunscreen, insect repellent, a fishing hat, a flashlight, and angler's clippers.

Visiting anglers are must usually purchase a non-resident fishing license. Check with your lodge as soon as you get there, or beforehand if possible.

ABOVE *Rainbow trout, so called because of the red stripe along their sides, are among the favorite North American fish. They love fast, rushing water, and pounce on dry flies like a cat on a mouse. They fight hard and leap often. Rainbow trout are not only found in the Rocky Mountains – indeed, they can be fished throughout North and South America, as well as in many other parts of the world.*

FLIES, CLOCKWISE FROM TOP *A Parachute Black Gnat; a Stonefly Creeper; an Elk Hair Hopper; a Gold-ribbed Hare's Ear; a Royal Wulff; and a Damselfly Nymph.*

The Miramichi River

Canada

Leonard M. Wright, Jr.

"Though the fish comes off at the second jump, I'm encouraged by the possibility that they may be starting to take and I begin covering the water at the top of the pool with renewed concentration. A half-hour later, well after my keenness has slackened again, I see a large boil out where my fly should be and feel a small tap. Too big a swirl to be made by a grilse. I stand stock still and check my wristwatch. He'll be back in his lie by now, but I'll give him three minutes to settle down."

In some ways, fly-fishing for Atlantic salmon (and that's the only way you can fish for them in the Canadian Maratimes) doesn't make any sense at all. For example, the fish don't feed on their upriver migration: their digestive juices dry up when they enter fresh water. So why expect them to mouth your poor counterfeit of something they aren't going to eat in the first place?

Then, too, the expense can be damnable. If you're going to fish private water – and most of the good pools are owned by individuals, lodges or outfitters – you can expect to pay from $1,500 to over $10,000 a week, not counting travel, tips, booze or poker losses. Since a catch of two or three fish a week is about par for the course, averaged over a season, you can figure out, without taking off your waders to count piggies, how much it's going to cost you to catch fish that your local fishmonger might pay you $20 to $30 for.

BELOW *A Silver Rat.*

And yet, both here and in Europe, salmon fishing is widely considered the stratospheric fishing experience. Men, otherwise sane, travel thousands of miles and spend princely sums, year after year, just to step into a river that, likely as not, will be either high and muddy or too warm and low when they arrive.

However, if you insist on going despite the arithmetic – and I confess I do at least once each season – you can increase your odds by doing what Leo Durocher used to call "playing the percentages." The obvious first move in this game is to find out where the fish are.

Every year, *The Atlantic Salmon Journal* publishes the recorded, rod-caught totals for each river in Canada's Maratime Provinces. But don't rush out and try to buy a copy. I can, as the admen say, save you time and money. Most years, New Brunswick's Miramichi river system produces a larger catch of salmon, all by itself, than all the rest of the rivers in that province plus the totals for Quebec, Nova Scotia, Labrador and Newfoundland combined. Yes, you heard me right, the Miramichi fishery usually accounts for at least half of all the Atlantic salmon caught by anglers in the entire Western hemisphere.

Following "The little shepherd of Coogan's Bluff" formula down to the last decimal point, it is of further self-interest to note that, of this total Miramichi system take, over 75 per cent of it comes out of the main Southwest arm. How'm I doing, Leo?

BELOW *A Ponoi Red.*

ABOVE *My own feet and rods as I stand on the bottom of a traditional cedar-strip canoe on a journey upriver.*

ABOVE *The exhausted angler after a hard morning's fishing on the Miramichi River in New Brunswick.*

I have a rather wealthy friend who owns a few, productive pools on this mainstream section. I once asked him why he settled on the Miramichi when he could easily have afforded water on the high-rent rivers to the north such as the Restigouche or the Grand Cascapedia.

"On this river, the reported catches are 30,000 to 50,000 a year. How big a run is that? On the few European rivers where they have fish-counting chambers at the head of tide, they've found that the up-river rods take only about twenty per cent of a run. If the same holds true here – and there's no reason why it shouldn't – from 150,000 to 200,000 must run up this river during the average year. Do you know what that means? It means that, during the open season of a little more than three months, an average of over 1,000 salmon per day have to be passing through my pools. Where else can I get odds like that?"

The Miramichi has another major asset: it is extremely user-friendly. Since it's medium-sized, as salmon rivers go, boats are rarely called for and, at average river-levels, the wading angler can handily cross it in the riffles at the heads of pools. The river-bottom, in most places, is paved with gravel or small stones which provide safe and comfortable wading.

It is also a relatively shallow river. The average fish holding lie is only three to five feet deep so only small-ish flies are needed, mainly #6s and #8s – flies about an inch long. On the larger, deeper rivers, anglers often have to resort to huge #1/0s or #3/0s to get the salmon's attention. Such lures look like humming-birds impaled on meat-hooks and are brutes to cast.

And casting is the name of the game when you're salmon fishing. There's an old saying that it takes a thousand casts to raise a fish – and even that may refer to the good old days. If you figure three or four casts a minute, that adds up to one stingy rise in a hard, half-day of fishing, and landing, or even hooking, that one riser is far from a sure thing.

The standard presentation is to cast an underwater or wet fly across and downstream at a 45-degree angle and allow it to swing in an arc until it dangles directly below you. Then you take a giant-step downstream and repeat the process until you've covered all the likely fish-holding water in the pool. Of course, if the water is quite slow, you cast at a wider angle to hurry it along and you cut a smaller slice in fast water to slow it down. The trick is that, no matter what the current may be

BELOW *A Bomber.*

BELOW *A Silver Stoat.*

ABOVE *On a frosty morning, frustrations are aired, quite literally, on a streamside picnic table.*

RIGHT *A composition of flies, reels, and lines, created as I wait patiently for a fish to bite.*

doing, you should control your fly so that it moves at that special, impossible-to-describe speed of travel salmon seem to prefer.

Having said that this is a handy-sized river to fish, I don't want to imply that it's a Mickey Mouse one. Even in its middle reaches, riffles and runs average over a hundred feet wide and pools run from 150 to over 200 feet.

The main Southwest stretches some hundred miles above its head of tide at Quarryville so it's an extensive waterway. And its major tributaries – the Northwest, the Little Southwest, the Dungarvon, the Renous and the Cains – average about fifty miles long and are respectable fisheries in their own rights.

While the local scenery lacks the more dramatic contours of Nova Scotia to the east, it is, nonetheless, pleasant, rolling country with well-wooded hills and meadows, which were once working farms, carpeting the valley floor. This is productive hunting, as well as fishing, terrain. There are plenty of grouse and woodcocks in the thickets. You see moose occasionally, deer frequently, and black bear almost certainly if you visit a town dump at dusk.

The Miramichi has always been the nearest-to-affordable salmon river in Canada because it is known as a "little fish" river that is decidedly "grilsey." A grilse is a salmon weighing only three to five pounds because it has spent only a single winter packing on weight in the Arctic feeding grounds. A mature salmon, which will usually weigh about ten pounds and occasionally reaches fifty, has spent two or more winters up north gorging on shrimp, capelin, and herring. The

ABOVE TOP *A high-jumping salmon throws off spray at Sutter's Pool on the Miramichi River.*

Miramichi delivers at least three grilse for every true salmon and the majority of its adult fish fall into the modest, eight-to-twelve-pound range, so Miramichi fish can't average over five or six pounds.

The bigger, more pricey rivers to the north show a far higher salmon-to-grilse ratio and the salmon themselves average much heavier. The median weight of fish taken on the Moise or the Grand Cascapedia, for example, would be about twenty pounds and fish well over thirty pounds are not uncommon. Moise angler and famed adman, Ted Bates, once killed three salmon, each over 35 pounds, before lunch one day. Traditionally, big-fish rivers can command extortionate prices.

Recent regulations may change all this, however, and riparian owners on the Miramichi may see their fortunes rising. In the Province of New Brunswick, all fish over 25 inches long – meaning all mature, two-winter salmon – must be returned to the river, unharmed. In Quebec, only one fish a day may be landed and that one

RIGHT *Bill Taylor of the Atlantic Salmon Federation playing a large salmon on the Grand Cascapedia River in Quebec. The guide stands by with the net.*

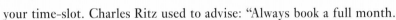

must be kept. Suppose an angler on, say, the Matapedia, lands a small grilse at nine in the morning. He's out of the river for the rest of the day with not much to show for his big-fish fee.

A Miramichi angler, on the other hand, can land four fish in a day – release two and keep two – before he limits out. True, he can't keep any of his larger fish, but he can enjoy the excitement of hooking and playing them which is really what most anglers go up there for in the first place.

One of the drawbacks to salmon fishing anywhere in the world is that schools of salmon enter rivers in pulses – mainly triggered by rises in water – and, since you usually have to book months in advance, there's no way of fore-seeing whether the river will be full or nearly empty during your time-slot. Charles Ritz used to advise: "Always book a full month.

BELOW *A moment of great relief: Bill Taylor's fish is in the net – and what a fish it is!*

LEFT *The release of a beautiful hen fish caught on the Bonaventure River. This river has the cleanest water on the Gaspé Bay peninsula.*

That way you can be sure you have at least one good week." Thanks a lot, Charlie – I'll do just that when they abolish the IRS.

While we're back on the subject of money, I should point out that there are ways to fish the Miramichi on the cheap. About a third of the pools are "Crown water" – an obsolete term because they used to be considered the property of the "Bloody Queen" but are now provincial property and open to all licensed anglers resident or non-resident.

If you fish this open water, your costs can be modest. Your non-resident license is $50 per week – $100 for the season – and you must, by law, engage a local guide for $50 a day, plus tip. However, he may guide three fishermen so the cost to an individual is hardly ruinous. Hotel rooms and meals cost about the same as in the States. If you really want to bare-bones it, your guide will probably tell you which families in town will take in angler/boarders.

Be warned that this will not provide a "gracious living" experience. If there's a run of salmon coming through, and you always hope for one, an open-water pool may be lined by ten to fifteen anglers on each side spaced less than fifty feet apart. Each conga-line moves slowly down the pool, the bottom end continually peeling off to start in again at the top. If you move down too slowly, the man behind you will noisily rip his fly out of the water within inches of your precious waders. You'll get the pace, and the message, quickly enough.

If you stay at a lodge with private water, however, you'll have far greater

LEFT (TOP TO BOTTOM) *A Muddler; a Ponoi Green; a Yellow Wiggler; a Cosseboom; and a Blue Doctor.*

freedom of movement. You won't have to race to a pool at daybreak hoping to get in a couple of run-throughs before the stampede begins, either. At most camps, breakfasts are hearty, leisurely meals and the morning fishing usually starts at the civilized hour of 9 am and ends before a 1 pm lunch.

Typically, four rods will be assigned to a pool, two on each side, which allows plenty of elbow-room when fished in the usual, cast-step-down-cast manner. If, say, four of the fish resting up in the pool that morning are in a mood to take, your odds are far better than if you're sharing them with twenty to thirty others. You probably get what you pay for.

Results of a morning's fishing are totally unpredictable because nobody can foretell how many salmon will be lying up in the pool you're going to fish or what sort of mood they'll be in. A lot depends on water levels and weather patterns. My first morning's salmon fishing during early July last year was fairly typical.

The water is clear, but about a foot higher than normal summer level due to a soaking rain two days earlier. A few fish may travel on through without stopping with this much water, but most will take up resting lies in the pool rather than running the shallow bar at the head of the pool in bright sunlight.

The guide suggests that I start, half-way down in the pool, and walks 100 yards up to the head of it to coach the other angler who has never fished for salmon before. He knows I've been at it for years and have fished this particular pool dozens of times, so he leaves me to fend for myself.

Which fly should I tie on? I have three boxes in my vest containing an over-kill of 250 flies even though I know I'll tie on only six to eight old favorites during the entire week. I finger a #8 Conrad – a time-tested, hairwing pattern that's all black except for a green butt – but decide that, with the river up, a slightly larger #6 would be a shrewder choice.

I start angling seventy-foot casts about sixty degrees across stream, watching the end of my line to gauge the speed of my fly. When I get it right, I am full of anticipation, expecting a fish to tighten my line at any moment.

Forty-five minutes later, however, my acute expectation is sagging. As I reel in at the tail end of the beat, I hear a shout upriver, then see a grilse leap two feet out of water. The rookie has hooked a fish in water I'd just covered. So much for years of experience!

Though the fish comes off at the second jump, I'm encouraged by the possibility that they may be starting to take and I begin covering the water at the top of the

BELOW *Richard Adams, probably the most famous fishing guide in Atlantic salmon history, has fished and guided on his beloved Matapedia river for over sixty years. He is truly a legend in his own time.*

pool with renewed concentration. A half-hour later, well after my keenness has slackened again, I see a large boil out where my fly should be and feel a small tap. Too big a swirl to be made by a grilse. I stand stock still and check my wristwatch. He'll be back in his lie by now, but I'll give him three minutes to settle down.

I shoot out a cast of exactly the same length and angle as the previous one and hold my breath as the fly starts its swing. Nothing. I repeat three times without result, then strip in the line and change to a smaller #8 of the same pattern. No action. I change again to a brighter Jock Scott of the same size. Nothing doing. I admit defeat and switch back to my original pattern and start on down the pool.

My concentration wanes again and I cover the water mechanically. When I reach this "nth" degree of boredom, old songs or even nursery rhymes often pop into my head, playing over and over again like a broken record. Today is "The-bear-went-over-the-mountain" day and, try as I will, I can't turn the music off. I am down to the lowest, slowest part of the pool and finishing my hundredth "to see what he could see" when my line slowly begins to rise, my rod-tip starts to bend and then I feel solid weight as my line starts cutting upriver. Salmon have a habit of taking when your mind is elsewhere and you least expect them.

It's another grilse, but a big, fat one that will push five pounds and, three jumps and five minutes later, the guide has him in the net. There's still a half-hour till lunchtime, but there's no more action.

Walking back up the hill to the lodge, I ask myself the eternal salmon-fishing question: why did that fish take? Was it because I had chosen the right pattern and swung it past him at the proper speed? Or was it pure, blind luck? In a rare burst of honesty, I have to concede that it was probably fifty-fifty.

Well, that's salmon fishing for you. Like flying coast to coast, it's hours of utter monotony punctuated by moments when your heart is in your mouth.

Knowing all this, do you still want to try it? All right, but be warned that salmon fishing is like "that first, fatal glass of beer" or that first teenage puff on a cigarette. If you catch a fish, you're at risk. Kill several and you're most certainly a goner.

But maybe I'm not too objective on the subject. After all – and shame on me – I've never been able to quit smoking, either.

LEFT *A proud angler hand-tails a salmon on the Grand Cascapedia River. Note the two-handed rod. These rods are gaining in popularity for their ease of line handling and efficiency in covering the water.*

BELOW *Hope springs eternal in the hearts and minds of fishermen.*

On Wesley's River

Canada

TOM McGUANE

"I arose from bed in the wonderful music of the birds in the forest surrounding the camp. To western ears, the sliding notes of the redstart made a summery mystery. I thought of the warm haze in the skies, the nearness of the sea, the plain thrill of fishing for strong North Atlantic ocean fish whose legend required their seasonal presence in what otherwise was a woodland trout stream. The mind of an angler is stretched to account for this."

Recently, and among people we didn't know that well, my eleven-year-old daughter said something that made jaws drop. She had heard the phrase "the F-word," possibly from a potty-mouthed sibling, and assuming in our house that it must mean fishing, said to a group of guests, "*All my dad cares about is the F-word.*" In the astonished silence that followed this showstopper, she added, "When he's not doing it, he's reading about it."

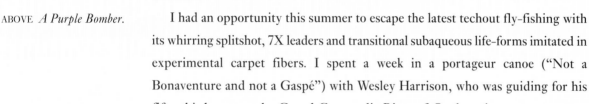

Well, it's true; but I don't like every kind of it and some of the latest forms of trout fishing as applied in my home state of Montana make me loath to bump into any of its practitioners for fear I will again see the tall man on the banks of Poindexter Slough who was tinting his neutral-colored flies with Magic Markers to match the mayflies rising around him. There's always some little rivulet no one else wants, a brushy bend, a pond back from the road under wild apple trees. Go there.

ABOVE *A Purple Bomber.*

I had an opportunity this summer to escape the latest techout fly-fishing with its whirring splitshot, 7X leaders and transitional subaqueous life-forms imitated in experimental carpet fibers. I spent a week in a portageur canoe ("Not a Bonaventure and not a Gaspé") with Wesley Harrison, who was guiding for his fifty-third year on the Grand Cascapedia River of Quebec. A portageur canoe, which is what Wesley called it, is a broad-bottomed and commodious rivercraft big enough to carry nets and rain gear, that can be driven by a light outboard, and can slip along quietly in the river from drop to drop, as the precise settings of the killock or anchor are called. A bowman is called for to handle the anchor, in this case

a cheerful young Canadian named Jeff, who deferentially helped Wesley move the boat through its daylong ballet on the rapids and meanders of the great river.

I was warned that if I did not fish seriously the entire time that I was on the river, if I repeatedly misstruck fish or failed to turn over my leader in the wind, Wesley would return to shore and put me off the boat. He has taken more than one sport in early with the recommendation that he go elsewhere to learn to fish before coming back. I was tuned up by such admonitions forty years ago on the Pere Marquette River by my father and my "uncle" Ben Ruhl; and there was a certain solace in having the majesty of a great river presumed as a place of seriousness, if not solemnity. These men grew up before the advent of Jet Skis and other entertainment doodads of this suckhole age. The river was your great wife and the very hem of her skirt must be honored.

I arose from bed in the wonderful music of the birds in the forest surrounding the camp. To western ears, the sliding notes of the redstart made a summery mystery. I thought of the warm haze in the skies, the nearness of the sea, the plain thrill of fishing for strong North Atlantic ocean fish whose legend required their seasonal presence in what otherwise was a woodland trout stream. The mind of an angler is stretched to account for this.

I had breakfast with my hosts who aren't particularly anxious for you to know who they are: homemade pastries, homemade jams, tawny local bacon and farm eggs. I gathered my rod and sweater, a book of low-water salmon flies on Patridge Wilson-style hooks, some hard candy to suck at tense moments; then walked across fields of wild strawberries swept by a warm, balsamic breeze. My only fears were

ABOVE *A father and son hook up on the Grand Cascapedia, one of the premier salmon rivers of Quebec, while the local Native American guides steady the boat and prepare to net the fish.*

that I would be struck by lightning or that news of a world war would come over the little radio in the kitchen or that Wesley would kick me out of the canoe.

I met Wesley Harrison and his bowman Jeff. Wesley was a tall, strongly made and cheerful man in his seventies, flannel sleeves rolled over arms that had poled his canoe thousands of miles. Jeff was that rare, quick-witted youngster, without a phony bone in his body. He kept one eye on Wesley to be sure of the right syncopation of effort.

The river was a little dark and I mentioned this to Wesley. He shook his head

ABOVE *The fish of a thousand casts: that's what they call Atlantic salmon when it seems nothing is moving. But just as your thoughts start to wander — bingo! There he is!*

faintly. "Not good," he said. "The old Indian calls this p'ison water." We pushed off and started the motor. I sat in the middle of the canoe and rested my fingertips on my fly rod, laid across the thwarts. I kept one eye on the unscrolling river behind and one on Wesley whose billed cap shifted left and right as he sized up our course.

We passed another canoe on the way with two Mic Mac Indians guiding a well-dressed sport who failed to acknowledge our passing. "Oh, that old Indian feller

Wesley walked over to me, looked at my straight rod. It was silent. Then he asked, quite coolly I thought, "What happened?"

Now he wanted to look over my tackle. The leader, a finely tapered thing, he actively disliked. I buried my own views of leaders and took one of his, tied on another fly, and began fishing the next drop below the one where the salmon, a big salmon, had taken the fly. I knew how it was. The next take could be a week away. There was a cavernous silence in the canoe. I resumed my methodical fishing of the drop, cast, lengthen, cast, lengthen. The waterspeed was picking up lower in the pool and required more careful mending of the line. I kept seeing the fish in the air, hearing the erratic screech of the reel, feeling that slump as the dead rod straightened. And Wesley's question, "What happened?" I wasn't happy.

BELOW *A golden sunset over the Miramichi finds an angler fishing the riffles for running fish moving upstream.*

BELOW *A Green Machine.*

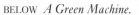

But then I hooked another fish, a hard-running ocean-bright fish; and this one, after several wonderful leaps, ended up in Wesley's net, a big deep hanging silver arc. With a wide smile that confirmed my absolution, Wesley said, "A fresh one, right from the garden!"

We bounced along the river toward the camp, tall ferns thrust through the gunwales to announce our fish. When we landed, Wesley shook my hand and said he'd see me in the morning. "You can't leave us now," he told me. "We're well acquainted from fighting the salmon together!"

I headed back up through the banks of wild strawberries considering a nap, the river poems of Michael Drayton, considering the notion that no one owed me anything.

BELOW *What fly to use for the last pool before supper?*

LEFT *A big, wonderful hen-fish of 24 lb is released back into the clear, clean waters of the Bonaventure.*

CANADA: FACTFILE

BACKGROUND

From Nova Scotia through New Brunswick, Quebec, Labrador and Newfoundland, the Maritime Provinces of Canada can boast more than 400 salmon rivers. These are some of the world's prettiest Atlantic salmon waters and the fish that run them are noted as acrobatic and resilient fighters. A number of the more remote catchments were not fished by fishermen until well into this century, when the advent of floatplanes made them more accessible. Many of the pioneering expeditions were the work of the legendary fly-fisherman Lee Wulff, who was also responsible for revolutionizing several techniques and practices associated with Atlantic salmon fishing, including the "portland" or "riffled hitch" (a method of fishing a conventional wet fly so that it skates across the surface of the water).

The catchments of the Maritime Provinces may not produce the vast numbers of fish that they used to, but many of their names are synonymous with large fish. Rivers such as the Grand Cascapedia, Moisie, Restigouche and Matapedia still produce fish in the 30–40 lb class. Canada is also tireless in trying to improve the runs of salmon to its waters. In May 1998 the Atlantic Salmon Federation's Quebec Council announced a buy-out of the province's remaining commercial nets, and many now feel that the Federation is very close to a buy-out of the last commercial Canadian netting operation. With a long history of strong catch restraints being placed on rod and line fishermen, which has proven effective in improving the number of returning fish, a buy-out of these remaining nets would further enhance all of the province's river catches.

For fly-fishermen thinking of going to these fantastic rivers, the future looks increasingly bright.

WHEN TO GO

As with most Atlantic Salmon destinations, early season fishing can suffer from high water levels and cold temperatures. But by mid-June most Canadian rivers are receiving the first runs of larger mature fish. In mid-July the bulk of the grilse run will have started. While low water and bright sunny conditions can make fish despondent in August, fishing normally picks up again in September, when the last runs of fresh fish enter the rivers. On some of the region's systems, these late-returning fish can be some of the largest of the year.

TACKLE

RODS: Single-handed 9 ft rod for 7–9 wt line. Double-handed 12–14 ft rods for 8–10 wt lines.
REELS: Direct-drive large arbor reels with capacity for 150 yards of backing plus fly line.

LINES: Mostly floating, though intermediate and sink-tip may be useful in the early season.

LEADERS: At least 8 lb test line; perhaps up to 15 lb.

FLIES: Dry flies – Bombers, Wulffs, Muddlers, Brown Bi-visible and Macintosh. Wet flies – Rusty Rat, Silver Rat, Cosseboom, Blue Charm, Jock Scott, Thunder and Lightning and Black Dose.

FLIES *A selection of Bombers – by no means the only flies used in Canadian salmon fishing, but perhaps the most exciting because the salmon's take is visible.*

Dances with Trout

Alaska

JOHN GIERACH

"*Most days we spent two or three hours flying over genuinely trackless country, often at altitudes of two hundred feet or less, which is low enough to see bears, caribou, and even tundra swans clearly, not to mention stream after stream running red from spawning sockeye salmon. I must have asked a dozen people why the salmon turn red in the rivers, and the only one who knew was a native guy. 'It's so the bears can see 'em,' he said.*"

The backcountry of Alaska is a perfect silence broken by the sound of motors: generators, outboards and especially the droning of float planes. Up there the single-engine plane is the equivalent of the pickup truck. Once you're away from the state's handful of roads – in the bush where the fishing is really good – a plane is your only way of getting anywhere, not to mention getting back.

I was in Alaska not too long ago with my friends DeWitt Daggett and Dan Heiner. DeWitt is a publisher and Dan is the managing field editor of an outdoor magazine (which means he manages to get into the field as much as possible).

We fished from three different lodges – technically, two lodges and a hotel – and spent a lot of time in the air, which is standard procedure. There would be the flight in and then, most days, weather permitting, we'd fly out to this or that river in the morning to be left with a guide and maybe an inflatable raft or a boat stashed on site. Then we'd be picked up at a predetermined place and time to be flown back to the lodge in the evening. Or what passes for evening. In the Alaskan summer there's a little bit of duskiness in the wee hours, but nothing those of us from "down below," as they say, would call night.

Most days we spent two or three hours flying over genuinely trackless country, often at altitudes of 200 feet or less, which is low enough to see bears, moose, caribou, and even tundra swans clearly, not to mention stream after stream running red from spawning sockeye salmon. I must have asked a dozen people why the salmon turn red in the rivers, and the only one who knew was a native guy. "It's so the bears can see 'em," he said.

ABOVE *Early-morning activity centers around the dock at Bristol Bay, where planes and boats prepare for the day's fishing.*

We often had the rivers we'd chosen entirely to ourselves, and that sense of loneliness was enhanced by the knowledge that now and then the plane doesn't show up to take you back to the nice, cozy lodge. This doesn't happen often (it never happened to us) but there is weather to consider, or engine trouble, and every now and then a pilot will get sick or even just forget that he was supposed to pick you up, only to slap his forehead in a bar two days later, turn to the guy on the next stool, and say, "Oh, shit." Fishermen are seldom lost for ever, but they've been known to get stranded for a while.

At the time it seemed like an outrageous odyssey, but back in Anchorage I found that we'd only gone a couple of inches down the Alaska Peninsula on a map

of the state that would cover the average kitchen table. I went out on the front porch and tried to extrapolate the feeling of vastness from our own little trip to all the rest of that game- and fish-infested, largely roadless open land as an exercise in meditation. I sat there through two cans of beer and couldn't do it, but I did remember something Wallace Stegner had said on an audio-tape DeWitt's company produced – something about how you don't even have to go into the wilderness to get its benefits, just knowing it's out there is a great comfort.

When we boarded the Alaska Airlines flight from Anchorage to Iliamna, the stewardess got on the intercom and said, "Fasten your seat belts and, yes, the reds are running." That was welcome news because I was psyched to catch salmon, as was everyone else on the plane. There were sixty-something passengers and exactly that many rod cases. No briefcases, no lap-top computers. We were there in late

ABOVE *Twilight falls on Nonvianuk Lake in Katmai National Park. This is as dark as it gets in mid-summer. The sound of loons calling echoes across the waters in the dusk.*

ABOVE *Some popular Alaskan flies. The colorful patters are for salmon. The deer hair mice are for rainbows. Note the eyes and ears on the mice.*

July so any salmon caught would probably be sockeyes, aka "reds." These are a marginal fly rod fish, many people said, but that hardly mattered.

For one thing, I'd spent a week fishing for Atlantic salmon in Scotland that same summer and had gotten skunked. I wasn't exactly looking for revenge (although going after, but not catching, a certain kind of fish does give you a long-lasting itch), there was just the idea of those millions of big fish that live some-where out at sea and then run up into the rivers once a year, past orcas, and seals, and bears, to spawn and then die. When you come from a place where there are fewer fish and they pretty much stay put, that's romantic stuff.

I got into salmon on our first day on the water. We'd flown into the mouth of the Tazamina River and then motored upstream a mile or so. The water was full of sockeyes, but that didn't seem to interest anyone much except me. Dan, DeWitt, and the guide were calmly speculating on where the rainbows and grayling might be, while I kept leaning over the gunnels saying, "Jesus Christ, look at all the salmon. Stop the god damn boat!" Most of the fish were nice and silvery, still fresh from the sea.

When we finally beached on a sand bar the guide got the other two guys going with streamers and then led me to a huge pod of sockeyes. He told me to rig a pink Polar Shrimp with split shot, as if I were fishing for trout with a nymph. One thing about the Alaskans: unlike the Scots, they fish for salmon as if they actually want to catch them, with sink-tip lines and lead.

When the guide saw that I was rigging up an old Payne nine-and-a-half-foot light salmon rod with a brand-new Peerless #6 reel, he said he'd never seen one of those and asked to try it.

"Shoot," he said, "this is a little heavy, but it casts real nice."

There were fifty salmon in a pool not ten feet from where I was standing. "I'm glad you like the rod," I said, "but give it back."

I had a fish on for a minute or two and lost him. Then I got a good hookup, but the fish was snagged in the back. It weighed six or seven pounds and took longer to land than it should have.

I thought, yeah, I've heard about this. There are those who say the plankton-eating sockeyes don't take flies and the best you can do is foul hook them, and there are others who say they do too take flies if you do it right. The rules say the fish is a keeper if it's hooked somewhere in the face, ahead of the gill covers.

If I remember right, I landed seven salmon that afternoon, four of which were hooked in or so close to the mouth that I'd say they either ate or tried to eat the fly.

And that's as far as I care to delve into that controversy. I will say that when a sockeye is hooked near the front it fights real good, especially on a bamboo rod.

Those first few days we fished from the Iliaska Lodge owned by Ted and Mary Gerkin. There's a long story here, and if you'd like to hear it you should read Ted's book, *Gamble at Iliamna*, because he tells it much better than I could. Anyway, it was here that I began to understand how sockeye salmon were viewed by Alaskan fly-fishers.

The sockeyes, along with the kings, silvers, chums, and pinks, form the basis for the entire ecology of these watersheds. The number of fish in these runs is astonishing: six million in this drainage, nineteen million in that one, and there are hundreds of drainages.

Salmon often run all the way up into the smaller rivers and creeks, many of which are connected by large lakes. There are resident grayling and some Dolly Vardens in these streams, but the big rainbow trout and Arctic char are only in the flowing water in significant numbers when they follow the salmon runs up out of the lakes. Sometimes a fisherman will say that Such-and-Such River isn't good for big rainbows yet because the salmon aren't in. If you're new at this you'll have to ask him what the hell he's talking about.

The trout, char, and grayling feed on salmon eggs that are dribbled by the ripe hen salmon as they run up the rivers and then later on the ones that wash out of the spawning reeds. This sounds like an incidental dietary footnote until you multiply the salmon by millions and get tons of protein from stray eggs alone.

BELOW *An Orange Comet.*

The fish are really onto these things. It's said that big rainbows will swim over and nudge ripe hen salmon to dislodge eggs. Every guide and bush pilot I talked to claims to have seen that.

Still later, after the spawn when the salmon all die, these same gamefish feed on bits of rotted salmon meat dislodged by the current. It's hard to picture, but in this scheme the pretty rainbow trout, char and grayling fall into the same ecological niche as maggots and vultures.

The standard flies are salmon-egg patterns and sickly beige-colored "flesh flies," tied from rabbit fur. Naturally, these are fished on a dead drift. This may not be what you'd call classy stuff, but it does match the hatch perfectly.

The dying and dead salmon are also eaten by gulls, ravens, eagles, otters, and so on, not to mention aquatic insects, which then go on to feed the salmon parr and smolts before they return to the sea, as well as the grayling, trout, char and such during those times when there are no salmon in the rivers. Then the young salmon themselves form part of the diet for other gamefish. In the middle of all this, you can go to the places where rivers enter lakes and fish streamers for big char collected there to feed on migrating smolts. The schools of char are often under flocks of excited, hungry gulls and terns.

That's the obvious stuff you can see from a boat or while wading a river. There's also the plankton/salmon/seal/orca connection out at sea. In the grand scheme, that's what salmon do: they bring the nutrients from the ocean far up into the freshwater rivers, lakes, and streams and there's no way I can convey the magnitude of it. It's just something you have to see.

ABOVE *A Bead-eye Salmon Bugger.*

BELOW *An Orange Flash.*

And then there are the bears. Alaskan brown bears – along with rainbow trout – put on a large part of every year's growth gorging on salmon, and once you've stepped in a huge, steaming pile of bear crap you begin to see that their droppings are not an insignificant contribution to the fertilizer needed to grow the grasses that are fed upon by the caribou that are now and then eaten by the bears – and so on.

This is efficient, economical, messy, smelly, mystically circular, and temperamental. It's especially temperamental if you count the commercial netting of salmon – the "nylon curtain," they call it – that can screw things up seriously when it's not properly regulated, as most people will tell you it, in fact, is not. Take away

ABOVE *Susan Rockrise caught 79 salmon during her week at Bristol Bay Lodge in southwestern Alaska. She is shown here with one of them.*

ABOVE *A beautiful wilderness setting for an overnight camp.*

the salmon, as some would gladly do for a single year's profit, and the ecosystem would die.

They say that the silvers and, in some circumstances, the kings are the real fly rod salmon in Alaska. The sockeyes are loved as a food fish and for their overall contribution to the food chain, but in the circles we were traveling in – fly-fishers and fly-fishing guides – they don't seem to be too highly rated.

One morning at Iliaska when the weather was too shocked in for flying, some of the guides drove a crew of us over to the Newhalen River to join 75 or so other fishermen who were dredging for sockeyes. This is called "combat zone fishing," and one of the guides told me the Newhalen was nothing. "You should see the rivers you can drive to from Anchorage," he said.

I got into it after a while, even though I claim not to like fishing in a crowd or chunking lead. I mean, what the hell: these were big fish and this was Alaska, where things are sometimes done differently. In the true spirit of things, I got deeply interested in killing some fish to take home.

By the way, I believe that "chunking" is the proper, common term. It's onomatopoeic, coming from the distinctive "chunk" sound split shot makes when it hits the water.

When the ceiling lifted after a few hours, Ted and another pilot flew over to pick us up and take us to a secluded little river to catch big rainbow trout, possibly on dry flies. "You're about to go from the ridiculous to the sublime," Ted said.

Rainbows are what the guides and lodge owners brag about most – in terms of both numbers and size – and they're what many visiting fly-fishers are looking for. After all, this is one of the few places on earth where, at the right time, with some skill, a little luck and maybe the right guide, you can bag your ten- or twelve- or (if the stories can be believed) even your fifteen-pound rainbow on a fly rod. The fish will be scavenging behind a run of salmon instead of sipping mayflies but, if you connect, it will be a by-God, double-digit wallhanger.

Not far from Iliamna Lake by float plane, on a river the name of which I've been asked not to mention, I landed a six-pound rainbow on a dry fly. It was a nice fish, big enough to make the lodge book (volume III), in which, among other things, you can record for posterity any trout over four pounds caught on a dry.

It was a nice fish, but not a great one by Alaskan standards; memorable only because it was hooked on a floating caddis pattern instead of on a sunken salmon egg, flesh fly or streamer. On the other hand, it was probably the biggest trout I've ever caught on a dry fly.

People have written pages in that lodge book about a single, good fish – eloquent stories filled with keen observations and humour – but I couldn't think of anything more profound than, "Six-pound rainbow on a #14 olive Stimulator," dated and signed. It's not that I wasn't happy, I was just a little tongue-tied.

We caught salmon on wet flies and split shot, nice-sized Arctic char on eggs and Woolly Bugger streamers, rainbows on streamers and eggs, and one day I got into some pretty Dolly Vardens, once again on eggs. Apparently, you don't do a lot of dry fly-fishing in Alaska and I understand some fishermen on their first trip there are a little disillusioned by that.

I won't say I was actually disappointed, but there were a few times when I got

ABOVE *A Muddler Minnow.*

ABOVE *The weather can change rapidly in Alaska. This morning was sunny and virtually cloudless. Within twenty minutes of my admiring its beauty and taking this photograph, the sky had been overcome by dark clouds and I was watching the pouring rain.*

enough of lead and sink-tips and flies that looked less like bugs and more like bangles from a stripper's costume. And, yes, those did happen to be the few times when we weren't catching fish. I've noticed that certain fishing tactics seem a lot more acceptable when they're working.

Still, that day on the river that Ted Gerkin asked me not to write about – the one where the big rainbows would come up to a dry caddis fly – was a tremendous relief, and so was our first afternoon at Wood River Lodge on the Agulawok River.

There were fish rising in front of the cabin as we lugged our gear from the plane, and when we rushed down there we found that they were rainbows and grayling, both up to eighteen or twenty inches, rising to a this-and-that hatch of caddis, mayflies and small stoneflies. The fish weren't too picky, but we did have to fish flies that at least approximated the appearance of the real bugs. I was already in the water with my five-weight rod strung up, DeWitt was playing a fish and Dan had just missed a strike, when I learned that I had to run back to the cabin and dig my dry-fly boxes out of the bottom of the duffel bag. At that point in the trip I had caught countless big fish, but it almost killed me that, for five minutes, Dan and DeWitt were getting them while I was looking for those damned fly boxes.

The next day we could have flown out once again to catch great big something-or-others someplace else, but we unanimously voted to stay and fish the river right in front of the lodge. They gave us two guides with boats, and we fished from right after breakfast – say, eight in the morning – until dusk, which would have been going on midnight. Sure, we broke for a shore lunch and dinner at the lodge, but that's still a long day. In fact, this has happened to me at least once every time I've gone north. I say, "Jeeze, I'm kind of tired for some reason," and the bright-eyed guide says, "Well, we have been fishing for about sixteen hours now."

We caught rainbows, some nice big Arctic char, and my biggest sockeye of the trip (ten pounds) on streamers, but what I remember most clearly now are the grayling.

They were almost all good-sized, maybe fifteen to twenty inches, and throughout the day we'd find pods of them rising in the slack water beside faster currents. "That's because they're a lazy fish," Duncan said. That's Duncan Oswald, one of several guides at Wood River who specialize in fly-fishing. He also ties the flies for the lodge and knows the river's hatches. That's significant because in Alaska you don't have to know the hatches to catch fish.

I fished for the grayling with a seven-foot, nine-inch Mike Clark bamboo rod and Dan broke out a sweet little Pezon & Michelle Parabolic. Neither rod raised any eyebrows and, in fact, I was surprised at how many cane rods I saw on that trip.

Apparently, many Alaskan fly-fishers have a darling little bamboo stashed away for just these kinds of occasions.

As I said, the hatches were scattered, but the best was a fall of size fourteen dark stoneflies. The grayling would execute a refusal rise to a #14 Royal Wulff, sometimes eat an Elk Hair Caddis, Irresistible or Stimulator, and absolutely hammer an elegantly simple deer hair and calf tail stonefly of Duncan's own design. I brought a few of these home with me to copy.

Some people will tell you that grayling are easy fish – the bluegills of the north – but I've never found them to be like that. The few times I've fished for them in their native range, they've been catchable, but far from pushovers: easy enough that you can usually get some, but still hard enough that each fish is an event. And, of course, they're unbelievably, iridescently beautiful. The perfect gamefish, in other words.

That night at the lodge over gin and tonics, one of the other guides said it was too bad we hadn't gone off with him to catch the "pigs" but, more for Duncan's benefit than ours, I think, he said he did realize that a salmon egg is "chunked," while a dry fly is "presented."

We saw lots of bears in Alaska. They were following the salmon runs, as we were – inadvertently or otherwise – so it was unavoidable. These animals are called Alaskan brown bears, although there's some disagreement among the scientists about whether they're a separate species from the grizzly. The main difference is size. A big brown bear looks just like a grizzly, but stands a foot taller and weighs as much as 600 pounds more. When you're sharing a gravel bar with one, size does seem to be the defining factor.

A big sow and a yearling cub came down to the Newhalen River the first day we fished it. I was about fourth in the line of fishermen upstream from the spot the bears wanted. When one of the guides hooted "Bear!" I looked, broke off the eight-pound salmon I was playing without a second thought and began wading slowly but deliberately upstream, as they tell you to do. Dan, who doesn't like bears much, was just ahead of me. He didn't say anything, but he was making a quiet noise deep in his throat that sounded like the cooing of a pigeon.

Later, DeWitt said it was interesting to see the "ripple of recognition" go through us when the bears waded out into the river.

We saw bears almost everyday, and there are three things people tell you about them: that, nine times out of ten, the bear will decline a confrontation; that if he doesn't decline, it's probably your fault; and that a bear's personal space is no less than fifty yards. That seemed awfully close. I found that I had to be at about 200 before it would occur to me that the adults were handsome and the cubs were actually pretty cute. Bears scare me badly, but I still like them a lot, which I take as evidence that I've negotiated something heavy.

We had only a couple of ticklish bear encounters, one of which we had in a spot where a small creek entered a lake. The plan was to wade up the creek a half mile or so to a place where, we'd been assured, there were huge rainbows and grayling, but there was a sow and two cubs around the first bend, so we had to turn back and work the inlet, where there didn't seem to be too many fish.

I won't try to describe the whole, grim dance in detail, but eventually a young male bear came down to the inlet and made it known that we had blundered into his personal space and that he wasn't pleased. Since he was on shore and we were

BELOW *A father and son, together with their guide, proudly display yet another bright silver salmon, fresh from the sea.*

BELOW *Early morning coffee in the camp, and a toast to another great day in paradise.*

RIGHT *Brown bears fishing for salmon at Brooks Falls in Katmai National Park. From the safety of an elevated wooden platform, anglers and tourists can watch as many as a dozen bears catch dinner.*

already up to our armpits in the lake, we had a little trouble getting out of his way, although we tried. At one point the bear gave us some negative body language – lowered head, flattened ears. This doesn't sound like much on paper, but on site it's pretty damned impressive.

Throughout the whole thing our guide, Nanci Morris, spoke in a charming voice, first to the bear, then to us, and she never unholstered her Smith and Wesson .44 Magnum. She was the picture of composure and said later she was more worried about that sow getting nervous because boars are known to attack cubs.

It turned out okay, but I was glad to hear the deep, unmistakable drone of the DeHavilland Beaver Nanci calls the Cream Puff coming to pick us up. It occurred to me that having an airplane come and save you from a bear is a great way to get over your fear of flying. When the plane taxied in, Dan waded out and kissed a pontoon, able to kid around now because it seemed we'd live.

Nanci is the head guide (excuse me, "Director of Sportfishing") at the Quinnat Landing Hotel in the town of King Salmon. Her specialty is trophy-sized kings, and in some magazine article or brochure she was once dubbed "the queen of the king salmon guides." Naturally, that stuck, as embarrassing publicity always does.

When I said something about getting to be head guide at a place like that at an obviously tender age, Nanci said, "Yeah, and, not to put too fine a point on it, try doing it as a woman."

I could see that. Competence is admired in a place like King Salmon, but men

far outnumber women and at times the horniness is almost palpable. And it's a little rough – in a pleasant way for a tourist, but rough nonetheless. Over some beers in the hotel bar a pilot named Red told me, "We try to make a year's living here in five or six months, so we fight sleep deprivation half the year and depression the other half." He also said, gazing wistfully out at the Naknik River, "Ah, Alaska. She seduces you every summer and then abandons you every winter."

Anyway, Nanci does seem to love that plane with something close to a passion. As head guide, she almost always manages to schedule it for her own trips and, although she talked about other things in the two days we all spent together, she kept coming back to the Cream Puff. When we walked down to the dock to board it or when it banked in to land and pick us up, she'd say, "Just look at it. God!"

The first time I saw the Cream Puff it was sitting at a dock on the Naknik River and we were sitting in the bar at Quinnat Landing, near the big picture windows, eating thick steaks and talking about the fishing. During a lull in the conversation, Nanci gazed out at the Beaver and said, "See that plane out there? I love that plane. If that plane was a man, I just might say 'I do.' "

At which point every man in the joint looked out the window at the lovely old purple Beaver. Its big radial engine was idling. At that range it sounded like the purring of a large, happy cat.

I Know a Good Place

Alaska

CLIVE GAMMON

"And now, though this is my seventh morning on the Karluk, the fly rod shakes in my hand as I scramble up the loose pebbles to watch the army that's surging into the Karluk's mouth – the day's new wave of coho salmon streams out of the Pacific on the turn of the tide, thousands of bright-struck fish leaping, cavorting like circus clowns."

ABOVE *A Sculpin.*

ABOVE LEFT *Although brown bears are a fairly common sight in Alaska, up close and personal they never fail to command a healthy respect.*

Sometime in the mid-nineteenth century, when the Oregon Territory was still in dispute between Great Britain and the USA, a Royal Commission headed out from London to inspect the damn place, see if it was worth having. It reported back to Parliament in a strongly negative style, the nobleman who was its chairman having been disgusted to discover that the salmon in the Columbia River did not rise to the fly like those of the Tweed. This, conceivably, altered the history of North America. It was also a slander on noble fish, as you will see.

Over the Shelikof Strait the morning sky had the iridescent sheen of the shell of a freshly shucked oyster, steel gray suffused with pink and blue lights that took fire on the snows of the Valley of Ten Thousand Smokes and on Mount Katmai,

ABOVE *The first flight out in the morning from Enchanted Lake Lodge in Katmai National Park, south of Iliamna Lake on the Aleutian Peninsula.*

a 6,700-foot-high volcano forty-five miles away on mainland Alaska.

The sea was an oyster shell, too, blue with rose highlights, calm, barely moving until it broke lazily against the monolithic cliff of Tanglefoot, stirring the kelp, pushing by Mary's Creek until the water swirling out of the Karluk River checked and roiled it. This was slack tide, with the water as idle as the fur seals riding the little swells, immobile as the three bald eagles settled on a stony spit in the river.

The Karluk itself, on the west coast of Kodiak Island in the Gulf of Alaska, looked barren; empty, translucent water slid fast over gray stones until it met the Shelikof in an acre or two of confused chop. On a ridge

above, I watched the water for a sign that the ocean was starting to bully its way in again. The seals had vanished, the eagles taken to the air before my senses picked up the change and the daily miracles that would come with it, foreshadowed now by a fretting of the calm water and the silver reflection in it, like the sun catching the shields of an ancient army's vanguard.

And now, though this is my seventh morning on the Karluk, the fly rod shakes in my hand as I scramble up the loose pebbles to watch the army that's surging into the Karluk's mouth – the day's new wave of coho salmon streams out of the Pacific on the turn of the tide, thousands of bright-struck fish leaping, cavorting like circus clowns.

Stripping line as I go, slithering down the stones, I wade clumsily out into the river, launch the garish green-and-purple streamer fly, flashy with tinsel, into the thick of them. My right hand, gripping the rod butt, is wrapped with half a dozen Band-Aids covering cuts of a week's worth of salmon battles. The past seven days have seen this fly rod bend into more than one hundred cohos. Still, I tremble. I am in the finest salmon river in the world, no matter what the people in the rustic lodges along Canada's Restigouche or the tweedy inns on Scotland's Tay or Spey or Dee might think. The Karluk is salmon fishing as known in heaven.

The great fly-fisherman G.E.M. Skues, father of modern nymph-fishing, once unbent enough to write a little fiction concerning the late Mr Castwell, a somewhat bumptious dry-fly purist who, as he thought, had ended up in heaven and been provided with a perfect streamside cottage, the finest tackle and an attendant water keeper. And perfect trout fishing, it seemed, until Mr Castwell began to grow uneasy after catching fish after splendid fish from the same spot. Skues concludes his tale with this bit of dialogue:

"How long is this confounded rise going to last?" inquired Mr Castwell. "I suppose it will stop soon?"

"No, sir," said the keeper.

"What, isn't there a slack hour in the afternoon?"

"No afternoon, sir."

"What? Then what about the evening rise?"

"No evening rise, sir," said the keeper.

"Well, I shall knock off now. I must have had about thirty brace from that corner."

"Beg pardon, sir, but his Holiness would not like that."

"What?" said Mr Castwell. "Mayn't I even stop at night?"

"No night here, sir," said the keeper.

81

"Then do you mean I have to go on catching these damned two-and-a-half-pounders at this corner for ever and ever?"

The keeper nodded.

"Hell!" said Mr Castwell.

"Yes," said his keeper.

Mr Castwell's hell, though, was confinement to a corner. There was no infinite variety of flies, of techniques, of locations as there was on the Karluk. Nevertheless, the reports of the spectacular fishing over the past year or two had seemed to suggest a kind of drawback that might best be summarized as the Chocolate Factory Syndrome. It's said that chocolate factories have no pilfering problem because employees are free to eat all they want. After a couple of days few of them retain a taste for sweets. Could salmon, then, turn out to be like chocolate? Was it possible to fish until success became satiety?

Journeying to Alaska in midsummer, that seemed unlikely. No fishing could be that good. There would be someone, you could bet your chest waders, who'd greet you at camp with such time-honored words as, "You should have been here last week." And, indeed, during a stopover at Anchorage, there came a foretaste of such a put-down.

That was in Northwest Outfitter's, the city's major tackle store, aglitter with trays of salmon flies. The sales clerk was confidently buoyant about the patterns, as such men always are – the Polar Shrimps, the Skykomish Sunrises, the Bosses, the Skunks. "Figure on one fly for every hour you fish," he said alarmingly, scooping up a dozen Purple Fishairs with Mylar. "You'll want a box for all these and …"

"Did you hear how the silvers are running?" I interrupted him – cohos are often called silvers.

"And you'll need something in green and orange," he said.

The silvers, he was reminded. "Uh, I didn't get word yet," he said offhandedly.

From a tackle salesman, this was the equivalent of a cynical laugh, an indication that the fish were still offshore. I got the same message at the departure lounge for Kodiak, where people were lugging rod cases around as they do garment bags in other airports. "Early for silvers," a rod-bearer said to me. "Where are you heading?" I told him the Karluk. He'd never heard of it.

I needn't have worried. The next morning, forty-five minutes after the light

LEFT *When I called out to Brian O'Keefe that there was a bear right on the bank behind him, he thought I was kidding.*

airplane headed out of Kodiak, over Women's Bay and across the hills and tundra, I looked down on to the thread of the Karluk as it broadened into a lagoon, down on to fish erupting everywhere on its placid surface. Hello, chocolate factory, I said to myself as we landed.

And a factory, it turned out, where there was no need to report for work unconscionably early. The lagoon fish, well, they were sort of semipermanent residents, said Robin Sikes, the elderly Alaskan (elderly at twenty-eight, that's to say, in a state where twenty-six is the median age) who greeted the group of which I was now one. Better to breakfast at leisure, wait for fresh fish to run in from the sea on the tide and enjoy the balmy summer's morning with the temperature in the sixties.

So there was time to make acquaintance with the other anglers in my charter: Drs Hamada, Habu, Hatasaka and Inouye and Mr Okazaki, all from northern

California, all but one dentists; more California dentists, Drs Cosca, Wagner and Angel, with his son Jacob; and the odd men out, Mr Channing, a physical therapist, once a trainer with the 49ers, Mr Sopwith from his Sacramento rice farm, and Mr Lidner and Mr Miley, retirees.

BELOW *Bus Bergman about to net a big char for his wife Lydia on a float down the Kanektok River.*

Later they would become Teds, Stans and Leos, et al. Now, as they assembled their gear on the grassy slope in front of the lodge, they divided neatly into two groups – the fly-fishers and the men with, well, the hardware, the spinning gear, the

heavy spoons. I was no fishing snob, I told myself, but I knew which group I would go to if it came to an emergency root-canal job during the week.

We strolled down to the river together to clock in. Salmon were breaking everywhere in the lower pools, and before I'd even made a first cast I could see one of the spin fishermen with his rod bent into a fish. I took my time, made a short throw or two to get the feel of a new graphite rod, then put out a long cast at the classic angle, across and downstream. The Skykomish Sunrise must have swung by a whole school of leaping fish.

An hour later the silvers were still passing it by, as they did the Purple Fishair I substituted later, and later again the Polar Shrimp. There was a moving belt of salmon, but I hadn't sampled one; nor, so far as I could judge, had the other fly-fishermen. Mortifyingly, the spinning rods were enjoying heavy action. Jacob,

BELOW Early morning fog greets the first anglers of the day at a wilderness camp on Lake Kagati.

ABOVE *Hutch, a Bristol Bay Lodge guide, in his mouse-decorated hat. Mouse flies are very effective for rainbow trout.*

eleven years old, was just about keeping his foothold on the pebble bank as a thick-bodied silver, fifteen pounds maybe, tried surging for the volcanoes on the far side of the strait.

When it was clear the run had ended for the morning, I walked back with Jacob to the lodge.

"He was kind of big," Jacob said. "I couldn't reel him in. I thought he was going to win."

"Oh, really," I said.

"I was kind of relieved when I had him on the shore."

"Oh, you landed him, then," I said.

"I wanted to keep him," said Jacob. "Very much. But, see, there's an Eskimo legend that if you kiss the first fish you catch and then you throw it back, it tells its buddies and you can catch more fish."

"And did you kiss it?" I asked Jacob.

"Yeah," he said.

I told him that was terrific as I glanced at the fat spoon now clipped to the keeper-ring on his spinning rod. I tried to smile, but I'm fairly certain it came out like one of those tortured Humphrey Bogart grimaces.

Sikes had said there was a good chance of taking salmon that afternoon in the big lagoon higher up on the Karluk, but the prospect of blind casting into the deep holes up there was unappealing to one nurtured in the white turbulence of northern Atlantic rivers. So I hiked yet farther upstream where the Karluk became a river again.

ABOVE *A Sculpin.*

And a different river, the obverse of the tidal water downstream through which the bright battalions of cohos from the sea had poured in the morning. This was a battlefield in its hideous aftermath. Salmon, dead and dying, leprously white, patchworked in virulent yellows and reds, lolled and drifted in the slack water close to the banks. Fish, sockeyes and humpbacks, that had spawned, and were now spent, finished. And hanging on the flanks of this broken salmon army were river guerillas, Dolly Varden char, pink flecked on their sides, predacious, vicious-hitting, in character absurdly unlike Dickens's delicate heroine of *Barnaby Rudge*, for whose pink-spotted gown the species is named. They gobbled now on the profusion of ripe salmon eggs that dribbled from the stony redds, as four weeks later they would gobble salmon fry. They gobbled also any small bright fly I threw at them, like Mr Castwell's trout, two- and three-pounders hitting on every cast. I had released maybe thirty of them, and I was ready to admit that this wasn't even a chocolate factory. It was a peanut farm.

ABOVE *A happy group portrait. Note the difference in coloration between the silver fish on the right and the red one on the left. The latter has been in the river longer and is closer to spawning.*

ABOVE *Freshly grilled silver salmon with garlic butter and lemon is hard to beat.*

That evening after supper there were no dentists to be seen, for a seminar was in progress. In businesslike style they had chosen the Karluk River for a convention. Left in the clubroom, among a few others, was a gentle-featured man of sixty-five, Bob Miley from Red Bluff, California, a retired telephone company repairman, who said he had saved for two years for this trip. Now he was hunched over a vise in a corner, under a reading lamp, tying flies, notwithstanding the fact that he'd brought two hundred or so with him.

It was a mild emollient to one's self-esteem to discover that Miley, almost fifty years a fly-fisherman, had also found the Karluk no chocolate factory, at least on the first day. "What are we doing wrong?" I asked him.

Miley gave his answer some thought. "Don't believe it's the pattern," he said. "Just tying these 'cause I like tying flies." He thought again. "We've got to go deeper," he said. "Those fish we're casting to, the ones leaping and slashing on top?

They're not the hitters. Hitting fish are underneath. Those men got 'em on heavy spoons, right? We got to get our flies scratching the bottom. Reckon that's the way they want it."

What I'd been doing, what we'd been doing, was fishing conventionally downstream, forgetting that the cohos and the mighty chinook salmon of the Pacific were a different kettle of fish from Atlantics. At this moment I couldn't help feeling nostalgia for the fish of that other ocean, the ones the Romans, in admiration, had named *salar*, the leaper. "Trouble is," I said, suddenly, petulantly and illogically, "these damn silvers have no history."

Robin Sikes overheard me and said, "Come with me a minute."

This August evening there was light to spare. We walked away from the lodge to a steep earth bank. He took out a knife and started to probe at its side. Soon he had worked free a small, smooth oval stone, flat with a broad groove at each end. He handed it to me.

"Fishing equipment," Sikes said. "A sinker – six thousand years old maybe." He pointed at the cutaway bank. "See the layers?" he asked. "That's a kitchen midden. We had five anthropologists up here this summer from Bryn Mawr. They found slate knives, axheads and sinkers. They reckoned the early people, the Koniags, moved in here right after the first glaciers had gone through, found the big fish run and stayed." Sikes took some string from his pocket and stretched it round the stone. A sinker, self-evidently. "No history?" he asked. "Man, this has been one of the hottest fishing areas in the entire world for hundreds of years now."

Thousands, more precisely. Sikes warmed to his lecture. The native people had had it to themselves, he said, for most of those six thousand years, until the Russians came in the eighteenth century, pushing the Empire forged by Peter the Great to its ultimate eastern frontier. In particular, it was Alexander Baranvo who first swashbuckled on to Kodiak Island and the Karluk, seeking fur-bearing sea otters. What he found was perhaps the mightiest salmon run in the world – chinooks, sockeyes, humpbacks (pink salmon), dogs (chum salmon) and cohos – which lasted from May until September. "There must have been twenty million fish moving into the river," said Sikes. "And there were no laws."

Massacring many of the Koniags as a prologue, the Russians salted salmon in barrels, then shipped them west. Later they were joined by freebooting Americans, and then came two events that almost destroyed the most prolific salmon resource on earth. The canning process was invented in the 1790s and in 1867 the US purchased Alaska.

When that purchase became known, men fought with crowbars.

RIGHT *The view from the Bristol Bay Lodge dock on a quiet morning epitomizes the Alaskan great outdoors.*

ALASKA: FACTFILE

BACKGROUND

Of all the destinations featured in this book, Alaska offers the most diverse range of quarry to the fly-fisherman. As well as five species of Pacific salmon, there are giant rainbow trout, Arctic grayling, Dolly Varden, Arctic char, lake trout and northern pike. Alaska's inaccessibility makes it a haven for these fish and almost nowhere else in the world are fly-fishermen offered such pristine wilderness conditions in which to fish. While all the fish species in Alaska have their devotees, the different types of Pacific salmon generate the most interest. Visiting fishermen from all over the world flock to the forty-ninth State from June to September to sample some of the world's most prolific salmon runs.

King, or chinook, salmon are the largest Pacific salmon and perhaps the most demanding. On most rivers they average a little over 20 lb; 30 lb is nothing to write home about; and 40–50 lb fish are not uncommon. Kings over twice this size have been taken in nets, although a much more modest fish will test your tackle to the full, especially if it is fresh run. Sockeyes, which can be difficult to tempt to the fly, are probably the hardest-fighting Pacific salmon pound for pound; while the silver salmon, with its looks and its propensity for dramatic jumping fights, most closely resembles the Atlantic salmon. Humpback and chum are the least fished-for of all the Pacific species: they are the smallest and lose condition quicker than some of their larger relatives. The sparkling silver of their flanks quickly fades and in its place spawning livery appears, almost as soon as the fish enter fresh water.

WHEN TO GO

Spring in Alaska is the time of snow melt and heavy runoff for most of the river systems. As soon as the flows start to stabilize and the water temperatures to rise, the first runs of king salmon start to enter the river; in a normal year they'll arrive around the second week of June and continue to run until around the end of July. In early July the first runs of

LEFT *A collection of rods and reels at rest for the evening during a wilderness float trip.*

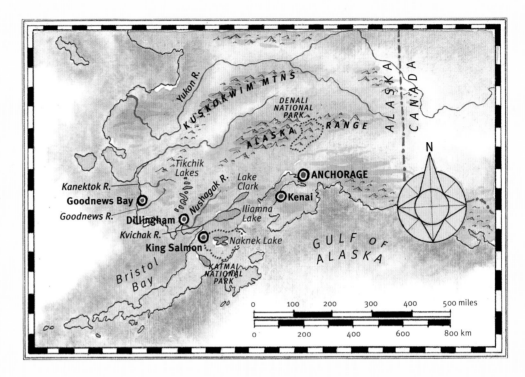

sockeye will be forging upstream, soon to start taking on the dramatic red-and-green spawning dress for which they are so well known. August sees the beginning of the run that so many fishermen await: the dynamic silvers start to enter most watersheds by the second week of August, and may well continue to run right into September.

TACKLE

RODS: For king salmon – single-handed 9 ft for 9–10 wt lines. For sockeyes and silvers – single-handed 9 ft for 6–8 wt lines.

REELS: Large arbor direct-drive with capacity for 150 yards backing.

FLIES 1 *Orange Krystaliser* 2 *Black Matuka* 3 *Babine Special* 4 *Orange Super Comet* 5 *Black Krystaliser* 6 *Green Boss* 7 *Sculpin* 8 *Olive Sculpin* 9 *Eggsucking Leech* 10 *Olive Matuka*

LINES: Fast sinking lines for kings in heavy early water. Sink-tips and floaters for sockeyes and silvers.

LEADERS: 10–15 lb for kings; 8–10 lb for sockeyes and silvers.

FLIES: Matukas, Wooly Buggers, Zonkers, Gray Ghosts, Mickey Finns and Orange-and-White or Red-and-White Bucktails.

My Platform of Despair

Iceland

ART LEE

"Here the broad Laxá narrows dramatically, with churning rapids at the head, below which the pool plumps a bit and has dug deep enough into the lava bedrock bottom to provide good holding lies (although you might not think so to see the rush of water over the top), but just as quickly narrows again to pour with incredible power over a plate of lava no more than twenty feet wide, under a bridge and into a maelstrom of frothing white water below."

Among the many reasons Iceland's Laxá I Adaldal is my favorite Atlantic salmon river is that just as when you shoot ducks, you do well to hit. Five hundred in baseball – that is, land one-half of the salmon you hook. The greater your skill, the higher your average may turn out to be; but overall, year in and year out, that's more or less the way it goes. Make a mistake and your fish is gone. Isn't that the way salmon fishing really ought to be? You bet.

But what makes Laxá different than, say, New Brunswick's Miramichi or most Gaspé rivers, the "name" rivers of Scotland, or for that matter, the general run of Icelandic salmon rivers and streams? After all, at first glance Laxá isn't a brute by any means. In fact, though wide and carrying a lot of water, its spring creek appearance, reminiscent of Idaho's Henry's Fork, might even con you into thinking that landing Laxá salmon will be a piece of cake.

But there's the weed, for instance, especially late in the season. Ever try to control a twenty-pound salmon with ten pounds of weeds draped over the leader and line? No mean feat, believe me. And then there's all that submerged lava, always abrasive and sometimes as sharp as razor blades, and so tough as hell on leaders. Let a fish fool around near the bottom of most Laxá pools, and you're in big trouble, brother, to say the least.

There's also the size of the fish. Each year several salmon of thirty pounds and more are hooked on Laxá, not only on flies, but on bait and spoons, but precious few are landed. I've taken a pair of 29's and a few 28's, but only one of more than thirty pounds – a 33-pounder which, as I wrote elsewhere several years ago, is the only salmon I've ever caught to which I claim "braggin' rights." The small flies often necessary to attract Laxá salmon, even when the water is high, are also a crucial factor. Sizes six to fourteen are usually more effective than larger flies. Liphook a fifteen-pounder on a size twelve Hairy Mary Orange, then permit a gob of weed to slide down the leader against the hook, and you're done like a dinner.

An unforgiving river is this Laxá I Adaldal, and that's why, at least in part, in a country of so many "Laxás," this one warrants its special designation "the Laxá."

As far as I know, I'm the only American who has fished every salmon pool on the river, and I hope no one will find it unduly immodest when I say that over the years I've given as good as I've got. Except on one pool: Núpafossbrún, which has been "kickin' my ass" for more than twenty years. This is the one place on Laxá where, as the late hotelier-sportsman Charles Ritz lamented of his misadventures with the always colorful Count Denissoff on the Russian exile's Åaro and its

RIGHT *The blue boat on upper beat number three, moored in the wet grass, allows anglers to fish the deeper parts of the pool, which can't be reached from the shore. The boat waits there year after year in exactly the same spot. Some things never change.*

ABOVE *A traditional sheepskin fly wallet shows off a variety of Icelandic flies, both single hook and double. An old saying, "bright day, bright fly; dark day, dark fly," helps with selection.*

"Platforms of Despair," I have been "pursued by continuous bad luck."

For sheer power, Núpafossbrún, interestingly enough, is the one pool on Laxá which might contend with the tumultuous Åaro and its famed (or infamous) "Platforms." Since most Americans who fish Laxá know the pool only as "the bridge at [beat] number seven," it may not matter, but for the record, translated from the Icelandic, Núpafossbrún means "brink of the falls beneath a steep hill," with the Núpa complicating things a bit, being the dative case of an old Icelandic word (*núpur*) which also situates the pool on the farmstead to which it belongs.

Here the broad Laxá narrows dramatically, with churning rapids at the head, below which the pool plumps a bit and has dug deep enough into the lava bedrock bottom to provide good holding lies (although you might not think so to see the rush of water over the top), but just as quickly narrows again to pour with incredible power over a plate of lava no more than twenty feet wide, under a bridge and into a maelstrom of frothing white water below. So powerful is this compacted flow, in fact, were it not for a tight, but deep, crevasse, left by nature in the lava plate near the east bank, I doubt that any salmon, even salmon as powerful as those for which Laxá is famous, could ascend this foss.

As luck would have it, Núpafossbrún isn't at all difficult to fish from the west

95

RIGHT
This pool, known as the Channel, on beat number three, is one of the river's most productive and beautiful. Ponies graze against a backdrop of snow-capped peaks, while the gentle currents flow through ribbons of grass, making this a magical place.

side, or low side of the river, except that relatively few salmon tend to lie to that side of a potent whitewater current which more or less bisects the pool. And while it's also easy enough for a skillful angler to cast most of the way across the meat of the pool, that midstream surge causes your flies to bolt so quickly from east to west that it's unlikely many salmon in the prime lies even see the flies, much less are inclined to chase them. So, for your best shot at Núpafossbrún salmon, you have no choice but to fish from three flat-topped *hraunpallar*, or "platforms" of lava which are part of the *höfði*, or bluff, which, in turn, is part of that *núpur*, or hill of grass, rock and blueberry bushes which rises steeply several hundred feet behind you on the east side of the pool. Or to fish *klöppunum*, that is, "from the cliffs," as some Icelanders like to put it, which loom over Núpafossbrún's real hotspots.

Now, except for the fact that you have to cast about as much up-and-down as sideways just to reach the water, to fish Núpafossbrún effectively – unless maybe you're a severe acrophobe – is probably not as difficult as mastering enough of the Icelandic language to describe the setting at all colorfully and make yourself read smartly. You can't see them, even from such height, but the salmon are always lying right there in front of you, and unless you try to cast too far, which would defeat your purpose for fishing from there in the first place, there's plenty of room between the *hraunpallar* and the *núpur* for a backcast.

Picture yourself standing high over this water, tight to a salmon and knowing that should that salmon decide to leave the pool, either it's gone, simple as that, or you're in for the adventure of your lifetime when you try to scramble down the rocks and under the bridge on a narrow catwalk immediately adjacent to the reality of death in the form of furious water and potentially murderous boulders. That will give you some idea of why taking a fish at Núpafossbrún has to be Laxá's ultimate thrill and crowning achievement, not for the awkward afoot or faint of heart.

And given this, you can probably also understand why I'm so goddamned frustrated by the fact that virtually everyone with whom I've fished Núpafossbrún over the last quarter century – from my first Laxá fishing partner, the late Dave Danzig, back in 1972, to my present fishing partner, Galen Mercer, just a couple of years ago – has tasted that experience. Everyone, that is, except yours truly.

Hell, Dave took a pair of 22-pound males in one week, both perfect "gentlemen" who fought the good fight but never even threatened to depart the premises, while Galen hooked and landed a nice sixteen-pound cock the very first time he ever laid eyes on the spot. Then, to add insult to injury, I began raising a good

ABOVE *Pétur Steingrímsson, a famous Icelandic guide, shares a few of his secrets with a visiting fisherman. He often "wears" his favorite patterns.*

Núpafossbrún salmon just seconds after Galen's fish was safely in guide Volundur Hermodsson's net, a salmon that "looked" eight times at an array of flies without taking before I finally had to call it a night (notwithstanding all onlookers kindly ignoring their wristwatches), since the blinkin' fish was still teasing me a full fifteen minutes after Iceland's statutory 10 pm quitting time. Even when desperate, you can only stretch the rules so far.

But I'm a confident salmon fisherman in the main and have always believed, despite a superstitious streak rooted no doubt either in the sod of Ireland or the clans which fought the border wars between England and Scotland, or both, that one day I'd hook my Núpafossbrún salmon while "standin' tall" on one of those *hraunpallar* high over the pool, and that my fish would be a "whopper." I blush to think how many times I've envisioned the perfect take, the ensuing battle of such epic proportions, including, of course, the risk of life and limb, as to one day prompt some brooding Icelandic poet on a dark winter day to pen the Artúr Núpafossbrún Saga which would forever after take its leatherbound place alongside the Njálssaga, the most famous of them all, the Gisla saga Súrssonar, on which a nifty period flick called *The Outlaw* was made, and the forty-odd other sagas for which this island nation of Viking heirs is renowned.

However, dreams are dreams and reality is reality, and so it was when I found myself faced with Núpafossbrún once again last August, I allowed my soul to slip from the former place to the latter, something a salmon fisherman should never, never do, at least not entirely. In other words, I took to the *hraunpallar* with more emphasis on the exercise of memory of past failures than on the exercise of hope, and aren't "the infinite opportunities to exercise hope," after all, as John Buchan reminded us so brilliantly, why we're really doing it in the first place?

BELOW *A Garry Dog.*

I had two rigged rods in the rod racks on the car roof: one a fourteen-footer for a number ten line and a 2.5-to-1 multiplying reel with the most potent drag I've ever used; the second, a rod of the same length but for a number nine line and carrying a reel with a basic, though certainly sound, pawl drag. Riding in the car, I had already asked Galen to permit me first shot at the *hraunpallar* side of Núpafossbrún and had decided to tackle it with the stouter stuff for obvious reasons. But something also told me that I wanted to fish a Stardust fly, a pattern of my own design, the one on which I'd taken the 33-pounder from Laxá several years earlier. At this point, I'd have to guess now, my soul was still more or less in trim.

But then upon alighting from the car, I looked up at the roof and what fly pattern do you suppose was already cinched pretty as you please to the lighter

outfit? Yup, a Stardust, a new one sparkling in a shaft of sunshine that burst through a hole in the clouds of this generally overcast afternoon. How distinctly I remember looking at the fly which seemed to sing in the bright light, then at both rods and knowing what I ought to do. But instead of taking the, what, one minute necessary to transfer the Stardust from one tippet to the other, I opted to utter the unforgivable, "Might as well grab the light rod, Steini [Steini Stefansson, my guide]. You and I both know I never catch any salmon here anyhow."

Galen and I may have discussed the what–iffiness of my decision for a moment. I don't recall now. What I do know is that there was no Sibyl present, either within or without me, to remind me as Virgil wrote in *The Aeneid*: "Easy is the descent to hell . . . but to return, to regain the outer air, now that is the rub, that is the task."

And so I crossed the narrow bridge over the torrent at the tailout of Núpafossbrún with light rod and pawl reel at shoulder arms, probably humming a Sinatra tune. Oblivious.

ABOVE *The boat pool on lower beat number one bathes in hillside reflections on a quiet summer evening.*

Reaching the first *hraunpallar*, the favorite lava platform of Icelandic wormers, the water looked black as always beneath me and wildly white at midstream. I stripped just enough line off the reel to reach the water perhaps fifteen feet below and began fishing much as one would do when covering any salmon pool with a wet fly – short to long – until after ten or so arm-length pulls of line, my Stardust was landing all the way out in the heavy current, then sweeping smoothly inboard towards me. Nothing showed and so I reeled in and picked my way along the precarious dirt path between the rocks to *hraunpallar* number two, the platform from which every angler in the universe, it seemed to me, had hooked a Núpafossbrún salmon but me.

Again, I stripped the five or six pulls of line needed to reach Laxá's surface, and once again began extending one pull per cast after the fly had swept the water to the base of the lava *höfði*, the bluff. From high over the water I could clearly see the fly, its dark silhouette planing just below the surface.

Whether it was on line-pull number four or number five that she came, I cannot tell you now for sure. But I can tell you that it was on a very short line and that I could see her clearly, polished silver rising out of the pitch to inhale my swinging fly. So close that I could also see that she was a she not a he, that she weighed at least 25 pounds, and that she was as fresh from the sea as fresh could be. So close that even as I tightened on her, I had that first inkling, born of fighting more salmon than it might be seemly to say, that I was in big trouble as the result of having made a big mistake. In fact, perhaps the best way to sum up my position, even as early as this moment, lies in guide Steini's concise assessment: "Oh shit."

Now before proceeding to center ring, much less into the clinches or against the ropes, there are a few things you ought to know about the August salmon of Laxá I Adaldal in general and those which hold in Núpafossbrún in particular.

First, is that most of big Laxá's females arrive early, or from late June through mid-July. A fresh August female is real rarity, not to mention a real prize. Second, is that Laxá hens exceeding twenty pounds are also relatively uncommon, regardless of the period. Third, most of the Laxá's largest salmon are males which, for whatever reason, whether they're fresh or not, simply don't fight nearly as hard as the river's females. Or put another way, to play a twenty-plus pound Laxá female is arguably comparable to doing battle with a fresh forty-pounder on most great salmon rivers, no mean feat, even when optimally tackled.

That's the "downside." The "upside" is that gaining entrance to Núpafossbrún is so hard-earned for any salmon that once in the pool, most are

FAR LEFT *One afternoon I tore myself away from the fishing and climbed into the hills for a bird's-eye view of the spectacular surrounding countryside.*

BELOW *A discussion of tackle and technique draws a curious crowd. The pool in the background is that described by Art Lee in the essay. The falls drop away under the bridge.*

LEFT *A Rusty Rat.*

RIGHT *A Silver Doctor.*

disinclined to leave it, even in the heat of battle. Time and again, I've seen fish tear right to the brink, only to suddenly reverse course as if to say: "Even getting caught is better than going through that again." And so if your salmon is small enough to be easily handled or a typical fish, though big perhaps, you have a reasonable chance of ultimately seeing it in the net.

Given a big, fresh female fish, however, all bets are off, a reality I recognized only too well from the outset.

The early rounds of this fight were at once promising and sobering in that, after a few head shakes characteristic of most salmon after the take, the fish ripped off across the river and upstream, rather than down – indicating on the one hand she might hang around, while on the other, instantly underscoring my blunder back at the car, as my pawl reel, drag-tightened to the max – was literally shrieking, even as I burned my fingertips while trying desperately to slow her down a little by creating additional break.

What is more, though I was stationed over the water, she had already managed to bury my line, which became acutely evident when, high in the pool, she leapt through the foam – a glorious sight – then turned and tore downstream again to a point not far from that at which she had taken the fly. Me? At that moment my total preoccupation was trying desperately to get back some line.

Planted as I was atop a *hraunpallar*, I had nowhere to go, after all, not as you do when you're playing big fish under "normal" circumstances, say from a gravel beach or grassy bank. Certainly no putting the rod over your shoulder and walking upstream, your fish following like an obedient pooch. All I could do was to hold on and think, use rod pitch and angles and adjustments of hook pressure points in hopes of convincing her that what I wanted, no, *needed* her to do – to stay abreast or above me – also represented her best chance of escape.

But talk about chancy. Which way do you go? Do you angle your rod to the left, that is, upstream, for instance, fancying that she'll take the hint; or go for broke and angle it downstream, or toward the tail of the pool and

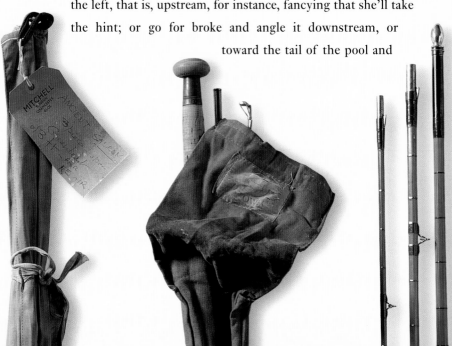

the maelstrom below, praying she'll believe you want her to go that way and so play into your hands by doing the opposite?

I opted for the former, but it made no difference, as she went neither up nor down, but instead raced directly across the pool where she made two more stunning jumps before once more allowing me to pump and reel her back almost to the point at which we'd first met.

And then she did what I guess I somehow knew she would do from the very outset. Side-on to me, she began to edge away, until at about midstream, she turned slowly inboard, that is, toward me, then suddenly bolted downstream for the tail of the pool. There, after only the briefest hesitation during which time she turned again to face upstream deep in the hole just ahead of the crevasse up through which she had no doubt swum into Núpafossbrún perhaps as recently as that very day, she turned once more and rushed down the shoot into the churning white water below. I can only wish now that you could have heard my reel beg for mercy as fly line and backing melted away, seemingly heading for sea faster that you'd want to drive a car on a good lava road.

I hope I wasn't born on the back of the train, and so by the time Steini and Galen were at my side, I had already struggled my way down the rocks to a point no more than five or six feet from the water raging over the lava plate, even as

BELOW *This is the moment of truth and high anxiety. Can the angler apply enough pressure to draw the fish into the net without breaking the leader?*

backing continued to seethe from my reel. There was no sign of fly line at all anymore. But it's funny, isn't it, how your mind can focus on two things at once without drifting, even in a crisis? And so whereas I was confident I could get the fish if I could just make it under that bridge, I was struck by a vivid memory of my longtime Icelandic friend Ingvi Jónsson, or Ingvi Rafn ("Black Raven") as we still call him, wending his way under the bridge with great difficulty when we were both 25 years younger and considerably less copious at the midriff.

"I've got to try to follow her," I told Galen nonetheless.

"You can't," Galen shouted over the roar of the foss. "The catwalk is too narrow, and if you go in, you could be done for. I'm not sure I could do it." Galen is twenty years younger than me and agile as a cat.

"I've got Steini," I shouted. Steini, a nickname related to the Icelandic word *steinn*, or stone, fits the moniker perfectly. In his late twenties, he looks like an NFL Pro-Bowl guard and is well known as the "bouncer" upon whom the local police rely to bail them out when they get into trouble trying to handle the worst offenders among huge crowds of boozing young people drawn from miles around to local dances. "He can hang onto me."

"And you'll probably both go in. Steini's strong, but he's no ballet dancer," Galen said just loud enough for me to hear. But his jaw was set. "If you want, I'll take the rod and try to go under, but you, no way."

ABOVE *This happy angler proudly displays his first Laxá salmon – a memorable moment.*

All anglers, it would be hoped, have certain quasi-religious principles, and one of mine is, "Thou shalt never pass a rod." Whether bluegill or blue marlin, if it's not one-on-one, it isn't sport. To pass a rod disgraces both fisherman and fish. But on the other hand, I had never lost a fly line to a fish of any species or size and this, too, had taken on some religious significance over the years. So perhaps you can sympathize with my quandary, as staring downstream, the only fish on earth that mattered a whit to me at that moment was adding insult to injury by taking her Nemesis' colors as she widened the distance between us. But the most depressing part of all was the realization that Galen had been absolutely correct – that for the first time in my long career astream, there was something truly beyond me, something I could no longer do and be sure of living to scribble the tale for you to read later.

Meantime I had not even noticed my reel's sudden silence, and as I glanced down the bank at the very brink of the shoot, there was Steini, my backing in hand, pulling it toward him hand over hand with all his strength. "It does not matter," he called back over his shoulder with the look of the greatest kindness and deepest

sympathy I have ever witnessed on the face of a guide. "The fish did cut off on the rocks down there and has been gone for a long time. Shit."

"I wonder how often Denissoff felt like I do when he owned the Åaro 'Platforms'?" I muttered to no one in particular as the three of us crossed the bridge on our way back to the car. Beneath us the funneled-down Laxá continued to rage toward a broad and gentle pool not far downstream.

"Sometimes, but for him, there was always tomorrow," Galen answered over Laxá's roar, and Steini nodded, although it's unlikely the young Icelander had ever heard of the onetime finance minister to Russia's last Czar, or the salmon of the short but mighty Norwegian river which had tested his will and tortured his tackle until the day he died.

ABOVE *Guide Pétur Steingrímsson and visiting angler Bill Young share a moment of camaraderie on the walk back to the lodge. It's been a good day.*

105

Grimsa Journal

Iceland

NICK LYONS

"Each day you learn a bit more. The salmon react in a new way, striking in the lower end of the pool, in the slick; you learn the slow and steady Crossfield retrieve for water without sufficient current to swing the fly, or how to vibrate your rod horizontally to induce a take. You cast a bit better and you learn the virtue of careful casting by the increased interest the fish show when your flies land three inches rather than ten from the far bank. When the salmon roll or jump you think of dry flies – but they won't work here any more than you'll find a mosquito: bad trade."

SUNDAY NIGHT: Salmon. There are salmon everywhere: salmon leaping the falls behind the lodge, their force astonishing; salmon and salmon rivers – this year's, last year's – in everyone's talk; smoked and poached salmon on the table; on the wall, old and new photographs of men with notable salmon; salmon statistics in the log, with pool, fly, and size listed; salmon in my dreams.

And at dinner, at eleven o'clock, after the first evening of fishing, almost everyone said they had taken a few. Schwiebert took one ten minutes after we got to the river – a bright six-pounder in one of the lower pools. Dick Talleur said he was no longer "a virgin": he had taken his first, lost a second. Joe Rosch, who had never fished for them, brought back two – one better than twelve pounds. He said his hands and knees were shaking after it was netted; he said that, from the excitement, he had fallen flush into the river.

The Grimsa is low but it is filled with salmon. Ten times this afternoon, before we fished, I walked back to the falls, where salmon – some small, some perhaps ten to fifteen pounds – were making their headlong, vital, terrible, exultant leaps at the top of the rush of white water. In the foam and swirl below the falls you could see a tail, a back, flick black out of the white boil. How bright and powerful they are. One four-pounder kept missing the falls and leaping smack into wet lava. I do silly things, too, when caught in the spawning urge.

I have never fished for salmon, but I am catching salmon fever. Perhaps I won't get any. Tonight I was bewildered. I made cast after cast with my #10 rod and double-hooked Blue Charm: across and downstream, then a little half-step and another cast across and downstream. Nothing. Nothing whatsoever. The worst of it was that fish were jumping, coming clear of the water and falling back every few minutes. Big fish. Bigger fish than I had ever seen in a river. Sleek, silver, determined fish. I had not a tick. I went back over my beat four times and moved not one fish.

After a spell, inching downriver along the lava and lava-rubble bottom, watching the crystalline water that appears devoid of all life but for the salmon, you begin

BELOW *Doug Larsen casting a long line in the wading pool of Beat 1 on a morning when the river was full of fish.*

BELOW *A Blue Charm.*

RIGHT *The blue boat in midstream casts a Laxá Blue or maybe a Hairy Mary for the reluctant salmon.*

RIGHT *A beautiful summer day on the river – hot and still – good for pictures, not for fishing.*

to think you will never catch one of these fish. There seems so little logic to it. Sparse once told me: "By God, the beggar isn't even feeding when he's in the river. If a fish rises to my fly, I want to know why." I have not the slightest notion how to get these mysterious fish to move. Even the flies have strange names: Blue Charm, Black Fairy, Thunder and Lightning, Hairy Mary, Green Butt, Silver Rat. In sizes #6 to #10, double-hooked. Which to use?

Still, what a lot of fun we have had so far. We got to Reykjavik at nine Saturday morning, slept, and walked through the closed town (except for Talleur, who is training for the Montreal marathon and *ran* a short ten miles). The city, built mostly of concrete, since there are few trees, is quaint, even charming. Woolens, silverwork, and ceramics are the chief wares – and they're very handsome. Then we had dinner at Naust, which Ernest said was the finest restaurant in Iceland. The place is like an old sailing ship, with round windows and nameplates of old ships at each table. We ate graflax – which is raw salmon treated with herbs, buried in the earth, then served with mustard and brown-sugar sauce – and then the others chose grilled baby-lobster tails, an Icelandic specialty; I had British beef and we all drank a lot of wine and then had ice cream and brandy. Ernest told us about the early witch hunts in Iceland, which ended when someone said: "Hey, you fellows are killing off the most interesting girls in town." And Dan Callaghan told one about a guy who ate a couple of stoneflies, washed them down with a glass of wine, paused, and said, "The wine's not right." Talleur was there, and Bob Dodge (who's paired with me for the week), and Bob Buckmaster, who has read and loved Plunket-Greene's *Where the Bright Waters*

Meet, and any man who's liked that book I know I am going to like. Anne and Dick Strain, the Perry Joneses, and Joe Rosch, the others in our party, ate elsewhere. We are from Iowa and Albany, New York City and Bellefontaine, North Carolina and Oregon, and we are all in pursuit of this fish bright from the sea, about which I know less than nothing.

The two-hour bus trip from Reykjavik to the Grimsa Lodge this morning wound past the Hvalfjord, which served as an American naval base during the war, and into the Iceland landscape, which is stark, treeless, and curiously beautiful.

Now it is 11.30 and we are settled into the well-appointed lodge that Schwiebert built and there is still light in the sky and I am exhausted. I am also high-keyed, tense. I know this kind of intense fishing. It will be necessary to catch a fish or two before the edge is off. Maybe tomorrow.

MONDAY AFTERNOON: Got my first salmon late this morning on Beat 3, the Strengir. I had fished hard since seven o'clock, casting across and downstream time after time. Buckmaster had given me a crash course on how to tie and fish the riffle hitch. An interesting technique. Since the fly is visible, the take is more dramatic than when the fly is fished conventionally. After a few hours I tried it and an hour later saw a good fish flash. I held back my impulse to strike, then struck and felt him.

The fish went to the bottom of a heavy riffle, shook its head, and sulked for five minutes. I could not budge it. Then it went a bit upstream, then down into the next pool. And in ten more minutes, Gumi, our gillie, netted it. I was thrilled to get a first salmon, a seven-pounder, but, except for the force of the thing, disappointed in the fight. It had not jumped. It had not taken me into the backing. "Brown salmon," said Buckmaster at lunch. "He's been in the river too long. They don't eat, you know, and lose something every day." This not-eating inspired me. I wished I could learn how to not-eat for three months at a stretch. But the food at the lodge – heaping plates of lamb, halibut, salmon, potatoes, and irresistible desserts – is too good.

I got another fish soon after the first, about four pounds, then struck a fish bright from the sea. It went off like a firecracker, leaped, got below me, let me get below it, and finally I beached it. A good morning. The edge is off.

Fished with Buckmaster this afternoon. What a lot of fun he is to be with. Peppery. Wise about salmon. Full of stories. We were on a difficult pool called, with good reason, "Horrible." Bob uses only a fly he ties called the Iowa Squirrel Tail, in fairly large sizes, with a riffle hitch, and he was determined to get one. He cast long and with great skill and then riffled the fly into the slick before a falls. Nothing. Then we went upstream with Topy, his gillie, and the two of them coached me into catching a small sea trout. Bob went back to "Horrible" and worked hard for more than an hour but caught nothing. Still, we'd found a lot to laugh about and the company was awfully good, so the afternoon was a delight. "There's more to fishing than to fish."

"What you're looking for," Schwiebert said, "is a salmon with an itch." I have been looking awfully hard. I don't even know what day it is. My right hand is becoming locked in the casting position, and at night I can feel the thrust of the Grimsa against me and inside me that rhythmic, endless pattern of casting across and downstream, inching forward a half-step, then another cast, then watching the fly rise and sweep across with that pretty little "vee." I've caught nothing in several sessions now, and the wind has become raw, snarling. My casting hand is blotched and swollen from sun and wind and a certain lunatic look has come into my eyes.

Anne and Dick Strain invited me to fish with them this afternoon and I did, on the Strengir again. Anne is avidly looking for new species of birds and is a fount of information about them and about the flora. She pointed out the alpine thyme

BELOW *Mike Fitzgerald casting a long line over the reflecting waters of the Laxá I Adaldal.*

clustered in small patches of bright purple everywhere, cotton-grass, yellow hawk-weed, and pink thrift. I can recognize the whimbrel, with its long curved bill, and the arctic tern.

Dick took two good fish in the last of the five Strengir runs, then, exhausted from casting my heavy rod into the wind, I lent it to him: whereupon he promptly took a third salmon. I tried for another hour but raised not a fish. Then Sven, their gillie, came by and I lent him the rod: whereupon he promptly hooked a good salmon. They called it the Lucky Rod. I have begun to wonder if my first three salmon weren't flukes. Will I ever get another?

Fishing intensely, you grow not to see yourself. Ernest told me at lunch that salmon fishing makes manic-depressives of us all. I feel low. Is it because Bob Dodge got such a fine bright fish this morning, then another, while I got none? I hope not. I enjoyed watching him fight that fish for nearly a half-hour, then net it. It was about nine pounds and terribly strong, and it jumped and ran and when he finally had it his hands were trembling. We took a dozen photographs of him there on Beat 1, holding the fish by the tail, with the falls and the lodge in the background. His excitement was irrepressible. He went up to the lodge, got some scotch, which we all drank riverside, and said, "If I don't get another fish this week, I'll be satisfied."

But this afternoon I feel low, and it is apparently visible, and I still wonder if I'll ever get another salmon.

More snarling wind and cold but no rain. I got one seven-pound fish, the only salmon of the afternoon by anyone in the party. Is it Tuesday?

Every morning we breakfast, a few at a time, as we get up. A buffet of bread, butter, marmalade, sardines in tomato sauce, cereal, and black coffee is laid out, and we can add two eggs cooked to order with ham or bacon. I always sit facing the window, where I can watch the water and the falls. Fewer salmon are leaping now. We need rain.

Then we rouse our partner, head to the wet room, and put on waders and vest. It is cold in the morning and I have been wearing a cotton shirt, a Cambrian Flyfisher's sweater, and an ochre guide's shirt; yesterday I had to add a scarf. Everyone else has felt soles on their waders, which hold well on the lava; I wear my cleated soft-aluminum and felt rubbers, which have proved excellent.

RIGHT *The quiet peacefulness of the lovely Laxá I Adaldal will linger for ever in your memory.*

Our gear is virtually what you would use for large trout: a rod for an 8 line (which I have switched to from my 10), 18-pound test backing (which no one has needed yet), and a heavy leader, 12-pound test and up. The best flies have been the Blue Charm, Rusty Rat, Collie Dog, and Black Tube, all on a double hook, in the smaller sizes.

You learn to fish the lies, not the rise. You begin to *see* the line in your dreams as the week progresses and you rotate beats. Fishing until ten, then talking another few hours, then rising early and spending long hours on your feet, everyone gets tired. Joe has started to skip supper. Some of us have skipped part of a morning's fishing, others rest when their turn at "Horrible" comes. Talleur rested by running sixteen miles yesterday.

In the mornings at seven, and then again at four, the gillies wait outside the wet room. Most of them speak English reasonably well; only Ernest, among us, speaks some Icelandic, which someone told me is not a language but a throat disease.

Each day you learn a bit more. The salmon react in a new way, striking in the lower end of the pool, in the slick; you learn the slow and steady Crossfield retrieve for water without sufficient current to swing the fly, or how to vibrate your rod horizontally to induce a take. You cast a bit better and you learn the virtue of careful casting by the increased interest the fish show when your flies land three inches rather than ten from the far bank. When the salmon roll or jump you think of dry flies – but they won't work here any more than you'll find a mosquito: bad trade. You learn to shorten your leader to seven feet, 16-pound test, against stiff wind, and that this does not bother the fish a whit. When a salmon is on, you have a fish with saltwater size and power in trout-stream conditions, and you remember that Earl West told you to play these fish hard, that a half-minute's rest and you have a fresh salmon on again – so you add more pressure and are amazed that you have not yet lost a fish among the five – or is it six? – you've caught so far.

You watch Schwiebert carefully. He is deft, economical, wise about this river. He teaches you the lies and how much skill truly matters. He knows the history of each pool.

And, knowing the river itself more intimately each day, you look forward with greater expectation to the rotation of the beat. You know the beats better and you have more confidence that you can do this thing. This morning we have Beat 5, which has been fishing extremely well. I think about that as I step out of the wet room and walk with Bob toward Gumi's car.

Joe looked shaken tonight. He had lost a big salmon. Very big. He had seen the fish roll just above the falls of Beat 3 and had tied on a small Blue Charm, cast slightly

upstream, mended twice, and watched the huge fish take it solidly. The salmon leaped, raced upriver, settled into the pool, then, after ten minutes, leaped again and headed for the falls. Joe decided to try to turn him and the fly pulled free. Now he thinks he should have let the fish go down the falls; he charted the route and thinks he could have followed it. There was much talk and the consensus was that this would have been wisest. The gillie thought the fish would have gone twenty pounds, perhaps more.

Joe was shaken but he has caught an unforgettable memory.

I am fishing his beat tomorrow and asked him to map out the spot. Still no rain.

An interesting afternoon with Bob Dodge. We fished a long flat stretch the others call "The Lake." Perhaps sixty or more salmon are stacked up here, waiting for higher water, and Dan Callaghan and Perry Jones have taken good fish here. Bob went across stream, inched over to the lip of the bluff, and served as "point man" for me. But I could not, though I cast over the salmon many times, move any of them.

Later we went upriver and each took a good fish in broken water. We are beginning to know a bit more about the river and about salmon fishing, and we have at least some confidence that anyone who can use a fly rod reasonably well can take fish. Iceland is not the moon and salmon fishing is not astro-physics.

A flash of bright silver. The fly turning out of the eddy, buffaloing downstream. The tooled lunge. Up, out of the black near the rock he came, into white water, his back curved and turning. Up and out and then down on the fly as it gained speed and began to zip. I waited. And waited. There! I struck, felt the fish throb, and then he careened off, down toward the rapids. Forty, fifty feet of line. Sixty. The first foot of backing came through my fingers.

Then he stopped, shook his head, started off again, and leaped, smashing the water, shaking, and falling back.

Fifteen minutes later I had him on my side of the river. I looked up and saw a dozen cars lined along the bridge, watching. The salmon jumped again, ten feet from me. Ten minutes later he turned to his side and I led him to shallow water. The fish was ten pounds, bright silver, and bolted off when I disengaged the fly.

It is Thursday.

FRIDAY NIGHT: I tailed my first salmon today, a nine-pounder from Beat 5. Dick Talleur was there and got out his camera.

"No!" I called to him, hiding my face. "I've made my reputation by not-catching fish."

"No one deserves a fish like that more than you, Nicky," he said, "after all your family disasters."

"My reputation …"

"I won't blackmail you," he said, clicking off a couple of shots.

When I had gotten a good grip on the salmon's tail, I raised the fish high and kept it high, and kept smiling, long after Dick had stopped shooting.

A little later, upriver, I had four good strikes and could not come up with a fish. Buckmaster kept asking if I was striking too fast. "No," I said, after checking my fly, after discovering that I had busted off both points on the double-hooked fly, "just fishing not wisely but too true to form."

Anne Strain has seen and identified twenty-six different birds, including the gyr-falcon, red-necked phalarope, black-tailed godwit, white wagtail, turnstone, merlin, arctic redpoll, and wheatear. I like the names. I should watch the water a bit less, the sky more. It is strangely beautiful here – spare, the meadows in varying shades of green, spotted, white, and brown Icelandic ponies drinking at the river, the gray streaks of lava everywhere, the snow-splotched mountains, the vast Montana-like space, that little red-roofed Lutheran church on the hillside, the neat farms, sheep everywhere, places where you can look up a valley at four, five water-falls, one over the other, silver in the sunshine, sunsets the color of salmon flesh, and the light, the light that is always here, even late into the night, making the days longer, fuller.

ABOVE *Full of expectation, an angler walks out to the river on his last evening.*

SUNDAY MORNING: I am exhausted. We leave for the plane in an hour.

Last night Talleur and Buckmaster asked me to go to a local dance with them. Bob wanted to know more about the people. I realized that all I know of Iceland was Snorri Sturluson and *Egil's Saga*, read in graduate school, and that the country had 222,000 people, rampant inflation, gorgeous sweaters, and great salmon rivers. We left at one o'clock at night, in a Land Rover packed with young gillies, the cook, and a couple of pretty girls working at the lodge.

BELOW *A Sweep.*

Images: the jammed dancehall and Bob Buckmaster, who is past sixty-five, doing a convincing hustle or rope or robot or whatever it's called; the blinking lights; rock in Icelandic; the young eager faces; Talleur breaking training with a vengeance; the trip back at five in the morning, as the light broke, drinking bitter Brennivin (known locally, and for good reason, as "the black death"), watch-ing thermal geysers and meandering salmon rivers taking the first glints of light, and all singing, at the top of our lungs, in English, "When the Saints Come Marching In."

Then Bob Dodge and I were out at seven, because we had the most productive beat, and I could hardly stand. But I took a good salmon quickly and that seemed a good way to end matters. "Take up your swords," I rumbled, "the morning dew shall rust them," gave my rod to Gumi, and leaned back in the car to dream of the terrible swift strike of the salmon.

Meanwhile, Bob hit into a slew of salmon with an itch, had ten good strikes, missed a few, hooked and lost a few, and took four fish. A better way to end matters.

Now we're packed and ready to leave. It has been a splendid, memorable week. Too brief. Schwiebert and Callaghan caught the most fish, over twenty each, and Anne Strain got a magnificent nineteen-pounder that struck at ten o'clock and fought her until after eleven last night. I got enough.

There is already talk of coming back. The phrase "trip of a life-time" has been used. There is talk about the effect of this place.

But is Talleur really serious about training on graflax and peanut butter?

BELOW The rocky ledges of the Grimsa River epitomize the stark, barren, windswept image of Icelandic salmon fishing.

ICELAND: FACTFILE

BACKGROUND

"The Land of Ice and Fire", as Iceland is some-times known, is an extraordinary country. In this raw and desolate landscape, it feels very much as though the forces that shaped it are still at work. There are some hundred or so rivers in Iceland that hold salmon, the best of which are located on the north and west coasts, with a handful on the south coast. Almost half of these are classified as first-class rivers, capable of yielding prodigious numbers of fish to rod and line.

While many rivers are privately owned, the Government places its own regulations on the fish-ing. For example, strict controls govern the number of fishermen allowed to fish each river. So when analysing catch statistics, fishermen should always enquire how many "rod-days" are actually fished in a season.

As the world has noticed diminishing catches of Atlantic salmon, so the Icelanders have become ever more aware of the measures necessary to conserve them. "Catch and release" is no longer an alien phrase in Iceland; the law requires you to disinfect your tackle on entering the country to reduce risk of disease; and the hatchery work here is among the most advanced in the world. The Atlantic salmon-fishing world also owes one Icelander in particular a great debt: Orri Vigfussen has tirelessly cam-paigned for the removal of open sea and coastal nets throughout the salmon's range, resulting in a new worldwide public awareness of the plight of salmon.

Perhaps the most fascinating aspect of fishing in Iceland is that most of its rivers are crystal clear for much of the season. This offers fly-fishermen unrivalled opportunities actually to gauge the fish's reaction to each successive fly offered. There can be few greater thrills in Atlantic salmon fishing than watching the fish rise through water as clear as air and inspect the fly before inhaling it gently. Ner-vous first-timers often strike too soon, removing the fly from the fish's mouth.

WHEN TO GO

The season in Iceland varies from river to river, but generally starts at the beginning of June and ends in late August. The first two weeks of the season are

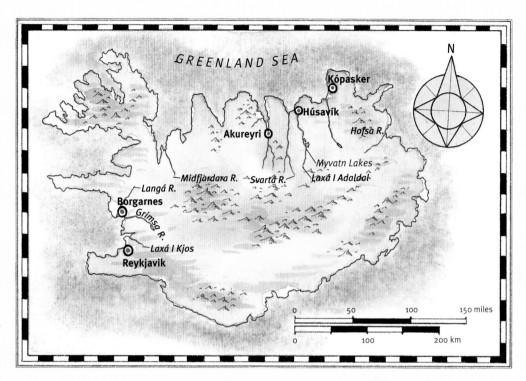

normally associated with high water levels and cold water temperatures owing to melting snow and ice from the catchment of each river. Conditions early on may require heavier sinking lines and big flies, but soon this fishing gives way to the more tra-ditional Icelandic style of floating-line fishing with small flies.

TACKLE

RODS: Single-handed 9 ft rods for 7–9 wt lines. Double-handed 12–14 ft rods for 8–10 wt lines.

REELS: Large arbor direct-drive fly reel with capac-ity for 150 yards of backing plus fly line.

LINES: Predominantly floating lines, but sinking lines early in the season.

LEADERS: 8–12 lb leaders are fine on most rivers.

FLIES: Black and Red Francis, small Collie Dog tubes, Hairy Mary, Blue Charm, Stoat's Tail, Munroe Killer, Red Butt, Green Butt, and an assortment of micro-tubes 0.25–0.5 cm.

FLIES 1 *Collie Dog* 2 *Curry's Shrimp* 3 *Orange Bucktail Shrimp* 4 *Ally's Shrimp (Tube)* 5 *Green Francis (Tube)* 6 *Sheila* 7 *Sunray Shadow* 8 *Sweep* 9 *Blue Charm* 10 *Red Francis*

OPPOSITE *A salmon for dinner lies in the moist green grass of the Laxá valley.*

Never on Sundays

Scotland

DAVID PROFUMO

"Running a fly down Rocky Cast one evening, there was a flash of grey flank and my small Stoat just below the surface was cancelled like a typing error. The Hardy Perfect made its corncrake rasp as the fish led us down to Fir Dam, where the universe opened along one of its seams and threw out a huge salmon into the air; the sun had gone as we arrived at the place called Paradise, then Mr Murray removed the champagne cork from his gaff-point and leaned over, there was a great convulsion in the margins, and he'd cleeked my prize."

ABOVE *An upstream view of the stunning Glencalvie beat of the River Carron in the Scottish Highlands.*

It didn't start with a salmon, it started with an eel – and I can recall it distinctly because it was the same year we almost burned the castle to the ground, and a French governess pushed my face into some scalding porridge. I was five, and my family had rented this place on Royal Deeside for the holidays. The night of the fire may have gone down in local history but for me the highlight of that summer was the day I first held a rod in my hands. It was a Japanese thing with a red plastic handle, and I lowered a lobworm into a little burn that was spating like gravy: the bootlace eel I hoiked out was my first fish, proudly displayed in the basin of the castle washroom until some adult demanded its removal.

Since then, although I am English, I have spent a happy proportion of my life up North and now I have a home just a raven's flight over the hills from the Dee. I have been lucky enough to fish for salmon in over thirty different Scottish rivers and loch

124

ABOVE *An afternoon break at the fishing hut on Fir Park pool on the River Dee.*

systems, and I have become an *aficionado*, an amateur, a lover of the sport (what I am not is an expert – a man who knows eighty-seven ways of making love, but can't find himself a girl). These days perhaps I feel a bit unfaithful when I conjure up salmon from an Icelandic foss, or even some chum bar in Alaska, but I always return to Scotland because this is where so much I associate with the culture of angling originally evolved – the floating line, the Spey throw, those malts – and whilst I admit her salmon are getting a bit thin on the ground I believe it is anyway the minor triumphs rather than the huge days that actually make fishing worthwhile.

To many people, fish are unappealing – coldblooded and uncuddly, even in the smaller sizes – but you can see why the salmon is one of the few to share the charisma of some of the terrestrial megafauna such as the elephant or deer. It is a glamorous creature, a nomad struggling up from the dark tides, swapping its silver

BELOW *A Sweep.*

BELOW *Gillie and fisherman discuss strategies on the River Oykel.*

for sackcloth, eventually wasting away in the headwaters of its own birth. Most societies require their fluvial myths, and this is heroic stuff – small wonder that the township of Peebles should derive its motto *Contra nando incrementum* ("There is increase by swimming against") from the spawning run of its local fish. Indeed, there are many parts of Scotland where the harvest of migratory fish once essential for the survival of tribes remains just as crucial to the health of local economies.

You can see this importance ritualized if we go to the very top of the River Tay in mid-January, where the long season opens with a blessing of the fleet. Kenmore, home of Scotland's oldest inn, is a little part of Scotland that the twentieth century forgot to spoil, and each wintry Opening Day there is a sizeable procession of folk marching down to the landing-stage accompanied by skirling pipes. As a sportsman I have a fondness for superstitious sequences designed to make things happen – from the icthyomancy of the Ancient Greeks to the custom of the Wonkgongaru Aborigines that requires their head man to pierce himself somewhere very painful and masculine, ceremonies before the hunt by water were once quite usual; there's no bodypiercing required at Kenmore, just the ladling into the stream of a dram from an ornate *quaich*. Then dozens of anglers can hurry off.

As our piscicidal century creeps to its close, the quest for a Scottish springer has become a bit of a unicorn hunt, but in its heyday the *locus classicus* for these big beauties was Loch Tay itself; I think the record for this hotel was Colonel Murray's thirty-one fresh fish averaging eighteen pounds (you used to pay the gillie three shillings and eightpence a day, plus a modest "allouance" of whisky to fuel him as he trolled you round the loch). These days as you send your wooden Devon strumming over some desirable residence in the river you're more likely to be rewarded with a pull from a spent *kelt*, or *baggart* (a salmon that has not shed her ova, sometimes known as a *thwarted matron*), but although these must naturally be returned unscathed they still give a thrill in the chill as they offer that first pulsing resistance against the current. I'm not one of those purists who'd rather stick his arm in an industrial log-chipper than use anything except a fly, but I do like to wave my rod about and I find the *harling* that goes on here a little dull. Mind you, this is Scotland's largest river and it can be a job to cover, especially in the lower reaches below Macbeth country, where its pools rejoice in names such as Fire Shot, Kill Moo and Rumbling Stane.

The Tay also has a history of huge fish unrivalled in Britain (the Wye in the 1930s might just have pipped it to the post), and it was here of course that our record salmon was landed by Miss Georgina Ballantine, a gillie's daughter, on October 7 1922; she killed it in the Boat Pool on Glendelvine Water after a struggle lasting two hours. She liked to recount how it was displayed in the window of Malloch's tackle shop in Perth and she overheard a local man say, "Nae woman ever took a fish like this … that's a lee, anyway!" Almost as intriguing is the saga of the fish lost by G.F. Browne, Bishop of Bristol, in 1868 just by the junction with the Earn. After ten hours the gut parted: one account ends, "Jimmy rows home without a word, and neither he nor the fisherman will ever get over it." It is said a fish was later netted downstream with the episcopal minnow in its mouth, and weighed seventy-one pounds.

I don't get to do much serious fishing in the summer, because we spend our time in the Outer Hebrides with our children, rummaging around in rockpools or pursuing sticklebacks with butterfly nets. But when I was growing up I had two wonderful angling mentors, and the summers meant salmon in Sutherland.

My uncle was a formidable, pipe-smoking sportsman practically stone deaf from flying open-cockpit aircraft in the Great War. He possessed a cartridge bag fashioned from the skin of a rogue lion he had once been obliged to shoot during his gubernatorial days in West Africa, and a hipflask capable of containing almost an entire bottle of whisky (he left both these heirlooms to me). Through his estate near the east coast ran the Fleet, one of those modest, unkempt spate rivers in which the Highlands abound, with a succession of bonsai pools that fished well for a few hours after each flood from July onwards, the grand total for that beat being perhaps a dozen salmon per season. Here at the age of twelve, after two summers of trying, I caught my first salmon – rather a tired grilse – from The Stepping Stones, using a Grant Vibration greenheart rod spliced with leather bindings. In attendance was the second mentor, Mr George Murray, my uncle's personal gillie.

As fishing guides go, the Scottish gillie is famously a race apart: some are genuinely water wizards, others are no better than reluctant caddies eager to guzzle your Scotch. Mr Murray – as I always called him – was a companion from Central Casting. His poker face, long considered the badge of a true Highland professional, hid both a sunny disposition and a pawky wit. During my teenage years as his sorcerer's apprentice I learned much from him – that you always refer to a salmon as "a fish", that a big fly can sometimes be effective in low water – but most of all he showed by example how one should always enjoy time spent on the water, irrespective of how the sport is going. This sounds obvious, but since then I've seen many anglers forget that the point is to have fun. From my hours spent with that quiet, gentle man I began to understand the paradox of fishing – how to accept both its illusion of treasure trove and the constant spectre of disappointment.

BELOW *A Crystal Ally's Shrimp.*

BELOW *A wee dram of fine whisky helps ease the pain of not catching a salmon on the Dee.*

OPPOSITE *A view downstream toward the Rock Pool on the River Oykel.*

Every other day – with the exception of Sundays, because of course no salmon fishing is allowed on the Sabbath – my uncle took a beat on the nearby Shin, a short hydro-controlled river that debouches into the Kyle of Sutherland alongside those other fine waters the Carron, Cassley and Oykel. Like them, it is a challenging river with formidable, bouldery pots and moiling chestnut-brown runs, not least of which is the celebrated Falls Pool itself, one of the most spectacular salmon leaps anywhere I know. To winkle out Shin fish you often had to hold your fly over a churning lie on a long rod (the sinuous Collie Dog lure was especially favoured), sometimes hanging off a rockface with your other hand. The salmon ran big for summer fish, too, and once you hooked one the commando tactics had only just begun. No fly-fishing could have been better designed to intrigue a fanatical teenager, and throughout those lank-locked, resentful years, when adults understood zilch and testosterone mood-swings clouded my vision, there was always the prospect of that river and its succession of roaring gorges.

Running a fly down Rocky Cast one evening, there was a flash of grey flank and my small Stoat just below the surface was cancelled like a typing error. The Hardy Perfect made its corncrake rasp as the fish led us down to Fir Dam, where the universe opened along one of its seams and threw out a huge salmon into the air; the sun had gone as we arrived at the place called Paradise, then Mr Murray removed the champagne cork from his gaff-point and leaned over, there was a great convulsion in the margins, and he'd cleeked my prize. It was a cock fish of twenty-one pounds, beaked like Punchinello. I have never forgotten the sight of him, squirming there on the metal, his great eye seeming to stare at me as he was hoist fatally into the half-light, a low gargling sound escaping from his throat. I was then fifteen years old.

Golden Ages are forever receding, and one can readily discover in the literature of the last century grumbles that the fishing is not what it was (the great fairy-tale collector Andrew Lang was at it, for instance, in his *Angling Sketches*, 1891); but few would deny that Scottish salmon fishing in the modern period is in a state of crisis. In addition to the high-seas netting, these stocks still have to contend with licensed drift-netters off the north-east coast of England, a disproportionate seal population, and now the threat of estuarial mariculture. The concentrations of parasitic lice around the salmon cages that clog the sea lochs of Scotland seem to be capable of damaging migratory fish in as yet unpredictable ways – several outbreaks of Infectious Salmon Anaemia were confirmed in 1998, the first ever in British fish farms.

ABOVE *George Ross, fishery manager on the River Oykel, puts the net under a fresh-run spring salmon.*

Meanwhile, to the amazement of many North American anglers who have been practising it for years, catch and release appears to be something that sharply divides the British game-fishing community, though our millions of coarse anglers have never found much problem with the concept. Old habits certainly die hard, but let's hope the salmon doesn't die out completely first.

Such are the years of tradition behind salmon fishing here that when I am wading in certain Scottish waters I am peculiarly aware of both the quick and the dead. It might be Wood on the Dee, Ashley-Cooper on the Spey, or any number of more anonymous forebears who have stood in a certain spot and watched the water jump up behind the same rock, but I am alive to their historical presence. (Sometimes I vaguely wonder if, a century hence, a similarly minded chap might recall how the present writer used to cast here with his superannuated carbon poles and manual reels, in the days when there were still wild fish, but the prospect of borrowed time is a gloomy one.) This sensation is strongest during my autumn visits to a fabled beat of the Middle Tweed, a river I have been privileged enough to fish during one of its prime weeks for the past twenty-two years. My historical fancy does not need much of a spur, for these are the very pools where William Scrope often cast while working on his *Days and Nights of Salmon Fishing* (1843), one of the few genuine classics on the subject; indeed each year, like the page of King Wenceslas, I tread in his steps, mindful of his warning "never go into the water deeper than the fifth button of your waistcoat", and to cease wading when the legs turn black. Scrope dwelt at Melrose, and was a close friend of the Laird of Abbotsford, Sir Walter Scott, whose novels (such as *Waverley* and *Rob Roy*) had done so much to make Scotland a voguish destination for angler-Saxons, restoring its clannish image tarnished to Southern eyes since the days of Jacobitism.

Autumn is anyway my favourite season here, with the slow fire of its colours burning through the leafscapes of beech and birch and the big stream rattling beneath sandstone cliffs of Tuscan pink. These borderlands look deceptively serene, though, and the land is steeped in the blood of Roman legionaries, reivers, moss-troopers and other feuding bandits; nearby the Scots murdered the last two Picts, to get their recipe for heather ale; in the distance rise the Eildon Hills, split into three by the Devil at the behest of Auld Michael Scot, the wizard who languishes in Dante's *Purgatorio*. Something of all this surely lingers, making the hand shake and the bloodstream tingle as your puny lure sweeps across the dark pools. Unless there is a rare drought – in which case I have to amuse my party with picnics and John Barleycorn – you expect to fish large, slow, deepish flies at this time of year, often Tweed-style from the back of a rowed boat. And so it was that I caught my largest-ever Atlantic here, a fish weighing twenty-eight pounds: a photograph of us hangs in the Rogue's Gallery at the Ednam House Hotel in Kelso, and I was so pleased with this achievement that I once drove a Dutch translator all the way down from Edinburgh, just to see the picture. When the autumn runs are on, the hallway of this famous hotel is sometimes paved with silver bodies awaiting

ABOVE *To reach some very enticing fishing pools in the gorge on the upper Kirkaig River requires a strenuous scramble.*

dispatch to the smokery, for the back-end Tweed salmon when absolutely fresh are amongst the finest of all Scottish fish.

It is in the still charming market town of Kelso that there lies buried another of my angling author-heroes, Thomas Tod Stoddart, who in his time (he died in 1880) was reputed to have fished more Scottish waters than anyone else; his diaries over fifty years suggest the taking of 67,419 fish, of which some 928 were salmon. He qualified at the law, but never found time to practise. In later life he was asked by one of his friends, who had risen to the rank of sheriff, what he was now doing. "Doing? *Doing?*" came the reply. "Mon, I'm an angler."

There is no guaranteed bonanza every autumn, of course, and more likely would be the experience I had not long ago, with John our able boatman. Fish were scarce, the river was thin and the colour of bitter ale, morale was low. He took me down to the Braes pool around teatime, and almost at once we had a tunk on the line, but the take never developed; at such times I always apply SWAG methodology (Scientific Wild-Assed Guess), so we changed the tube, and something must have looked slightly more plausible because a couple of casts later, as that fly came off the spine of the current, I felt a decent draw, the loop of line slipped through my fingers, and I was able to set the iron. The fish thrashed at once on the surface – seldom the sign of a good hook-hold – displaying a chrome fuselage of agreeable proportions, and I began to play him as gingerly as if I'd never before been attached to a salmon. After ten minutes of emotionally elastic time John murmured, "That's about grand now, sir", lifted the iron hoop of his massive landing-net, and there we had him, a cock of eighteen pounds, tideliced, my only catch of the week. "Not bad for a couple of amateurs," grinned John, who has worked on rivers since he was a boy. We walked back up to the cottage for a drink, comrades in arms.

Fishing stories should have a beginning, a middle and an end – though not necessarily in that order. Last year I drove my wife up to Deeside to revisit Braemar Castle, now a museum. Its stone stairwell and Rapunzel towers looked so much smaller than when I was a boy, but inside the door on the right was a souvenir shop that I was pretty sure had been the place. Yes, the lady serving there confirmed, it was originally the washroom, and there was the old marble basin. I knew it must have been nearly forty years since any boy left an eel there.

As an angler I sometimes think I may be on a quest for something that was lost, of which perhaps the fish is only a symbol.

ABOVE *The tea-colored waters of the Kirkaig flow down from the Scottish Highlands to the sea.*

LEFT *A lone angler admires the beauty of the upper Dee valley, as he prepares to cast.*

SCOTLAND: FACTFILE

BACKGROUND

If the English chalkstreams represent the birthplace of modern trout fishing, then Scotland, without question, is the place where most of the accepted techniques of fly-fishing for Atlantic salmon were developed. With an enormous wealth and diversity of rivers, from small highland spate streams such as the Kirkaig or Inver, to mighty systems like the Tay or Tweed, Scotland has long been recognized as one of the world's premier destinations for Atlantic salmon fishing.

Although there have been worrying declines in the numbers of returning fish over the past couple of decades, Scotland remains for many fishermen the quintessential Atlantic salmon-fishing experience. There can be few moments as rewarding in a fisherman's life as toasting success with a friendly gillie over a dram of whisky, while listening to the grouse calling from the heathered hillsides bordering the river.

WHEN TO GO

Precise legal dates vary according to the catchment being fished, but generally speaking the season starts around mid-January and ends in late November. Returning salmon and grilse in Scotland arrive at varying points of the season. Traditionally, the spring fish were the ultimate challenge. These fish are mature salmon, normally of high average size, that run any time between January and June. However, "spring fishing" seems to have been affected most by the recent declines in Scotland, with the result that now it is the summer run of salmon and grilse that makes up the majority of the most reliable fishing. On some of the larger rivers the autumn run of mature salmon is the final highlight of the season and with good volumes of water in the rivers (on which the fish can ascend a system), sport can be prolific until the last days of the season.

On many rivers in Scotland this autumn run of big fish has almost entirely superseded spring fishing, and it is also likely that this period will demand the highest rent and be hardest to gain access to. It is always wise to enquire early on if you wish to buy fishing during this time.

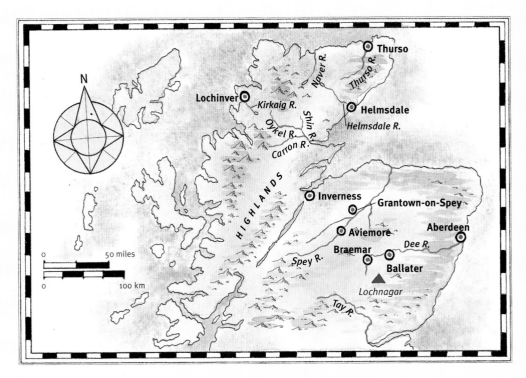

TACKLE

RODS: On smaller rivers, single-handed rods, 9–10½ ft for 7–9 wt lines. On larger rivers, double-handed rods, 12½–15 ft for 9–11 wt lines.

REELS: Large direct-drive reels with or without a drag system.

LINES: A broad selection (depending on water height and temperature), from floating through sink-tips and intermediate to fast sinking.

LEADERS: Lighter leaders, 8–12 lb, during the summer months, but as strong as 15–20 lb for heavier water and bigger fish in spring or autumn.

FLIES: Most rivers have favourites: speak to a local tackle shop or to your gillie. Size of fly is also a factor, dependent on water temperature and height. Keep a fly box stocked with small double- and single-hooked flies for summer, Waddingtons and tubes for spring/autumn. Patterns include Blue Charm, Black Ranger, Ally's Shrimp, Torrish, Dusty Miller, Munroe Killer, Silver Doctor and Green Highlander.

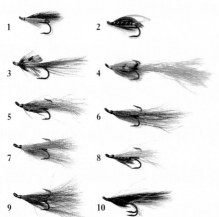

FLIES 1 *Arndilly Fancy* 2 *Sweep* 3 *Stewart Shrimp* 4 *Ally's Shrimp* 5 *Munroe Killer* 6 *Willie Gunn* 7 *Hairy Mary* 8 *Garry Dog* 9 *Silver Stoat* 10 *Crystal Sweep*

OPPOSITE *One evening while walking just below the junction of the Tweed and the Teviot, I spotted an angler with his rod bent double, obviously into a good fish. I ran down to the river bank just in time to capture this splendid picture of the hero and his prize.*

Mighty Mask

Ireland

DAVID STREET

"The wind was fine for dapping and patches of sunlight were starting to penetrate the clouds; if there was ever a time to fish the bluebottle, this was it. Bill changed rods and was soon dapping with the first of our two bluebottles. On the top of a rolling wave and against the vast expanses of the lough, it looked absurdly small, but, even at the distance he was fishing it, we could see the radiant splendours of its colours. Then, within minutes, a small circle showed on the wave's crest where the bluebottle had been riding – so quietly did the trout take."

ABOVE *A portrait of Dennis O'Keefe, my boatman and companion on Lough Sheelin, and his fly box. Both are truly exceptional – even brilliant – and I will never forget either one.*

LEFT *A Spent Gnat.*

Of the big limestone loughs on the western chain my favourite has to be Lough Mask to the north of Corrib – surely one of the world's great trout waters. On its eastern flank stretch the green plains of Mayo, which roll as pleasingly as the soft brogue on the local tongue. Above its western shore the blue Partry Mountains stand guard with the peaks of Joyce's Country showing clearly to the south. It is a vast expanse of water covering some 20,500 acres in all, ten miles long with an average width of around four miles.

It carries many enchanting islands as well as great reefs of rock which, being limestone, are jagged and needle-sharp, and some of these reach far into the middle waters of the lough, where one might expect the deepest places to be. Here they lie hidden just beneath the surface and sharp enough to pierce clean through the boat, making Mask no place for a newcomer to go charging about with an outboard engine.

There are days when the barometer rides high and the water looks innocuous enough, as it shimmers in a mirror-calm, but the weather can change quickly, as high winds sweep down from the Partry Mountains to transform it into a surging sea. The true Mask fisherman not only knows his lough in great detail, but also holds it always in a deep respect. It is, however, the presence of these reefs and shallows that makes the fishing, for they provide those superb long drifts over waters, varying in depth from three to ten feet, where trout to four pounds and more come readily to the fly.

It was Bill's invitation to join him at Ballinrobe for a week's fishing at the end of June that was my first introduction to the joys of Mask. Ballinrobe is a typical Irish country market town of much character and, by virtue of its position, in the middle of the eastern shore with its extensive shallows and rocky outcrops, is the natural centre for the fishing.

I joined him in Dublin and together we drove across Ireland, arriving in time to secure a boat for the week – Bill had his own outboard – and pick up a cylinder of Calor gas before pitching our tent in the soft evening rain by Caher Bay. Our routine was pretty basic and designed to give us maximum fishing time. The morning shave, bacon and egg breakfast, followed by a quick run into town to keep the camp larder stocked. I say "stocked" because our adversary turned out to be a stray dog, who prowled around our tent like the hosts of Midian, his mission to turn over our bin and to unstock our larder as quickly as he could. He had a great appetite for our steak suppers. With the chores completed, sandwiches made, camp secured and dog seen off, we would spend the day fishing our teams of wet flies down the long drifts of the lough.

Lunch would be taken on one of the many islands where we brewed the tea and sat amongst the random scatterings of limestone chips, which lay all around us, sharp and deeply fissured, and in all kinds of grotesque shapes. Cleaned and nicely mounted, some could have passed as works of modern sculpture. Bill, who has never lacked an eye for a quick bargain, set one up in the sand behind the fire and proclaimed it "The Violin Player", an early piece by Henry Moore, and I could see exactly what he meant. Sometimes other boats would be taking lunch as well, and it was good to compare notes on the morning's sport, and listen to improbable stories. Tea was always brewed in the "Volcano", an aptly named contraption that I have only ever found in Ireland. It is made of tin, the top part being filled with water from the lough and the base containing the little stick fire. Even on wet days the water comes quickly to the boil with the help of a little petrol from the outboard; the fresh tea has a tang about it that is far superior to the stuff from a thermos flask. I am sure the old Irish tinkers used to make them, and I would dearly love to get my hands on one. In my mind they are an integral part of a day's boat-fishing on the lough.

From his earlier exploits Bill had come to know the local boatmen – he was one of their number – as well as most of the fishing fraternity in the town, many of whom would gather for the evening jar in Luke's bar; and it was there that our footsteps would lead us before the day was out.

By the time we arrived at Luke's pub, it was as busy and full as ever. Luke was a fine-looking man of a somewhat military appearance and both he and his wife, Eileen, were excellent hosts. The bar they kept was full of character too, always dimly lit with ancient firearms glinting from the walls, for Luke was a keen collector of curios. It was a place of warmth and friendliness where conversation was what mattered – no nonsense here of fruit-machines or piped music. Luke was also a keen fisherman – he could hardly have been otherwise – with a special fondness for Lough Carra, a much smaller lough half a mile to the north-east of Mask.

ABOVE *An antique mayfly box, used originally for collecting live insects for dapping.*

I have heard Carra described as the most alkaline lake in Europe and I can well believe it. Its water is exceedingly clear, which is often disconcerting when you are fishing, as you tend to see the fish before they take the fly. The lough floor is a white sand and the rocks in the water are covered by a thick deposit of a soft, spongy marl, as if nature had fitted them with fenders. If you happen to hit a rock on Lough Mask it will possibly pierce the boat, but on Carra it is the rock that will be dented. The overall colour of the water is a yellowy green, like weak lime-juice, with the shades varying according to the depth, and much of the shoreline is fringed with large beds of reed.

RIGHT *Nick Zoll and Alex Mitchell engage in a tactical discussion in the* Sheelin Lady.

There were other evenings when Bill and I went straight to the pub after supper, before setting out once more on Mask to fish the sedge. After the day-time fishing it was somewhat eerie to be creeping under silent oars into Ballinachalla Bay by the light of the stars, and almost frightening to hear the massive trout erupting as they came for these sedges – some of them would have been fish in the five- or six-pound class. We both tied on Green Peters and fished them dry, even though it was no longer possible to see them on the water. Sometimes we drew the fly across the top, in imitation of the living creature, as it jerked its way in stages across the surface. When it is too dark to see the fly, I suppose one ought to strike each time a fish rises in the area where one thinks one's fly to be, and failing to do this, I probably missed the one chance I had, but, exciting as it was, we were not successful and returned fishless to our tent.

Irish fishermen on these big loughs are a thoroughly conservative breed, who rely almost wholly on fishing down the drifts with a team of three wet flies, or else dapping with the live insect, whilst a smaller number seem content with the tedious employment of trolling. They are reluctant to experiment, try a variation of tactics or do anything that diverges from this norm, even on those occasions when the well-tried methods fail to bring results. The dry fly, for instance, is virtually ignored. There is, however, some justification for this, because, as a general rule, the dry fly is always likely to be more effective on the smaller loughs. On the huge expanses, such as Mask affords, what hatches of fly there may be will be very localized affairs, and, provided there is a wave on the water, fish which may be rising will come to the wet flies just as well.

There remain, however, certain types of conditions – calm, bright days – when small dry flies do provide for better (and sometimes the only) opportunities for fish. Bill and I discovered this on just such a day one late August when the surface of the lough reflected like a mirror. As we motored up to Lively Bay we could spot occasional rises here and there, but they were few and far between and suggested cruising fish. We had decided to try the very small flies off a rocky shoreline, where we had some help from the sporadic appearances of the faintest of breezes which, when it was there, was just enough to put a little pin-ripple on the water. Within the

ABOVE *I couldn't resist composing this shot in celebration of a great day's fishing out on the lough during the mayfly hatch.*

hour, we each had a trout of over two pounds – Bill's to a size 16 Ant and mine to an equally small Ginger Quill. On days like these, most boats remain tied up and the few that are out will be trolling, but we met up with one, which contained two of Mask's specialists, who had been persevering with traditional wet flies, if not with much hope, and they were amazed that such tiny flies had worked.

Lough Mask has now become firmly established as the venue for the annual World Cup Wet-Fly Trout Angling Championship, and 1985 witnessed the twenty-first running of this event on these waters. From fairly modest beginnings of eighty to ninety rods in the early years, the reputation and popularity of these championships have grown steadily, and a new record of 371 anglers, from many countries, competed in 1985.

A fly-fishing competition that supports such a grandiose title has to be something special, and this one certainly qualifies. A combination of two factors – one of the world's great wild trout waters, and skilled boatmen – makes for a promising enough beginning, and many of the boatmen are truly colourful characters, to fish in whose company is an experience in itself. Not only do they know the lough like they know the way upstairs, but the fact that they are themselves competing each day for the Best Boatman prize ensures that they will work hard for their fishermen. Boatmen and anglers are all there to win. Such competition fishing is not for me. I have nothing against it in principle; it is only that the art I learnt as a boy I now pursue for relaxation. It is my way of easing the tensions that build up, restoring the harmonies and finding wholeness where waters softly lap.

When the Almighty had done creating Corrib and Mask and all the other fine big loughs of Ireland, He then had to make people to fish on them. To achieve this He must first have shaped three moulds, one for the trolling man, one for the dapping man and one for the fisher of flies. The trolling man turned out broad in the shoulder with a distinctly hunched appearance, the dapping man carried more flesh and made excellent ballast in the boat, and the fly-caster was more lithe than either and much quicker in reaction. Of course, in the long chain of evolution, many of us have become true hybrids, multifarious fishermen.

The hero of my story is none other than the humble bluebottle or blowfly – call him what you will – and, though he sports no claim to be a classic dapping bait, he can nonetheless prove himself a very deadly man for trout, and he certainly has his day. Bill had known this all his life, for, as a lad in the English North Country, he had learnt his fishing on the many little rills and becks that run among the hills there.

He grew to know their secret places – deep holes beneath the bushes, where the dark waters had, in times of flood, eaten their way in under banks. These provided the most desirable residences in the streams and were occupied by the best trout, who grew fatter each summer as the breezes blew many insects on to the water from the boughs above. In such sanctuaries, though a worm or minnow trundled down the run might reach them, they were generally safe enough from the angler's fly.

With cat-like tread Bill had stalked these trout until he could just manage to poke his rod-tip through the branches and lower a natural bluebottle on to the water. Being only feet away from the quarry, this kind of fishing demanded great skill, perfect judgment and the patience of Job, as entanglements were frequent, to say nothing of the difficulties involved in landing a fish, once hooked. It was, never-theless, an excellent school, for those who can winkle out trout by such methods can surely catch them anywhere.

The bluebottle, of course, has earned himself a thoroughly bad name, and most people regard him as no more than a pest and a threat to the hygiene of the kitchen. He rouses up that killer instinct which is never far below the surface in any of us, though I sometimes wonder if those perfumed sprays, which the housewife now uses, are not more harmful still. Whether we like him or not, he remains a creature of great beauty, whose iridescent, green-blue body reflects like a jewel with the glint of sunlight upon it. Boyhood forays apart, we had neither of us thought seriously about the bluebottle from a fishing point of view until it happened more or less by accident.

Nearing the end of our week's fishing holiday, we decided one warm evening that we would go into Ballinrobe for our dinner, to give ourselves a break from the chores of cooking in the tent. Except for one other guest, we had the dining room at the Railway Hotel to ourselves and, with the meal finished, were taking our time over coffee and enjoying a cigar. The hotel waitress, presumably also enjoying a quiet evening, had not yet removed our dirty dinner plates, which soon attracted a large bluebottle, whose appearance must have kindled former triumphs in Bill's mind. After paying our bill, we left the hotel, taking with us two bluebottles in a matchbox.

We had completely forgotten about the wretched creatures when we set out on the lough next morning, where the trout proved hard to move; two undersized fish were all we took in the first two hours. We had just started a new drift down a shore not very far from the entrance to Caher Bay, when Bill looked for a match to light his cigar, and suddenly remembered that the box in his pocket had other tenants.

The wind was fine for dapping and patches of sunlight were starting to pene-trate the clouds; if there was ever a time to fish the bluebottle, this was it. Bill

ABOVE *Lunchtime on the Irish loughs is as much a part of the experience of trout fishing in Ireland as the fishing itself. It's a time for fishermen to gather and talk tactics and tall stories.*

143

changed rods and was soon dapping with the first of
our two bluebottles. On the top of a rolling wave and
against the vast expanses of the lough, it looked
absurdly small, but, even at the distance he was fishing it, we could see the radiant splendours of its
colours. Then, within minutes, a small circle showed
on the wave's crest where the bluebottle had been
riding – so quietly did the trout take. Bill did all the
right things, lowering his rod-point, allowing plenty
of time, and was soon playing a handsome fish, which
was safely boated.

Now he passed the rod to me, remarking curtly as
he did so, "Your turn, and remember we've only one
left, so don't go messing things up."

This second and last bluebottle produced what
was virtually a repeat performance, bringing me a fine
two-and-a-half-pound trout, which appeared to be an
identical twin to the one we already had in the boat. A
pair of blowflies from the dirty dinner plates, a
glimpse of sunshine, twenty minutes' fishing time and
five pounds of trout – that was not bad going.

We then landed for lunch and the search began for more bluebottles, but we
never even saw one, and, in any case, I would defy most people to catch one in the
open air. Our arrival, however, had attracted the local cows, which soon gathered
round to inspect us. The nearest thing we could get to a bluebottle was the cowdung
fly and these were there in plenty, but our efforts to catch them were also in vain.
Their name betrays their habitat, and all we succeeded in doing was to add a strange
new flavour to our sandwiches. Even if we had got one he would not have been the
same man at all.

The following day we went back into Ballinrobe just in order to stock up with
bluebottles, but had quite forgotten it was early closing, and all the shops were shut
when we arrived. We stood and stared longingly outside the butcher's window,
where the thickness of a pane of glass was all that separated us from the finest bluebottles one could have wished for. I suppose that was hardly surprising since they
must have been feeding on some of the best steaks in Mayo. A maggot-farmer
would have had to go a long way to find breeding stock of this kind of quality.

Perhaps it was just as well the shop was closed, for it is one thing to enter

LEFT *Stuart Mcteare,
fly-fisherman and host
extraordinaire, selects the
perfect mayfly.*

a butcher's and ask for meat, but probably quite another to ask for the blow-flies only. One man's shame can be another's gold, and, as we headed out into the lough, we carried no such gold. It was, of course, our final day, and one which the sun kept breaking through to gild, as if to tantalize still further the fishers of the humble bluebottle.

BELOW *Lough Sheelin in the magical last hour of light – when big trout start to prowl and a fisherman's pulse begins to race.*

IRELAND: FACTFILE

BACKGROUND

Piscator non solum piscatur: "There is more to fishing than catching fish." Or so goes the motto from the famous Flyfishers Club in London. None of the other destinations featured in this book encapsulates these sentiments so precisely as does Ireland, where the wit and wisdom of your boatman and the daily ritual of lunch and tea on an isolated island are as integral a part of the fishing as tying on your fly.

While Ireland has its fair share of salmon and trout rivers, it is perhaps for the trout loughs (lakes) in the midlands and on the west coast that it is best known. These great lakes lie in the limestone bedrock of Ireland and with their high pH factor create a proliferation of insect life which in turn nourishes the trout at an extraordinary rate. Sheelin is reckoned to have the highest natural growth rate for brown trout in a still-water, anywhere in Europe.

The average size of fish on most loughs is about 2 lb, but on some, such as Sheelin, it can be as high as 4 lb. These leopard-spotted, golden-bellied trout, though, do not become large by being stupid, and they can be extremely difficult to catch. Perhaps the best line of attack when they are proving dour is to retreat to one of the many lakeside pubs and think things through over a pint of Guinness. One thing is for sure: some of Europe's largest wild trout will be waiting for you and your boatman when you return to the lough.

WHEN TO GO

Main fly hatches on most of the loughs start off each year with midge hatches in March. Shortly afterwards, in April, come the duckfly and lake olive hatches. The fishing pace on all Irish trout loughs reaches its most frenetic around the second week of May, with the advent of the mayfly, which for many is the highlight of the season. The mayfly is mostly over by early June and the fish become difficult to tempt to the surface as they start to hunt the schools of fry that abound in most loughs. Not

LEFT *Myself with a beautiful 5 lb Lough Sheelin brown, caught at twilight on a Murrough with the first cast.*

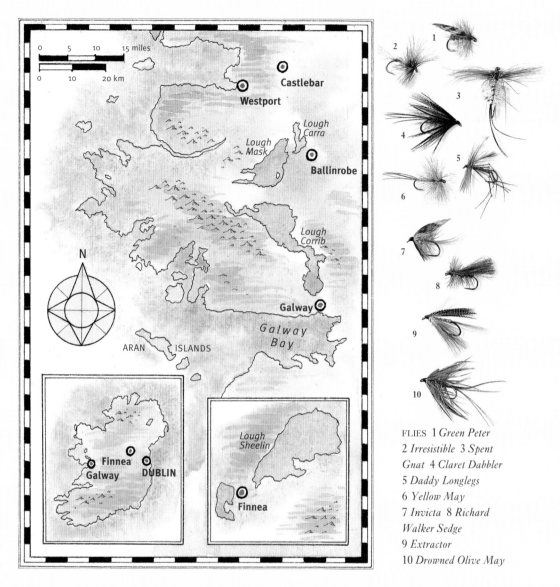

FLIES 1 *Green Peter*
2 *Irresistible* 3 *Spent Gnat* 4 *Claret Dabbler*
5 *Daddy Longlegs*
6 *Yellow May*
7 *Invicta* 8 *Richard Walker Sedge*
9 *Extractor*
10 *Drowned Olive May*

until late July, August and September can they once again be teased up to partake of the bloodworm, large sedges (caddis), daddy longlegs (craneflies) and grasshoppers. It is relatively easy to arrange for a boat on all the loughs, but it is wise to book accommodation in advance, particularly in May.

TACKLE

RODS: Single-handed 9–11 ft for 5–7 wt lines.

REELS: Direct-drive reels to balance with rod.

LINES: Almost exclusively floating line but take intermediate and sinking-tips.

LEADERS: Not less than 6 lb and up to 10 lb.

FLIES: Seasonal variations will, naturally, apply, but proven favourites include: Duckfly, Mayfly (Wulff or Shadow), Green Peter and Murrough Sedges, Bumble patterns (Claret, Golden and Olive), Fiery Brown, Kingsmill, Invicta, Teal Blue and Silver, Bloodworm, Hoppers and Daddy Longlegs.

His Biggest Trout

England

J.W. HILLS

"I was about to reel up when a fish rose ten yards above, close under my bank. It was one of those small movements difficult to place. It might be a very large fish or a very small one. A wild thought swept through me that this was my big one: but no, I said to myself, it cannot be. This is not where he was rising. Besides, things do not happen like that, except in books: it is only in books that you make a fearful bungle and go back later and see a small break which you think is a dace, and cast carelessly and hook something the size of an autumn salmon ..."

Those who fish rivers where mayfly come will agree that, though with it you get a higher average weight, yet actually the biggest fish are killed on the sedge. In 1903 on the Kennet [it] was a great mayfly season for heavy fish, and a friend of mine who had the Ramsbury water got the truly remarkable bag of six fish in one day which weighed over nineteen pounds: and yet the two heaviest fish of the year were got on the sedge. I got the heaviest. It was the 26 July 1903, a cloudy, gusty day, with a downstream wind, and I was on the water from eleven to five without seeing a rise. My friend and I then had tea and walked up the river at a quarter past six. Olives began to appear and trout to move; and suddenly a really large one started rising. We stood and watched, with growing excitement. He was taking every fly, in solid and determined fashion, and the oftener he appeared the bigger he looked, and the faster beat our hearts. It was settled that I was to try for him. I was nervous and uncomfortable. He was very big: it was a long throw and the wind horrible: I could not reach him, and like a fool I got rattled and pulled off too much line: there was an agonized groan from my friend behind me when a great curl of it was slapped on the water exactly over the trout's nose. We looked at each other without speaking, and he silently walked away up the river, leaving me staring stupidly at the spot where the trout had been rising. Of course he was gone.

The next two hours can be passed over. The small fly rise came and went. I caught a trout on a No. 2 silver sedge and finally, at about a quarter past eight, found myself gazing gloomily at the place where I had bungled. The wild wind had

BELOW *A Green Drake.*

OPPOSITE BELOW *An old stone bridge over the River Avon in Wiltshire has harbored many large trout in its shadows.*

BELOW *A quiet woodland pool on the upper Bourne in Hampshire offers a chance for a reflective moment to a passing angler.*

blown itself out and had swept the sky bare of cloud. Silence had come, and stillness. The willows, which all through the long summer day had bowed and
chattered in the wind, were straightened and motionless, each individual leaf hanging down as though carved in jade: the forest of great sedges, which the gusts had
swept into wave after wave of a roaring sea of emerald, was now calm and level,
each stalk standing straight and stiff as on a Japanese screen. There had occurred
that transition, that transmutation from noise and movement to silence and peace,
which would be more wonderful were we not so accustomed to it, when a windy
summer day turns over to a moveless summer night: when the swing and clatter
and rush of the day is arrested and lifted from the world, and you get the sense that
the great hollow of the air is filled with stillness and quiet, as with a tangible presence. They are peaceful things, these summer evenings after wild days, and I
remember particularly that this was one of the most peaceful; more so indeed than
my thoughts, which were still in a turmoil. I stood watching mechanically, and
then, tempting fate to help me, made a cast or two over the spot where the fish had
been. How easy it was to reach it now, how lightly my fly settled on the water, how
gracefully it swung over the place. All to no purpose, of course, for nothing
happened, and I was about to reel up when a fish rose ten yards above, close under
my bank. It was one of those small movements difficult to place. It might be a very
large fish or a very small one. A wild thought swept through me that this was my big
one: but no, I said to myself, it cannot be. This is not where he was rising. Besides,
things do not happen like that, except in books: it is only in books that you make a
fearful bungle and go back later and see a small break which you think is a dace, and

cast carelessly and hook something the size of an autumn salmon: it is only in books that fate works in such fashion. Why, I know it all so well that I could write it out by heart, every move of it. But this is myself by a river, not reading in a chair. This is the real world, where such things do not happen: that is the rise of a half-pound trout.

I cast. I was looking right into the west, and the water was coloured like skim milk by reflection from where the sun had set. My silver sedge was as visible as by day. It floated down, there was a rise, I struck, and something rushed upstream. Then I knew.

Above me was open water for some twenty-five yards, and above that again a solid block of weed, stretching right across. My fish made for this, by short, irresistible runs. To let him get into it would have been folly: he must be stopped: either he is well hooked or lightly, the gut is either sound or rotten: kill or cure, he must be turned, if turned he can be: so I pulled hard, and fortunately got his head round and led him down. He played deep and heavy and I had to handle him roughly, but I brought him down with a smash, and I began to breathe again. But then another terror appeared. In the place we had reached the only clear water

152

was a channel under my bank, and the rest of the river was choked with weed. Should I try to pull him down this channel, about three or four yards wide, to the open water below? No. It was much too dangerous, for the fish was uncontrollable, and if he really wanted to get to weed he would either get there or break me: even with a beaten fish it would be extremely risky, and with an unbeaten one it was unthinkable. Well, if he would not come down he must go up, and up he went willingly enough, for when I released pressure he made a long rush up to the higher weed bed, whilst I ran up the meadow after him, and with even greater difficulty turned him once more. This time I thought he was really going right through it, so fast and so heavy was his pull, and I think he was making for a hatch hole above: but once more my gallant gut stood the strain and, resisting vigorously, he was led down again. This proceeding was repeated either two or three times more, I forget which: either three or four times we fought up and down that twenty-five yards of river. By then he was tiring, and I took up my station in the middle of the stretch, where I hoped to bring him in: my hand was actually on the sling of the net when he suddenly awoke and rushed up. He reached the weed bed at a pace at which it was impossible to stop, shot into it like a torpedo, and I had the sickening certainty that I should lose him after all. To hold him hard now would be to make a smash certain, so I slacked off: when he stopped I tightened again, expecting miserably to feel the dead, lifeless drag of a weeded line. Instead, to my delight, I found I was still in contact with the fish, and he was pulling hard. How he had carried the line through the weeds I do not know. To look at it seemed impossible.... But the line was clear, and the fish proved it by careering wildly on towards the hatch, making the reel sing. I believe he meant to go through into the carrier, as fish have done

ABOVE *Spotting a quietly rising trout on the River Itchen, Hampshire, in the shade of a willow requires patience and a keen eye.*

BELOW *Thomas Yellow May.*

153

before and after, but I turned him. However, we could not stay where we were. The hatch was open at the bottom, there was a strong draw through it, and if a heavy, beaten fish got into this, no gut would hold him up. At all risks he must be taken over the weed into the clear water. I pulled him up to the top and ran him down. Then, for the first time after so many perils, came the conviction that I should land him. He was obviously big, but how big could not be known, for I had not had a clear sight of him yet. He still pulled with that immovable, quivering solidity only shown by a very heavy fish. But at last even his great strength tired. He gave a wobble or two, yielded, and suddenly he was splashing on the top, looking huge in the dusk. There ensued that agonizing time when you have a big fish nearly beat,

LEFT *Checking out the big ones under the bridge – they're really there.*

BELOW *The challenge of casting on a heavily wooded stream is to keep your fly in the water instead of the trees.*

but he is still too heavy to pull in, and nothing you can do gets him to the net. At last I pulled him over to it, but I lifted too soon, the ring caught in the middle of the body, he wavered a moment in the air and then toppled back into the water with a sickening splash. A judgment, I thought, and for a shattering second I believed he had broken the gut, but he was still on. I was pretty well rattled by then and, in the half light, made two more bad shots, but the end came at last, he was in the net and on the bank.

How big was he? Three pounds? Yes, and more. Four pounds? Yes, and more. Five? He might be, he might. My knees shook and my fingers trembled as I got him on the hook of the steelyard. He weighed a fraction over four pounds eight ounces.

The Chalkstream Idyll

England

NEIL PATTERSON

"That mysterious hole under the willow, that dark pool where the weed tresses wave like flags, under that old farm bridge. The chances of a big trout living there are so high, you'd never find my passing these places by in a hurry. As I think back to the big fish I've taken in the past, not one of them came from a place I wouldn't have expected to find them. The places you instinctively feel should hold big fish are the places you should head for with your shooting-stick. This is the best and most honest advice anybody can give."

ABOVE TOP *Nick Zoll selects just the right pattern for a finicky Itchen River brown. Streamside benches help anglers with these moments of concentration.*

Above all else, perhaps even more than in pursuit of their contents, fly-fishermen visit English chalkstreams in search of solitude.

In contrast to the crashing, boulder-strewn gorges, the raging rapids and chit-chattering riffles of the rain-fed streams, the shady shallows, whispering glides and secretive depths of England's southern chalkstreams soothe the soul and calm the mind of the visiting angler, lowering his pulse rate considerably.

Surprising, then, that fly-fishers on chalkstreams walk too fast when they're astream. Indeed, I'd go further and say that it's not just the speed at which they travel that limits chances of catching trout (and occasionally their breath), it's the fact that they move at all.

On that sticky day in July, I arrived at the river to find that there were no cars at Sticklepath Bridge. I had the river to myself, again. The sun was hot and I began to wish I'd come down earlier. There might have been a small hatch of something at this time of year. But right now, there wasn't a fly to be seen, or heard. The air was silent. I was able to detect the tiniest wing beat. The thick, morning water rubbed round the brick bridge supports like lava.

I decided to patrol the Square Dance, a compact area of mixed waters, incorporating a stretch of the main river on one side – and Cake Wood. Carpeted with comfrey and ferns and wallpapered by ancient woodland, this shady stream is tucked away behind the Mad House – our small, bark-covered fishing lodge. Here, the sun never breaks through the trees until late morning.

One of the best anglers I met in my first year on the river always used to disappear into an area of stream with about enough carriers to confuse an Indian scout. He wasn't just a good fisherman, he consistently dragged the biggest fish back to the hut. When I saw him set off, my heart went out to the trout. Yet to see him in action, you'd think nothing worked from the knees down. A solicitor from Kent, he was the textbook chalkstream fisherman. Tweed jacket, cap, tackled-out by Hardy top to toe. He was as straight as straight could be. Straight out of E.A. Barton's *Album of a Chalk-Stream*. No one, nothing, could be straighter. I called him Curly.

With his Volvo parked at the hut (doors and boot locked), Curly would go straight to one of three spots – often the same one every trip. There Curly would stay. I had enough time to walk round every likely fish-holding position on the river before he even lifted his rod. But at the end of the day, he'd have taken a heavier bag. In those days, this trout enemy number one paid a princely sum each season for his fishing. I calculated he could have bought the amount of bank he actually fished for the price of a bottle of fly-flotant.

Why did Curly catch bigger trout than somebody who spends the day stream-walking? And why is it so unusual to come across anglers like the trout-slayer I've just mentioned, who fish from a fixed position?

This isn't such an odd question to ask if you think about other forms of angling – coarse, sea, salmon, wet-fly, stillwater trouting. This obsession with fishing on the move is unique to chalkstreams. Why?

Maybe chalkstream anglers are loathe to remain standing in one spot on a river because they have no need to exercise territorial instincts on their beat. With restricted access, their solitude is never threatened.

The beat is theirs. No coachload of anglers is likely to spew out a hoard of green umbrella-toting fishermen, hell-bent on making claims to the best swims on the beat. The fact that I had the river to myself again happily confirmed my theory. Exclusivity, the fact that on most chalkstream beats there are relatively few anglers per yard of bank, is the reason. This, linked with the general belief that fish are always better on the other side of the fence, somewhere else, so keep moving.

But like most of the good and bad habits connected with chalkstream fly-fishing, you can usually trace them back to Frederic Halford. As the prophet of the idea that fishing the water blind is about as sporting as shooting chickens in the yard, he introduced a new concept. Namely, that before you could even start to cast a fly to a trout, you first had to find the fish in question – at least see evidence that it was there and feeding, a rise, or some other movement on the surface. In a historical context, Mr Halford substituted the sense of feel, so important to the wet fly-fisherman of the time, with the sense of seeing.

To his downstream, lure-dragging contemporaries, who spent long monot-onous hours anchored to lively spots praying that an obliging trout might just hang on to their offerings (it's no wonder they packed up fishing after the Mayfly), Halford's thinking did more than offer an effective alternative to wet flies. It repre-sented an excuse for fishermen to stretch their seized-up leg muscles. And to this day, the ritual of going out and looking for an opportunity, rather than perhaps waiting for it to come to you, is still as much a part of chalkstream tradition as cast-ing a fly upstream.

At Beech Bridge, I stood and looked across to the trees on the other side of the river. The water runs deep and slow under the branches there and I tried to picture trout that might be tucked under the bank. Big trout, their fat bellies squeezed in between the damp, mossy roots.

This is a slow, strange, sipping area. An area of puckered lips, rather than snap-ping jaws. Lips sucking at microcosms. It has everything a chalkstream angler could ask of a stretch of stream – except for the chalkstream angler's favourite kind of trout – trout that show themselves, trout you can see.

I leant back on my hands and clasped the wooden bar connected to the concrete and flint footbridge by three metal supports. They twanged nervously. I held my position.

In my experience, the advantages of seat-of-the-pants fishing outweigh the advantages of sole-of-the-feet fishing. Stream-walkers disagree. They say, "How do I know I'm not sitting over an empty hole?" I have to admit there was a time when I could understand this line of think-ing. Every time I stayed still for five minutes I'd find myself asking the same question. But after I'd managed to fidget my way through the initial few minutes and settle down, it was amazing how fast these doubts dissolved with the arrival of a trout mere yards from my feet, or at the sight of a fin beckoning me from the edge of weed-bed. Fly-fishermen who use this "empty hole" theory to justify their stream-walking can never have travelled up their river on an electro-fish-ing boat during the closed season, greeting each scoop of the net with "Goodness, I'd never have guessed I'd find a trout there." It's really quite revealing.

But having said this, I agree that some places are better fish-holders than others. And some places hold bigger trout than others.

Where are these places? And how can you find them? I was standing looking over one now.

The metal railing twanged like a slack banjo string as I settled in for the duration. Strangely enough, I've yet to read a fishing writer who has been wholly enlightening about streamcraft. By that I mean you can't teach anybody to find fish off a page. Think over the chapters you've read entitled "Finding Fish". What can you remember? Like me, you probably only have memories of shaky maps of imaginary rivers covered with Xs marking the spot, the whole effect being that they were sketched at full gallop. The fact is, trout move around too much during the year to be pinned down in this way. From surface food-bearing lies in the spring, to

ABOVE *Waiting for a rise on the far bank, deep in the idyllic sanctuary of the Itchen River.*

161

nymph-bearing lies in the summer, to give an example. Even in the course of a day, a trout may be found in a totally different area in the evening to where it was that morning. It's too much like musical chairs to be coded and systemised. The fact is, finding fish is to do with understanding fish. This takes experience and more often than not, gut feel.

Personally, I go looking for likely fish-holding places with the same enthusiasm as when I was knee-high to a pair of waders. I still rely on the same schoolboy curiosity and ingenuity. I can confidently say that I'm no better a trout scout now than when I was twelve.

That mysterious hole under the willow, that dark pool where the weed tresses wave like flags, under that old farm bridge. The chances of a big trout living there are so high, you'd never find my passing these places by in a hurry. As I think back to the big fish I've taken in the past, not one of them came from a place I wouldn't have expected to find them. The places you instinctively feel should hold big fish are the places you should head for with your shooting-stick. This is the best and most honest advice anybody can give.

Having said this, you may at first pass a lot of spots that look potentially productive but have never produced trout in the past. I suggest you forget the past. The reason why these places don't produce their fair share of monsters is often to do with a lack of understanding of why big fish get to be so big. They manage this because they stay out of trouble. They don't sit out in the middle of the stream in full view of the casual stream-walker. As a result they are rarely pestered by them. But for the reasons I will now give, these piscatorial Howard Hugheses are in mortal danger from the man who sews leather patches on the seat of his breeches and adjusts his eyesight in the manner I will now describe.

Charles Ritz once said that a fish seen is a fish almost caught. Fly-fishermen tend to glide over the big, wild trout because they take this too literally. They look for whole fish, not parts of them. Nymph-fishermen, in particular, miss trout because they don't hone down their observation to look for trout portions, "extracts of trout". Tails, fins, snouts poking out of weed-beds, silver patches where scales are missing against gravelly, pinky warts. The more exacting fly-fisher looks into the river and asks himself, "When is a trout not a trout ?" He looks for imaginary trout and takes away the tail, the fins, the gills, the body, the head – hoping something in the tight area he scans

ABOVE *Hampshire chalkstreams are the epitome of tranquility. This is a scene on the Avon River, not far from the great stone circle at Stonehenge.*

holds one or more elements of a trout. Only then can he conclude that a trout is not a trout – when it was never there in first place.

As I mentioned earlier, trout tend to move about in the course of a typical day. Big trout are perhaps the only exception to this rule. But just because they don't commute from one position to another doesn't mean they don't move at all. From my shooting-stick, I've noticed that big trout tend to move to eat. An inch here, an inch there, drifting slowly back, or pulling to one side to intercept a shrimp passing close by. They also move when disturbed, prompted by the arrival of another fish in the same weed-clump, or at the shadow of a bird flying overhead. These tell-tale signs are often only blink-and-you'll-miss-'em glimpses. The angler not there, not waiting for these opportunities, misses them. But what about the dry-fly man watching the surface?

Again, from a sitting position he, too, is able to increase the amount he sees simply by training himself to stop looking for every spiralling rise-form. He must adjust his vision to register changes of light on the surface, inverted dents, shimmers, nervous water. Having done this, the smallest dimple becomes an eruption, and the most gentle, insignificant flicker of the film becomes an opportunity.

This way of seeing is especially relevant to summer on the chalkstreams, when long ago I came to the conclusion that the commonest and most walked-over daytime rise-form isn't really a rise-form at all. It's a sound: the muffled sipping of trout – like Victorian middle-class ladies drinking hot soup – delicately sucking at small insects and nymphs glued to the sticky film. To the man who has been sitting quietly studying his stretch, such a rise is as visually and audibly arresting as if somebody had slung a half-brick into the water.

The amount the eye is capable of seeing is in direct relation to the speed at which it is travelling. The faster you walk, the less you will see. The slower you walk, the more you will see. The longer you stay in one spot, the better the chances of you seeing (and hearing) everything you're ever likely to see (or hear).

This is the Shooting-Stick Philosophy.

In effect, by standing still, you automatically improve your vision. And it's being able to see more opportunities that I believe is the main advantage of fishing

from a strategically placed stick. The second advantage is something I've already touched on: acquaintance with the environment around you. After twenty minutes, you start to get to know your patch as if you were born and brought up there. Even subconsciously you are aware of surface and underwater currents, the pace of the water – all these things add up to better presentation. The current carrying the food to the trout, for example, may not be the current you imagine it to be. It may be one of many different currents on the surface flowing at a different pace, from a different direction. An artificial fly sailing down the wrong current may sound the alarm bells to the waiting trout. The natural drift of flies on the water is often more important than matching the hatch.

As a resident in the area, you're also an expert on the most prominent food-types on the menu in the trout's local restaurant. This is unavoidable. By rooting

yourself to the spot, you qualify as a bush and a good deal of what is flying around will land on you. This familiarity with the food in your area may seem a small point, but often different flies will be hatching off at different parts of the river.

This detail isn't always appreciated by the stream-walker simply scanning the water looking for trout. His scant interest in the relationship between locality and the trout's lifestyle and food-type is often the reason why the stream-walker's fly, which fooled a fish on one beat, fails to catch a fish on another.

But this telescoping-in on a relatively small area of water scores most on summer evenings when fish up and down the river are selecting different flies in different stages of development.

By remaining in one spot you are, in effect, behaving like a trout in a feeding position. Just like the trout you will be aware of what fly (and at what stage of its

ABOVE TOP *Rising and hooking the trout is only the first part of the game – keeping him out of all those weeds is the hard part. The River Test, shown here, is a good candidate for practicing your technique.*

165

development) is passing by in the most abundance and, therefore, the fly that the trout opposite you is most likely to be feeding on. It's this kind of understanding and intimacy with the trout that I believe can only be appreciated over a long period of time – a long period of time rooted to one place.

Finally, this approach has one other advantage on summer evenings. It stops you chasing from one trout to another and finishing the day with a pulse rate of 120 and a trout total of nil. I'm now totally convinced that it's not anglers that trout are allergic to. It's moving anglers. By staking out a spot, you have control over how much your area is disturbed, or left undisturbed. The latter is essential if big, shy trout are to come out of hiding.

On the hard-pounded public waters of the Croton River in New York State, where I once fished, the fly-fishers stand over their plots with the patience of loyal dogs sitting bent over their masters' graves. After ten minutes fishing, you start to understand this logic. With waves of spoon-slingers marauding up and down the bank, it's the only way you can ensure that the fish in your area are not knocked unconscious before they get a chance to see your fly. This kind of ground-hogging may not apply to the etiquette-ridden beats in the south of England, but on some club or regularly-frequented hotel waters, for example, it makes a lot of sense.

ABOVE *A discussion of the most appropriate pattern on the banks of the River Test.*

Half an hour passed. The heat had soldered my hands to the metal rail. As the sun moved over my head, the deep blue shadows intensified under the bushes and a single ring, a ring with no centre, ebbed out into the middle of the river. This was the half-brick I had been waiting for. Evidence of stirrings from one of the many invisible trout in this dark area. Trout paraded like a row of Doric columns, their metallic blue skulls flush with the underside of the skin of the film, as if holding up the surface of the river.

As if built of marble, these weighty trout, one of them at least three pounds, had proved impossible to move – either upwards, out of their element, to intercept something on the surface (a nose breaking the surface might break the silence), or downwards, and thus breaking rank (perhaps disturbing a neighbour) to snaffle a nymph. To the angler glued to the spot, who by now would have noted and inwardly digested all these details, it was time to draw conclusions – and get to work.

The grey specks in the late morning sunbeams, which gave the scene Seurat's pointillist quality to the angler on the move, had more significant implications to the man on a stick trained to notice, rather than simply see, all around him. They were midges – chironomids, just like the ones so familiar to the stillwater fly-fisher, only smaller.

ABOVE *A High Rider Cul-de-Canard Black Sedge.*

As, year on year, the water level of the river drops, the flow slows down, the water temperature rises and the river becomes more closely related to the contents of a water butt, midges have become a regular feature. You notice these things when you're sitting on a stick by the river, or when you're sleeping next-door to it. I had given these changes some thought. The midge pupa looks just like its wiggly-worm larva in many ways. But closer inspection reveals wings and legs tucked away at the thorax, like a parachute. You will also see small, fluffy white breathing filaments at the head and tail. Fully equipped with the most up-to-date means of accumulating oxygen, midge pupae make regular trips from their homes before hatching. They do this to build up their oxygen store so they can break out of their skin stockings and power back up to the top again.

At the surface, midge pupae either attach their respiratory tubes and hang horizontally, their thoraxes piercing the top of the water, or they rove, wriggling just beneath the water level.

Compared to a hatch of mayfly, a fall of spinner or an explosion of sedge, all this hanging-out beneath the surface may seem decidedly uneventful. Not so. These midge manoeuvres may not be able to move mountains, but they can shift Doric columns, if only slightly – just far enough for the trout to suck in these squirming danglers, and to register a thin, single ring on the water surface. To the fly-fisher, who is lounging on a stick or leaning on a bridge rail with nothing better to look at, this single ring is a shock wave. It's certainly sufficient to register an opportunity.

To help me locate trout on hot summer days, I cheat a little. As well as my Polaroid glasses, I hang a small pair of 8 x 20 Zeiss binoculars round my neck, measuring only four inches long. I put these between my eyes and my polaroids to shield the glare. It works. And it allows me to confirm any vague distant movement, helping me put a shape to a fin, or an approximate size to a fish.

A silver-skinned circle uncoiled and slithered its way across the river. I received the signal as I was still leaning back on the bridge. I knew where the trout was lying, but not where he was positioned, at least not precisely. He could be behind the low overhanging branch, or in front of it. If only to calculate the life-expectancy of the minute midge pupa pattern I named the Suspender, this mattered.

Devised in conjunction with the River God, the Suspender has a tiny ball of Ethafoam trapped in a little sack made from nylon stocking material and tied in at the head of the hook. This way I ensure that my midge pupa hangs suspended under the surface film like a ceiling lamp.

At the Beech Bridge, whatever problems lie ahead of you, you don't have any behind you. Just as long as you keep to the centre of the bridge. On the back-cast there's all the room you could ask for. Cake Wood meets the main river here; your back-cast opens out over open water. This is just as well, because to get a line across to the gladiators limbering under the bushes opposite means a lengthy cast, a minimum of fifteen yards. A line of that length picks up the gentlest hush of a breeze.

One of the trout tipped the surface again. I heard his stony skull chip the surface of the water and the peck of his beak sucking in a forbidden wisp of air. I hung a long line behind me. Pulling back down with my left hand, I hauled all the aerialised line forwards. Lifting my rod tip up smartly just before it alighted on the water, the line dropped with two deep curves set in it to cushion drag.

In the dark I could make out a tiny white dot. The Ethafoam periscope had surfaced. The course had been set. It was five seconds from its target.

I didn't see the rise. Instead I saw the Suspender down-periscope and dive. This was all the indication I was given to tell me that the fish – at least one of the fish – was taken. The periscope reappeared, this time in a cloud of spray, immediately plummeting down again like a stone. The metallic-skulled submarine was heading for the depths – and the roots.

I had suspected this would be the fish's first, and most dramatic move. I was ready with my response. As soon as I made connection, I began crab-walking off the bridge and down the bank, letting him feel the weight of my walk. With as tight a line as my eighteen inches of hollow, floating Shockgum allowed, I pulled him decisively into the sunlight and horsed him to my ankles. A wild fish with a bottle-green back splattered with a handful of polka-dots, it was one of the last in a long line of a particular strain of fish in the river, a cross between the original river stock and the Loch Levens that were introduced into the water fifteen to twenty years ago.

In the end, it was no surprise that I caught this trout. In the same way that it was inevitable that, from my static position, the trout caught my eye in the first place.

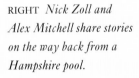

RIGHT *Nick Zoll and Alex Mitchell share stories on the way back from a Hampshire pool.*

ENGLAND: FACTFILE

BACKGROUND

The English chalkstreams are for many the true birthplace of modern methods of fishing with dry fly and nymph, now adopted by fishermen in rivers around the world. The chalkstreams still hold a certain magic in the minds of all fishermen, and fishing here you know that you are walking in the footsteps of some of fly-fishing's legends. Wild brown trout fishing can still be found here at its best and most demanding.

Though wild fish densities are not as high as they were in Izaak Walton's day and genetic purity is in some places challenged, it should not be forgotten that these fish are the forebears of many of the world's brown trout populations. The reputation that wild chalkstream brown trout have of testing the skill of a modern angler is well earned and has not diminished in the slightest. The beauty of the surroundings serves to create a fishing idyll that has existed for generations, and sitting on the bank of a chalkstream in June remains one of the highlights of fly-fishing.

WHEN TO GO

The season starts in mid-April, but generally the best of the fishing begins in May with the onset of summer and of the serious fly hatches. The classic mayfly hatch, on beats where it exists, generally occurs toward the end of May and the beginning of June. While this is the most popular and heavily fished hatch of the year, the trout develop a more discerning palate throughout the rest of the season.

Upstream fishing is the only legal method of fishing on most beats. Nymphs are generally forbidden until the middle of July, and on some beats their use is prohibited completely. The best of the season is over by the end of September, but fine autumn weather can prolong daytime hatches by another week or two.

TOP LEFT *A fishing party waits for the mayfly hatch to begin above Broadlands House on the River Test.*

BOTTOM LEFT *A beautiful wild Itchen brown about to be released.*

FLIES 1 *Claret Sedge*
2 *Spent Gnat*
3 *Thomas Yellow May*
4 *Houghton Ruby*
5 *Pink Shrimp*
6 *Richard Walker Sedge* 7 *Green Drake*
8 & 9 *Tup's Indispensables*
10 *Greenwell's Glory*

TACKLE

RODS: Depending on the size of the stream, 7–9 ft single-handed rods for a 2–4 wt line.

REELS: Basic direct-drive fly reel to balance with chosen rod.

LINES: Floating lines, 2–4 wt.

LEADERS: The lighter the better, and rarely more than 4X (4 lb) breaking strain is necessary.

FLIES: Match the hatch, which can change quickly. Proven favourites include: March Browns, Grannom and Hawthorns early in the year; Mayfly, Greenwell's Glory, Black Gnat, Tup's Indispensable, Olives, Sedge (caddis) patterns later in the year. Nymphs might include Hare's Ear, Pheasant Tail, Grey Goose and Shrimp.

There can be tremendous variation·in hatches of fly from one beat to another, as well as from river to river, and it is generally wise to enquire which hatches are predominating on your stretch prior to fishing it.

Raspberries in the Rain

Norway

ERNEST SCHWIEBERT

"The Laerdal drops through the meadows at Gammleboll, and sweeps past the

huge granite walls that buttress the Fagernes highway. Its currents churn against

these mossy battlements and dance into the depths of the Wallholen.

Salmon hold in its first sixty meters of current. They lie under swirling currents

of sapphire and spume, where the stream wells up silken and smooth, before the

river grows shallow over a tail of fine cobble. There are often sea trout in those

quiet margins, particularly in the weeks to come, but we were after bigger game."

"Oh good Sir, this is a war you sometimes win, and must sometimes expect to lose."

Izaak Walton, 1653

It rained softly through the night.

The mountains were completely shrouded in clouds just after daylight, and the street was wet when I crossed the gardens of the Hotel Lindstrom to breakfast. Great flocks of gulls were wheeling over the tidal reaches of the Laerdal.

The breakfast room was empty, but its cold table was laid and waiting, and the serving girls peered from the kitchen and giggled when I arrived. Breakfast was soft-boiled eggs and goat cheese and brislings in dill sauce, with sweet butter and black pumpernickel, and when I finished my coffee and a small dish of fresh strawberries, I returned to my room to dress for the river. It was chilly, and the Bergen radio promised cloudy weather and rain. There was an extra pullover in my duffle, and I rummaged for a rain jacket and scarf, since it was cool enough to see one's breath. The fresh hairwing Ackroyds and Orange Charms I had dressed before breakfast were lying on the tiny night table.

The morning ferry from Kaupanger arrived while I was loading the old Mercedes, and its ship's horn resounded through the lower valley, echoing from the steepwalled escarpments.

"Looks like a good morning," Andreas Olsen waved as I reached his cottage, and the famous old gillie clambered into the car.

"The fish like the rain?"

"It seems they do," he nodded thoughtfully, "and the river usually goes down when it rains."

"Goes down when it's raining?"

The veteran gillie smiled indulgently. "Cloudy weather stops the icefields from melting in the mountains," he explained, "and the river seems to fish better with less snow melt."

"Makes sense," I nodded. "Where are we fishing?"

"Kvelde," he said.

Andreas Olsen understood the Laerdal like no other gillie in the valley, since both his father and another legendary riverkeeper, Jens Klingenberg, were dead. Ole Olsen had been the keeper for Lord Henry Portman, and Klingenberg had served two other famous British experts, T.T. Phelps and J.C. Mottram. Andreas Olsen had dressed flies and gillied for the late Prince Axel of Denmark, and his

ABOVE *Anglers must follow the big salmon of the Alta River in a boat, but as the fish begin to tire the canoes are beached and the remainder of the fight is from the shore.*

FLY, OPPOSITE TOP
A Willie Gunn.

famous son, Olav Olsen, now dressed flies for Prince Harald of Norway.

The road winds south from Laerdalsoyri, past its tiny clapboard houses, and the old churchyard in a dense copse of pines, until there were scattered farmsteads above the town. The windshield wipers were dancing rhythmically as we passed the hayfields and casting platforms at Hunderi. The fields were empty and wet, and no one was building hay fences. Farmers in bright yellow slickers were loading milk cans at the Tonjum crossroads, and there were dairy cattle in the river bottoms. We left the car at the new bridge near the Kvelde Pool.

"Andreas, what did we draw this morning?" I asked.

"Wallholen," he said.

Thomas Falck was already fishing just above the bridge. He waved and shook his head to tell us there was no luck, and we clambered over the stiles and stone fences to reach the footpath along the river. The Wallholen lay several hundred meters far-ther upstream, and it was the pool we had drawn at Rikheim.

The footpath winds past fields of potatoes and cauliflowers and cabbages, and there were thickets of red raspberries at the stile crossings. The wet berries glistened with raindrops and were quite good. We continued along the river, in a corridor of silver birches, with the river tumbling just beyond the trees.

The Laerdal drops through the meadows at Gammleboll, and sweeps past the huge granite walls that buttress the Fagernes highway. Its currents churn against these mossy battlements and dance into the depths of the Wallholen.

Salmon hold in its first sixty meters of current. They lie under swirling currents of sapphire and spume, where the stream wells up silken and smooth, before the river grows shallow over a tail of fine cobble. There are often sea trout in those quiet margins, particularly in the weeks to come, but we were after bigger game.

Olsen was skeptical about my light rod, although he had seen me take a twenty-pound fish with it at Tonjum, with a brace of two-salt fish weighing thirteen.

"But we're fishing small flies," I protested.

"Pray for grilse," he sighed.

Olsen selected one of the traditional Jock Scotts from my Wheatley box, and cautiously knotted it to my tippet. The old gillie led me carefully up the rocky shingle toward the throat of the pool, and stopped to study the river, estimating its character at this height of water.

"Start here," he said.

"They're holding this high in the current?" I asked. "It still seems like pretty heavy water."

"They're holding under the current," he replied.

The false casts switched out, lengthening until they worked back and forth in the drizzling rain, and I dropped the fly well across the current tongue near the masonry abutments. I mended and lowered the rod to start the fly swimming, mended again and again, to slow it through the fast water in the belly of the swing, and began to work it with a teasing rhythm as it emerged from the tumbling spume. I took a step and cast again. Each cast sliced out through the rain, dropping well across the river, and came back enticingly through its concentric swing. Nothing. The heady anticipation of fishing an unfamiliar pool had begun to ebb, once I had fished halfway through its holding water.

"The river seems dead."

"Patience," the old gillie smiled. "There's still another twenty meters of good water to come."

Suddenly the current rhythms changed, seeming to bulge and swell imperceptibly, before two immense swirls came boiling up behind the fly. Olsen was refilling his battered pipe, cupping the bowl between his hands, to shelter it from the mist. "Cast again," he said.

I carefully repeated the cast, attempting to drop the fly in the same place, and mending again, to mute its speed into the belly of the swing. The salmon appeared again like a dark, pewtery apparition, boiling up behind the swimming fly, and the rod doubled over as it turned back with the Jock Scott in its jaws. It held quietly for a few moments, with a few sullen shakes of its great head, and suddenly bolted forty meters downstream, where it cartwheeled into the rain. There was a noisy screech of tires, as a passing motorist stopped to watch.

"How big?"

"Bigger than a grilse," the old man laughed.

Olsen believed it was better than thirty-five pounds. Other cars on the highway were stopping now, and the daily bus to Fagernes stopped too. People were gathering along the granite parapets of the highway, in a phalanx of black umbrellas, shouting encouragement and advice. The big fish jumped again, writhing into the rain like an acrobat, and the crowd gasped. The salmon bored deep into the belly of the pool, shaking its great hookbill viciously among the cobblestones and boulders, and it bolted again. It wallowed in the surface, threshing and throwing water, forcing me to surrender more and more line.

ABOVE *Red barns and birch trees punctuate the Norwegian countryside.*

RIGHT *An expectant angler fishes carefully down a pool on an early-season Laerdal River swollen with snow melt, outside the village of Laerdalsoyri.*

ABOVE *A pastoral view of the beautiful Namsen River valley. The Namsen has a reputation as a big-fish river.*

It was running now, as we scrambled along the rocky shoal, but it stopped again where the currents gathered in the tail shallows. The water bulged over its bulk, where it held like a big stone in the shallows. I prayed and waited. The great fish finally worked slowly back toward deep water, pulling stubbornly against the bellying slack, and returned slowly toward the throat of the pool. There was another clumsy jump that ended in an awkward splash, and the fish surfaced weakly at midstream.

"Getting tired!" I yelled.

The great fish seemed almost finished. Its huge tail fanned and fluttered now, and we worked cautiously upstream, furtively recovering precious lengths of line. I forced the salmon from the heaviest current tongues, until it rolled almost help-lessly against the pressure.

"Get ready!" I muttered prayerfully.

Olsen crouched and waited with the gaff, less visible to the struggling cockfish.

178

ABOVE *Thorpe McKenzie proudly displays the extraordinary 35-lb salmon he caught on the Alta River during a midsummer trip.*

The salmon rolled on its side, working its shiny gillplates with obvious fatigue, and I lowered the rod laterally to force it closer to the waiting gillie. Its great kype and immense shoulders and silvery flanks were visible in the pewtery light.

The veteran riverkeeper was reaching with the gaff, getting ready to strike, and the salmon lazily rolled over. The nylon raked across its pectorals and skull. It was almost within reach when the small Jock Scott came free. The great fish drifted just beyond the gaff, gathered itself in the shallows, and disappeared. The crowd of spectators gasped, and the flock of umbrellas returned to the bus.

"Damn!" I had been waiting to exhale.

The gillie came ashore wordlessly, collected our gear from the bench, and started back down the footpath through the birches. We were in poor spirits, crossing the stiles and fieldstone walls, and stopping to eat raspberries in the rain.

Sometimes a gillie's best skill is his silence.

BELOW *A Temple Dog.*

179

LEFT *A visiting American angler and his two Norwegian gillies proudly display an evening's catch.*

NORWAY: FACTFILE

BACKGROUND

Fly-fishing for the large Atlantic salmon that run Norwegian rivers was first introduced by the English in the early 1880s. Norway has long been able to boast the highest average size of Atlantic salmon on many of its rivers, and it was for these leviathans of the salmonoid world that the early explorers came. Many stories tell of huge fish caught or vast catches taken. What is extraordinary about Norway is that on the country's premier rivers these stories are still re-enacted. Rivers such as Alta, Namsen and Gaula, and others like them, still produce fish of 40 or even 50 lb every year.

It has not been a continual fishing idyll though. Norway was one of the first nations to close its estuarine nets, and its fish have been plagued by disease which has led to rivers such as the Driva and the Laerdal being closed for rod and line fishing until such time as salmon stocks have recovered.

However, it is still true that Norway must offer the best chance worldwide that fishermen have of hooking and landing the Atlantic salmon of their dreams. Fishing in the land of the midnight sun against a backdrop of stunning fjords, mountains and valleys while soaking up the tradition and history of the place is a special memory for those fishermen lucky enough to have been there.

WHEN TO GO

Above the 60th Parallel in summer, Norwegian nights are short, with perhaps only an hour or two of semi-dark conditions during most of June and July. Throughout Norway on May 31 fishermen feverishly tackle-up their rods in preparation for 12 o'clock midnight and the beginning of another season. It is generally reckoned that the largest fish will come in the first month of the season, with the smaller salmon and grilse run making up the majority of the fishing as the season advances. June and early July will also be the months in which the highest volume of water is in the rivers owing to snow melt from their mountainous catchment areas. On the larger rivers this heavier early water usually dictates a higher proportion of boat fishing. The season ends in August.

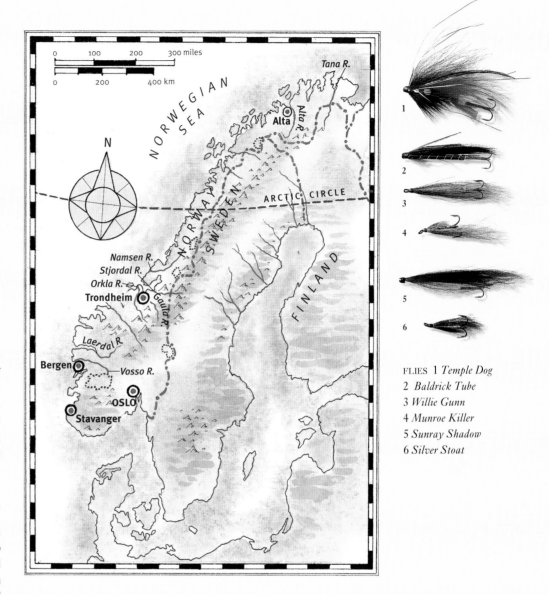

FLIES 1 *Temple Dog*
2 *Baldrick Tube*
3 *Willie Gunn*
4 *Munroe Killer*
5 *Sunray Shadow*
6 *Silver Stoat*

TACKLE

RODS: Double-handed rods, from 13 to 16 ft for 9–11 wt lines.

REELS: Large direct-drive adjustable disk-brake reels to hold fly line and at least 150 yards of 30 lb backing.

LINES: Fast sinking lines for early season fishing, through to intermediates and floaters by the end of the season.

LEADERS: 5–25 lb breaking strain leaders.

FLIES: Large hook sizes are the favourites for traditional hair- and feather-wing patterns such as Green Highlander, Akroyd, General Practitioner and Comally. Tubes and Waddingtons might include Baldricks, Sunray Shadows, Temple Dogs and Willie Gunns.

Fly-fishing in the Middle Ages

Russia

DAVID PROFUMO

"Sunlight suddenly lit the pool, and I had a surprising moment of certitude: the deep golden water gargled around my legs, and I felt a familiar, slight effervescence along my lower spine, that presentiment that something is going to happen. Arthur Ransome likened this to those strange occasions when silence descends on a crowded room, and at such moments in Czarist days they used to say, 'a policeman is being born'. To me, it is the 'fishological moment'."

elk and wild bull. In places – fresh or salt – where fish were to be found abundantly in season, spiral labyrinths of granite were arranged on the shoreline, some of them forty feet across. Such intricacy suggests a ritualistic purpose.

Excavations have revealed amber carvings of animals and fish, plus other zoomorphic figures in scattered sites: but then this culture apparently disappears, about 500 years before the birth of Christ.

The Umba had proved to be a dud, but my week on the Ponoi might have altered my entire perspective on salmon fishing. Of the forty or so rivers I've tried for Atlantics it was the most action-packed place I've ever wet a hook – and, to avoid brochurism and superlatives, I'd rather define it in terms of how it differed from my usual experiences of salmon fishing.

Most of my gamefishing is done in the British Isles and Ireland: for a start, we don't generally have sporting camps like this, where strangers commingle for a week or more. Our inns and hotels foster quite different group dynamics – doubtless weird to foreign visitors – but companionship is a crucial part of fishing, and I was lucky at Ryabaga to team up with Robert and Alistair, two expat Brits from Connecticut. My new friends were both energetic and experienced (Alistair had an incredible Alta salmon of 54 pounds on fly to his credit) and the triumvirate had its first day out on the Lower Tomba beat, guided by Jeff Vermillion. The river was a little high to be in perfect ply, but the guides were all positive and resourceful – this was the first difference for me, after decades of gillies, and the professional gloom of Celt or Gael. I lost a good, bright fish in the first pool we tried, after ten minutes struggling to bring it near the gravel bar along which I had waded, and it seemed virtually all day Jeff put us over fish. I was not used to this, either.

Long ago – and I can still picture the little Hebridean lodge where I came to this conclusion – I decided that arithmetic and salmon angling don't mix, and the man who is constantly hung up about the number of fish he has caught is really a guy anxious about his masculinity. Still, one can hardly describe a river like the Ponoi and avoid all mention of numbers. Between the three of us we played 24 salmon that day, and this was not considered a bonanza. The last one I had took me on the dangle, and, though I am quite hard on fish and tend to use stout tackle, it was almost twenty minutes before I brought her in – a silver darling of sixteen pounds, with that lavender sheen to her flanks, and for a moment all mine.

"Ain't it a neat river, though?" grinned Jeff, lighting his end-of-session smoke. I felt as triumphant as the champion crab-catcher of Kamchatka.

That night a bunch of us sat up late in the dining tent, sipping Stolichnaya, regaled by piscatory tales from Pierre (a French guest whose partner in life, Elaine, was a glamorous black jazz singer – a *rara avis* in this neck of the woods), and he told us of his experiences dry fly-fishing for crocodiles, using a live chicken. Before the Stolly stole all the remaining sense out of my ballpoint, I slunk to my tent to jot down initial impressions of this exceptional place.

With no licensed nets or poaching, and zero pollution, the Ponoi is frankly a privilege to fish in the modern age: the first twelve days of the season had rewarded anglers from the camp with almost 2,000 salmon. That would be a decade's tally from many of the rivers featuring in my fishing log. At times the runs are so prolific it gives one a rare glimpse of how things once were elsewhere: it's like fly-fishing in the Middle Ages.

ABOVE *One of the best pools on the Ponoi is the Home Pool, located only a hundred yards from camp. Anglers often visit it for a few casts after dinner.*

ABOVE *A panorama of the Ponoi River camp showing the tents, the river, and the vast wilderness beyond.*

The biggest of the region's 65 salmon rivers, the Ponoi may not be quite as torrential as some of its northern counterparts, but it can present a daunting prospect. At a hundred yards across, it's large even by our Tay standards, and the trick is to discern the distinct streams within the watercourse, and concentrate accordingly; whilst there is often some truth in the Spanish maxim *a rio revuelto, ganancia de pescadores* (meaning "in the troubled stream, gain for the fishermen"), aggressive wading is not always the key to more strikes, and it is possible to over-cast certain lies. Subtle strategies learned on smaller rivers can occasionally pay off here.

Mind you, with several miles of water at your disposal each day the average British angler – used to trying the same pools all week – will also feel spoiled for choice. It's pleasantly hard work covering your beat, clambering in and out of the boat and then wading your way amid the rocks, hour after hour, but you just fish through, for all you are worth – "Ride straight, and ride like hell", as the pig-stickers of the Raj used to advise newcomers to their peculiar pastime.

A word about "catch and release" (or *prise et remise*, as it is more stylishly known in Canada): many of us have been voluntarily practising this with salmon in certain

UK rivers for years, but it has to be said that the whole notion of "borrowing" a salmonid has not yet leached into the mainstream of our sport. The majority of our anglers kill salmon, if in good condition, and eat them. This was the tradition in which I was brought up – historically, it used to have something to do with private ownership of fishing rights – and I have to say there persists for me a palpable dif-ference in terms of passionate chemistry between losing near the net a fish you were anyway bound to release, and parting company just before the *moment critique* with one you might have decided to keep.

No doubt suitably funded philosophers are resolving this enigma as we sleep.

With virtually all our salmon waters privately husbanded and preserved, the British angler today enjoys little in the way of true wilderness experience. Most of our pools are particularised with names, and at least a hundred years of oral

189

ABOVE *A Thunder and Lightning.*

ABOVE *A Durham Ranger.*

history: the beat on the Tweed that I fish each autumn not only has fabled casts but individual rocks recorded in Victorian literature. By contrast, the Kola Peninsula was closed for military reasons until 1989, so its stones are as yet unstoried and its liquid mythology is still in the making.

The unwary European, used to footpaths along his beat, and bankside huts with soft furnishings (on the Tay there's rumoured to be one boasting a chandelier), might find all this wilderness occasionally overwhelming. Personally, I appreciate the joys of solitude: but I do recall a moment, wading deep around some dinosaur boulders at the mouth of the Pornache tributary, when I stepped into a dip where the stream churned below the rocks, and I realised I couldn't retreat. The rest of the party had boated away out of sight, and I felt a deep jolt of loneliness. (I was drying off on the bank, when they returned.)

The Ponoi salmon seem to behave more wildly, too. This may be because they are closer to their marine feeding grounds (I don't know), but they frequently charge the fly with a gusto rare on my home waters: sometimes the same fish will come three or four times before making up its mind, and the takes can be volcanic. If the temperatures are right, they also show well to a Muddler or dry fly; as a result, for every fish landed you probably enjoy some form of reaction from about four others. Except in fortuitous circumstances – such as a concentration of grilse briefly stopping in a pool, or a shoal of salmon entering a loch after a drought – this sort of sport no longer exists in Britain.

LEFT *Late August, and the beginning of fall, can put color in the leaves and frost on the rod rack.*

In the modern period, man has altered the weather and broken the wheel of the seasons. Many of the great migrations that used to articulate the year – bison, pigeon, even aquatic insects themselves – have become a thing of the past, and the runs of Atlantic salmon have been extinguished from hundreds of Europe's waterways. I am wary of nostalgia, but sometimes I stand on the banks of my local river, the Thames (which I have fished since I was a schoolboy), and imagine what England's ancient artery must have been like in its piscatorial heyday.

Legend has it that on the eve of the consecration of London's first church (in 616), St Peter himself promised good salmon fishing for ever to a ferryman and his family, provided they offered a tenth of all catches to the church – and records suggest that the Thames was for centuries a commercially viable fishery, with a healthy run of salmon. Hard up after the crusades, for example, Richard I sold off the salmon-netting rights to the City Corporation in 1197 for the measly sum of 1,500 marks – one of the first concessions of the sovereign's supreme prerogative in all English history. Shortly thereafter, Henry III began his menagerie in the Tower, and the king of Norway gave him a polar bear which was swum daily in the river on collar and leash, to catch salmon for its supper.

When I get my hands on that time machine, I shall take my Thomas & Thomas double-hander back to the medieval Thames, and start in just below the bridge.

The myth persists – though documentary corroboration is lacking – that at this period apprentices in London and elsewhere had inserted into their indentures an article specifying they should not be fed salmon more than once a week. This gives some idea of how common the fish once were, though I think the real reason was that leprosy was thought to be brought on by eating fish.

Right up until Regency times, professional fishermen on the Thames sent some 3,000 salmon to Billingsgate each season. Nemesis came with the discharge from gasworks, sewage, the building of pound-locks to make the river navigable, and greed. There have been recent efforts to re-salmonise the river, but whether the fish can reproduce is uncertain. George IV is said to have bought the last truly wild Thames salmon in 1820 for a guinea a pound, from a fisherman named Finmore.

By the Thursday, I had hooked more salmon in a week than I would normally encounter in a season, but the Kola gods had not forgotten my earlier arrogance.

We went downstream to Hard Curve – a stunning flight, only four metres above the water – and guide Rick said we just might be in for a bonanza; there had been a high tide and a full moon the previous day, and the first of the autumn fish were due any time (this was early September). Like a fool, I counted my chickens.

Back at the dock that evening there were general reports of a good day: one guy had landed a 23-pounder (a large fish for this system); our party had taken seven. "Hell, today I guess everyone caught a buncha fish," smiled Jack, a judge from Louisiana, who looked as if he were going to order me to get a haircut. I mumbled something polite. But I was the only person in camp who had caught nothing.

Slouching off to sulk alone in the sauna with the last of my whisky, I felt the black dog of despair snapping at my heels. I had fished badly that day, and I knew it – I'd missed the few offers that came my way, and my concentration had melted. Every cast should have an idea behind it, but by the afternoon I had become mechanical, resentful, hopeless. In psychic terms, the difference between no fish and one fish has got to be one of the greatest distances in the universe. And tomorrow was my last chance. Half-man half-scotch, I lumbered back to my tent in the dark like some beast of the Apocalypse.

Next day began with a roasting great hangover. It felt as if my mouth had been used as a pottery kiln all night, but I made it through breakfast and by the time the

ABOVE *Standing on a hillside, after dinner, I shot this picture of the camp. Its lights glow in the lingering twilight of one of summer's "white nights."*

boat had roared down to Gold Creek my crapula had been ventilated by the Arctic ozone. I had the beat to myself, as the others were fishing lower down, and I rolled a bright fish in the twisting water at the tail of our first run. He would not come again, but Dima my guide felt we were in business: "Maybe next pool is good, Dave," he said levelly, as he dropped the boat. I needed to believe him.

Wading in at the neck of the fast stream, I lengthened some line and made a goodish cast square across the current. Sunlight suddenly lit the pool, and I had a surprising moment of certitude: the deep golden water gargled around my legs, and I felt a familiar, slight effervescence along my lower spine, that presentiment that something is going to happen. Arthur Ransome likened this to those strange occasions when silence descends on a crowded room, and at such moments in Czarist days they used to say, "a policeman is being born". To me, it is the "fishological moment".

My Willie Gunn began to track round in an arc, and a fish flared off its lie and surged at it: in my excitement, I struck hard – and, against all the rules, this hooked it. That salmon did not come off, nor did the next five (I even had a brace of sea trout, as a bonus). "You're certainly making up for your blank day," observed Alistair pointedly into his soup – when we met up for lunch they'd had one apiece, and a smashed rod. We sipped a little Russian cabernet, and fended off looming thoughts of home. But I was still on a roll, and prayed silently to St Zeno – patron saint of fish hooks – that the fish would not all run through, or switch right off.

We swapped beats, but my luck held. At five to six, Dima histrionically consulted his watch. "One more drop," he announced. We had landed nine, and I had never managed double figures in the thirty years since I caught my first salmon.

A fish turned below the cliff, and with the third fly we tried there came a strangely gentle take, but he felt the steel and went into an aerial lambada. He made for the tailwater, and I braked him hard off my Bogdan: that fish weighed twelve pounds – I know, because we kept him for dinner.

They say you can't step into the same river twice, and I don't know if I'll ever make it back to the Ponoi. People ask if the experience of such plenty spoils you for the fishing elsewhere, but it does not. Ever since I caught my first salmon from a modest spate river in the Scottish Highlands – with a spliced greenheart rod and a line of dressed silk – I have become inured to droughts, dearth and disappointment. The opportunities offered by the Ponoi now seem slightly unreal. It was like a harem, but I know my natural place is back in the small-town dancehalls.

Prolific Eastern Margins

Russia

BILL CURRIE

"Rivers of the far north haunt you. They have an amazing numinous quality.

They draw you into their atmosphere and give you a marvellous feeling of

being, at last, in contact with wild tundra salmon. Ponoi has this quality. …

I have at times been very aware of the serenity of the wilderness. I have

fought a hard-pulling salmon while peregrines spiralled and screamed above

the pool. I have waded between great rocks under the midnight sun and

brought salmon in from the golden water."

Good salmon-fishing expeditions share many of the characteristics of pilgrimages. My first visit to the Ponoi had all the marks of that. It was certainly something more than a search for salmon abundance. It was an experience which drew on thirty years of waiting. When I was walking and fishing in the north of Finnish Lapland in the 1950s and '60s, I found my eyes and thoughts constantly turning to the east. From time to time I heard tales of the salmon rivers of the Kola. With a sweep of an arm and a glittering eye, travellers would say, "Over there lies the prolific eastern margin of the salmon world." It was heady stuff, but I was ready for it. I had no difficulty in believing that the Kola rivers were paradisal. There was one small practical problem, however; they were in forbidden territory. I was faced with what was in effect a war frontier between Finland and the USSR. This merely added spice to my longing to sample these Russian rivers and to see the lands of the Kola Peninsula through which they flowed. To whet my appetite, some of the rivers of the Kola tantalizingly had their headwaters in Finnish Lapland and, fishing and following them, I pressed on right to the frontier, catching large trout in pools among massive, ancient pines. Then, one day in the depths of the forest, I came across a salmon kelt (a spent fish) splashing in one of the headstreams of the Luttojoki. That river, not many kilometres downstream, crossed the frontier, took the Russian name Lotta and flowed to join the Kola River and meet the sea. Finding that solitary kelt was like meeting a messenger. It beckoned me and fermented my longing to fish for salmon in these eastern rivers of the peninsula.

Decades later, when relations between west and east had mellowed, I had the chance to go to the Kola and fish its largest river, the Ponoi. I savoured the prospects and they were compelling. The northern Kola rivers flow into what was, for me, the unknown Barents Sea – a northern and eastern ocean, salmon-rich, warmed by the tail of the Gulf Stream. The reported abundance of salmon in Ponoi was electrifying. The biologists were enthusiastic; they described important research into the salmon of this great wilderness river. Fishers who had been to the Ponoi excited me; they told me tales of salmon in plenty, wild takers, aggressive and full of wilderness spontaneity.

Ponoi is the longest of the Kola salmon rivers, over four hundred kilometres. It is also very strategically placed. It meets the sea at the most easterly point of the Kola Peninsula, where the northerly Murmanian Coast turns south and west to become the northern shores of the White Sea. The Ponoi valley divides the open, often rather stark, tundra of the northern peninsula, from the southern Kola where forests grow. There is another important difference between north and south, however. The northern rivers flow into the largely ice-free Barents Sea, while the

ABOVE *The end of a fine day's sport with good friends, a fresh fish for supper, and a helicopter ride home to the Ponoi River camp.*

rivers of the southern Kola flow to the White Sea, which freezes over in winter. Flying down from Murmansk in the helicopter – a two-and-a-half-hour journey – you get a view of the openness and heavily ice-scoured rock of the northern peninsula. It is a pre-Cambrian shield, rich in lakes, bearing only the sparsest signs of trees where valleys are sufficiently sheltered. Ponoi has cut a deep, beautiful valley into the hard rock of this shield. When you land at the camp, you will see this clearly. Well above the river, the tundra lies level and scoured; within the river valley, birch, aspen, pine, spruce and a host of Arctic wildflowers flourish. Summer migrant birds nest in the valley, falcons sweep above river pools, aquatic flies hatch and, above all, salmon in plenty run the river. In summer, Ponoi has a fecundity which can make it hard to believe that the river lies four degrees above the Arctic Circle.

The camp at Ryabaga sits among birches at the mouth of one of the smaller tributaries. A kilometre above that, the Purnache, a main feeder, joins. A short helicopter flight away the Acha flows in from the left bank. Both are memorable salmon rivers in their own right. From the Ryabaga camp, fishers cover a great swathe of excellent salmon water, embracing the two main tributaries and the wide, gliding, rich, streamy Ponoi all the way down to the estuary. Ponoi is, of course, in terms of the salmon and the delights of fishing for them, an *embarras de richesses*. For me, it always seems to be two rivers in one. The first is the panoramic Ponoi itself – a vast sweep of water hissing over the stones at Ryabaga, and two hundred and fifty metres away on the opposite bank you see the great sweep of the river gliding past cliffy red rocks and clinging birches. From the Ryabaga camp, upstream, right to the point of disappearance, the river presents a vast waterscape, punctuated in a rather theatrical way by two huge granite rocks which lie just downstream of the mouth of the Purnache. By day they glitter red; in the dusk they take on the appearance of primeval cut-outs. You look upstream to see the never-setting midnight sun. If you are fishing the Home Pool late after dinner, turn round and you will see the Ponoi above you flowing golden with its rocks and trees sombre with the darkness of silhouettes.

The second river lies at your feet as you wade. The water is tinged with peat, in summer looking like fino sherry. The streams curl round submerged stones and glide over beds of shingle, boulders and sand, forming a very active, very detailed and very fishy river. All the beats of Ponoi give you these two perspectives. On the one hand there is a vastness and on the other a detailed and intricate river within. There the river has formed a multitude of individual lies, like suite upon suite of salmon rooms, individually furnished. When I fish Ponoi I am always lifting my head to savour the panorama, then refocusing rapidly on the detail within casting distance, where my fly searches out pockets between boulders, curling streams butting off stone headlands or wide gliding sheets of water flowing over stones and sand. It is a wonderful salmon river.

You would expect a salmon-rich river like Ponoi to show fish constantly, but it does not. True, you do see salmon splashing here and there, but far less frequently than on Scottish rivers. I do not know why a river as full of fish as this is so secretive. The fish are no sluggards. They slash at your fly aggressively; they boil and lunge at dry and hitched flies and they are clearly enthusiastic and vigorous fish. But they do not show much. I grew to like this contrast between their covert behaviour and their sudden aggression. For example, fishing from the bank on Golden

BELOW *A Murmansk Munroe.*

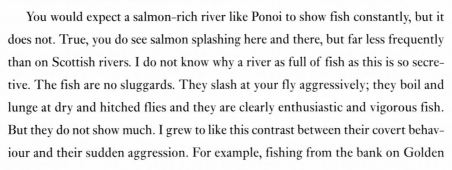

ABOVE *A lone angler fishes the Home Pool before breakfast.*

Beach with floating line was classic summer fly-fishing – exactly what A.H.E. Wood described on the Scottish Dee in the 1930s. At one point I was casting from the rocks, a little bit above the main stream, and I could see how the long line led the fly round, touring just below the surface as the current swung it in, making the leader straighten and the fly hover. Halfway down the stream, just as Sergei, my guide, was saying that he thought I would have had a take by that point, the fly disappeared inside a sudden swirl on the water, the line tightened and a salmon was on, heaving line out as it made for the heavier stream in the middle of the river.

ABOVE *An overview of the Ponoi River camp nestled in for the night, its lights the only ones for hundreds of miles.*

Then it happened again, as if the second fish had learned from the first. Both were eight- or nine-pound salmon, very fresh, great fish to raise and catch. From my position a little above the water I really was in the five-guinea seats. It was visually splendid. The sweep of the line, the touring and hovering fly and the sudden boil as the salmon took were the essence of good fly-fishing. I was just beginning to feel triumphalist when my fishing companion came downstream from the little bay above. He had also taken two. I would have launched into a eulogy about the stream I had just covered, but, before I could, he pointed upstream to the bay he had just fished and said, "A perfect place."

That visit was in mid-July. The spring salmon of Ponoi had been going well since late May, but had begun to tail off by July. Rods had accounted for four

thousand fish by the end of June. These earlier fish, many between ten and twenty pounds, were followed by a run of grilse – a vast run of one-sea-winter small fish – and with them came a run of two-sea-winter summer salmon – the eight- and ten-pounders (and better) which I have described. Later in the summer the runs of large autumn salmon come into the river, fish which might be anything from ten to twenty-five pounds. If it were merely a picture of these four runs – springers, grilse, summer fish and autumn salmon – each run bringing in large numbers, that would be a very satisfying picture of a salmon river in its prime. There is, on Ponoi,

ABOVE *Skating a bomber across the current is a great way of attracting Ponoi River salmon.*

however, another dimension. The normal order of things is that the salmon mature progressively while they are in fresh water, growing heavy with spawn which they will shed in the late autumn. On Ponoi, there is a class of fish which comes into the river in the late summer, stays in the river over the winter without spawning, stays on throughout the following summer and only then matures and spawns during the second autumn. The salmon, by that time a kelt, stays on further to over-winter in the river and it only leaves for the sea the following spring. This is a remarkable freshwater sojourn of eighteen months. It is incredible that salmon, which do not feed in fresh water, should be able to do this. What energy-packed fat and muscle they must have! This phenomenon has been clearly monitored and studied by the biological research team on Ponoi. Fish are tagged and logged and there can be no doubt that a proportion of Ponoi salmon record the longest period in fresh water known for the species.

You can fish bank, wading or boat on Ponoi. I like to have a ration of all three, but on certain beats there is some delicious fishing only to be had by using the boat. I do not just mean that the boat can take you out to cover water well beyond wading reach, to fish mid-river lies where the Ponoi curls over boulders, to long streams where the boat can let you drift down, choosing this or that angle over the water. I mean that the boat can, in a slightly contradictory way, let you fish close to the bank. The difference is that you are out fishing in, rather than in fishing out. On Clough Creek, just down from Golden Beach, and only an easy boat ride down-stream from the camp, there was a series of rocky headlands on the right bank. Glides sweep down on these and at the headland the stream breaks and, typically, forms a choppy stream below, easing off to a rippled glide over the deeper water where the headland stream has scoured out the bed. These are great places for salmon to lie. In the glides above the points you could present a steadily swinging fly coming off the lies and fish would follow and boil at it, turning and pulling and hooking themselves well as they did so. You would also find a fish – often a grilse – absolutely on the point itself, as if touching the rock point with its tail. In the broken stream and the long ripple below, you could swing or dangle the fly or make a hitched fly track over the surface as the conditions dictated. Fast streams like that were brilliant taking water. Fish would come fast to the fly, often appearing with great suddenness to take the floating-line fly or the hitch with a great surface splash followed by a hard pull.

The Ponoi guides were excellent and their knowledge of each pool was often critical. On Tomba, one of our lower beats, not far below the point at which the Tomba tributary runs in, the river slides deeply along a sheer rock face. It is the sort

BELOW *A Crystal Willie Gunn.*

ABOVE *An American visitor about to release a fresh-run spring salmon.*

BELOW *A memento of my week on the Ponoi River – 46 salmon released and 100 rolls of film captured. What a place!*

ABOVE *A moment of exhilaration for angler Dick Viall and Russian guide Misha Timoshenko as the net is safely under another Ponoi salmon.*

of lie I might not fish at all in Scotland, thinking that the water there would be deep, possibly very deep, and salmon might well lie under rock ledges and not be interested in the fly.

Alexi, my guide, said, "Cast your fly in, right to the rock face."

I cast and plopped my #4 Claret Shrimp about eighteen inches from the mini-cliff.

"Nearer," said the guide.

I hit the water a foot off the face.

"No, no!" said Alexi. "Hit the rock with the fly!"

"You must be joking," I said. But I did it.

The biggish single hit the rock face, dropped in and was immediately taken by a good fat grilse. Yes, I did it again. In all I took four fish from this lie using Alexi's technique of bouncing the fly off the rock face. Without his advice, I would have

201

fished this pool in the conventional way, keeping off the rock to save my flies, and I would probably not have moved a single fish.

Ponoi, like all good salmon rivers, is something of a schoolmaster. It opens new doors in the mind. My salmon fishing in Scotland does not use dry fly, for the sterling reason that it does not work. I do not mean it does not work ever. From time to time a trout fisher floating a size twelve Greenwell's Glory has a kind of happy accident and finds a salmon attached. I have once or twice seen a salmon take a sea trout dap. The classic experiment carried out by G.M. La Branche at A.H.E. Wood's invitation, trying out dry fly for the prolific salmon of the Dee was, alas, resoundingly unsuccessful. Riffled hitch work in Scotland, while it moves salmon sometimes to the waking fly, is a sticky and reluctant method, and is seldom practised. In Canada, Iceland and Russia I have fished both dry and hitched flies with success. Ponoi is a place where you soon discover how good the surface fly can be – dry flies, hitched flies and those astonishing non-creatures, bombers. Surface flies on Ponoi are great sport. Some of my friends go there to fish nothing else. It is very visual, often spectacular and can be a memorable way to take salmon. On the long glide of a pool on Alexevski, where the burn flows in, salmon which were studiously ignoring the conventional fly came vigorously to a hitched fly, showing great flanks and scattering spray in great rises. On a hitched bomber on Lower Tomba I had one particular, wonderful, mental snapshot of seeing a salmon's nose appear and just sip the fly down. That two-second glimpse, and the pull which followed it, triggered a sudden burst of recognition – boyhood dapping for big sea trout in West Highland lochs and dibbling for salmon in Sutherland rivers – a powerful and deeply pleasurable cocktail, sweetness and strength and sheer excitement blended. I have to record that these very memorable Ponoi surface events have given me a problem. Dry and wet are in tension in my mind. At home, I know one of these is a false mistress, but on Ponoi I suffer from what amounts to a confliction of urges.

Salmon fishing is very much a business of hands-on at one end and remote control at the other. Everything is interpreted. The rod in your hand and the line at your fingertips perform well-rooted skills, masterful acts, ones you can practise. The fly in the water is very different. Much of the time, we can only infer what it might be doing and, as far as the reactions of the fish to the fly are concerned, we hope and trust and imagine. You become very conscious of this on a new river like the Ponoi,

ABOVE *After dinner, with the light low on the hills, is the perfect time to enjoy the river and its solitude.*

especially one where salmon can be secretive. Of course, we all arrive at new waters carrying invisible baggage, preconceptions, experience of other waters. We travel to Ponoi hoping that wilderness Russian salmon will have read the right books.

I arrived with what might fairly be described as a small-fly prejudice. I fish the Scottish Dee a lot and, as spring turns into summer there, we fish small flies on a floating line. When I say small I mean size ten or twelve. To many these are trout sizes. I had heard that Ponoi salmon liked larger flies and brighter dressings, so at the beginning of my fishing I tried eights and even sixes, using conventional patterns like Garry Dog, tied with yellows and reds. The Ponoi salmon were half-hearted about these, on the whole. So, working as I say by remote control, as you might work if you had to cut a key and make it turn a lock by trial and error, I dressed a series of larger light-wire single hooks and found some of the answers I was looking for. The best pattern was a fly I have tied up for myself for years, the Claret Shrimp. It is an extremely simple fly and can be tied in one's fingers, even on the bank of the pool. It has a silver tinsel body and a long claret hair wing (I use

ABOVE RIGHT *Happy anglers pose for a group portrait with a fresh salmon for dinner just before the short chopper ride back to camp.*

dark hairs from a wine-coloured bucktail) which I push back over the head of the fly to form long trailing fronds above and below the fly body. But the key is the tail. It is of yellow bucktail and on Ponoi I made it very long, sparse and sinuous. I used the tail to double the length of the fly. (Fishers will recognize my debt to the remarkable Ally's Shrimp in this.) The Ponoi fish slashed at this fly with its long, sinuous tail. One salmon on Tomba sprang from the water and took the fly on its downward plunge as a brown trout might do to a dropper.

We travelled widely to our beats, often by helicopter, but one of the finest pools lay right behind the camp – the Home Pool. The head was the great sheet of water upstream of our camp but the important change of pace which made the pool memorable was right behind the camp where a bar of boulders broke the flat glide and formed a long powerful rippled flow which ran for hundreds of metres, past the moored boats and down to the bend which formed the head of Golden Beach. I fished there most evenings after dinner and on one occasion, fishing in the never-ending dusk of an Arctic night, I swung through the stream a size six Garry Dog with a long golden trailing wing and I hooked a fish which ran like no other Ponoi salmon I encountered. It leapt twice in the course of one formidable run and fought with great power through several other runs and solid pulling matches. I at last brought it in, a great silver fish, bright against the dark stones at the edge of the water. I watched it kick off into the current on release. In my tent that night, I pulled out the blue card with the Atlantic Salmon Federation "Salometer" Table and read off the rather generous fact that a thirty-nine-inch salmon would probably weigh twenty-two pounds.

ASF, you are too kind. I think that fish was eighteen and a half pounds, but what the salometer cannot compute is that it was absolutely memorable.

Rivers of the far north haunt you. They have an amazing numinous quality. They draw you into their atmosphere and give you a marvellous feeling of being, at last, in contact with wild tundra salmon. Ponoi has this quality. Of course, in its abundance, it can sometimes be very upfront and over-generous in its sport. On Ponoi I have at times been very aware of the serenity of the wilderness. I have fought a hard-pulling salmon while peregrines spiralled and screamed above the pool. I have waded between great rocks under the midnight sun and brought salmon in from the golden water. Moments like these seem close to the dream I had when I peered through the Iron Curtain and longed for the chance to fish a Kola salmon river. I am glad in one way that I had to wait to make the journey. In my youth, I would have treated the visit as an expedition. When my journey to the Ponoi eventually came, it felt much more in the nature of a pilgrimage.

RUSSIA: FACTFILE

BACKGROUND

Ask anyone who has fished in Russia (especially on one of the more prolific rivers) what it was like, and the answer is almost invariably the same: "more fish than you can shake a stick at", or "fishing like it was in the good old days". Statements like these provide a pretty good summary of what Russia has come to mean in the world of Atlantic salmon fishermen.

Owing to a high number of sensitive military sites throughout the Kola Peninsula, it was as late as 1989 – the period of *glasnost* and the end of the cold war – that reports first started to trickle in about the extraordinary content of the Kola's rivers. Salmon running the peninsula's rivers from the White and Barents Seas had never come under the kind of commercial fishing pressure that other nations' stocks had had to endure. Those who had led the initial exploratory trips were reporting unheard-of numbers of fish.

The team that first fished the Ponoi River was dropped near the headwaters with rubber Avon rafts, with the intention of fishing down the river to establish some known pools and a site for a base camp. After a short time it became apparent just how many fish there were in each pool. Rather than get out of the boat and fish every pool, they decided to stop only when five salmon could be seen in the air simultaneously as they entered a pool!

With such an abundance of Atlantic salmon throughout the Kola's rivers, it is possible not only for one angler to catch several fish in a day, but also to experiment with a wide variety of techniques. There is no doubt that the Kola Peninsula rivers have few equals, a fact that is unlikely to change in the near future.

WHEN TO GO

Nearly all of Russia's Atlantic salmon rivers are north of the Arctic Circle and the season is a relatively short one. The fishing starts in June and ends in September, and as with most Atlantic salmon destinations the returning fish ascend the different rivers in varying intensities through the season. The beginning and end of the season are most noted for larger fish, and the central months of the season for the largest schools of smaller salmon and grilse.

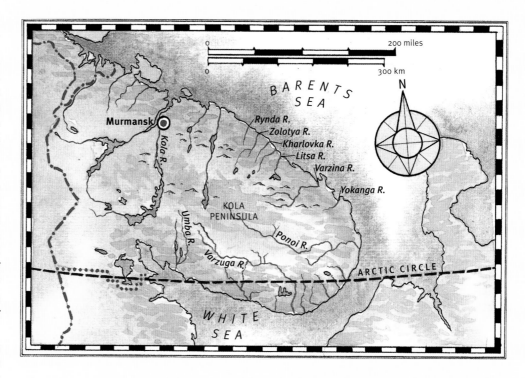

TACKLE

RODS: Single-handed rods, 9–11 ft for 7–9 wt lines. Double-handed rods, 12½–15 ft for 8–11 wt lines.

REELS: Large arbor direct-drive reels with drag systems capable of holding fly line and 150 yards of 25–30 lb backing.

LINES: A full selection of lines from floating to sinking. Most of the season will be fished with floaters and intermediates.

LEADERS: Depending on which river you fish and the size of the fish in it, 10–15 lb leader should be ample.

FLIES: Midsummer, dry flies are the most sporting: Bombers, Wulffs and Muddlers. Wet favourites are Ponoi Green, Allies and other Scottish traditional patterns.

FLIES 1 *Crystal Willie Gunn* 2 *Ponoi Red* 3 *Murmansk Munroe* 4 *Crystal Sweep* 5 *General Practitioner* 6 *Ally's Shrimp (Tube)* 7 *Garry Dog* 8 *Black & Red (Tube)* 9 *Willie Gunn (Tube)* 10 *Half & Half (Tube)*

OPPOSITE *Ponoi salmon respond aggressively to a waking bomber. In fact, some anglers prefer to use only dry flies, as it is so exciting to see the take.*

The Dreadnaught Pool

New Zealand

ZANE GREY

"The sun had set as I waded in again. A shimmering ethereal light moved over the pool. The reflection of the huge bluff resembled a battleship more than the bluff itself. Clear and black-purple rose the mountain range, and golden clouds grew more deeply gold. The river roared above and below, deep-toned and full of melody. A cool breeze drifted down from upstream. I cast over all the water I had previously covered without raising a fish. Farther out and down I saw trout rising, curling dark tails out of the gold gleam on the water."

"This pool here is called Dreadnaught," said [the Maori guide] Hoka, pointing to a huge steep bluff strikingly like the shape of a dismantled man-of-war. It stood up all alone. The surrounding banks were low and green. After one glance, I gave my attention to picking my steps among the boulders, while Hoka kept on talking. "My people once fought battles here. They had a *pa* on top of this bluff. I'll show you graves that are wearing away. The skulls roll down into the river. Yes, my people, the Maoris, were great fighters. They stood up face to face, and gave blow for blow, like men."

The lower and larger end of that pool grew fascinating to me. Under the opposite bank the water looked deep and dark. A few amber-colored rocks showed at the closer edge of the current. It shoaled toward the wide part, with here and there a golden boulder gleaming far under the water. What a wonderful pool!

I could see now how such a pool might reward a skillful far-casting angler, when the rainbows were running. After a long climb up rapids, what a pool to rest in! There might even be a trout resting there then. So I picked up my rod and strode down to the river.

A clean sand bar ran out thirty yards or more, shelving into deep green water. Here a gliding swirling current moved off to the center of the pool, and turned toward the glancing incline at the head of the narrow rapid. The second and heavier current worked farther across. By wading to the limit I imagined I might cast to the edge of that bed water. I meant to go leisurely and try the closer current first. It was my kind of a place. It kept growing upon me. I waded in to my knees, and cast half across this nearer current. My big fly sank and glided on. I followed it with my eye, and then gave it a slight jerky movement. Darker it became, and passed on out of my sight, where the light on the water made it impossible for me to see. I had scarcely forty feet of line out. It straightened below me, and then I whipped it back and cast again, taking a step or two farther on the sand bar.

My line curved and straightened. Mechanically I pulled a yard or so off my reel, then drew perhaps twice as much back, holding it in loops in my left hand. Then I cast again, letting all the loose line go. It swept out, unrolled and alighted straight, with the fly striking gently. Was that not a fine cast? I felt gratified. "Pretty poor, I don't think," I soliloquized, and stole a glance upriver to see if the Captain had observed my beautiful cast. Apparently he did not know I was on

ABOVE *With its high peaks, its heavily wooded country, and the ever-changing light that plays across its valleys, New Zealand is an inspiration to fishermen and photographers alike.*

the river. Then I looked quickly back at my fly.

It sank just at the edge of the light place on the water. I lost sight of it, but knew about where it floated. Suddenly right where I was looking on this glancing sunlit pool came a deep angry swirl. Simultaneously with this came a swift powerful pull, which ripped the line out of my left hand, and then jerked my rod down straight.

"Zee-eee!" shrieked my reel.

Then the water burst white, and a huge trout leaped in spasmodic action. He shot up, curved and black, his great jaws wide and sharp. I saw his spread tail quivering. Down he thumped, making splash and spray.

Then I seemed to do many things at once. I drew my rod up, despite the strain upon it; I backed toward the shore; I reeled frantically, for the trout ran upstream; I yelled for Morton and then for Captain Mitchell.

"Doc, he's a wolloper!" yelled the Captain.

"Oh, biggest trout I ever saw!" I returned wildly.

Once out of the water I ran up the beach toward Captain Mitchell, who was wading to meet me. I got even with my fish, and regained all but part of the bag in my line. What a weight! I could scarcely hold the six-ounce rod erect. The tip bent far over, and wagged like a buggy whip.

211

"Look out when he turns!" called Mitchell.

When the fish struck the swift current, he leaped right before me. I saw him with vivid distinctness – the largest trout that I ever saw on line of mine – a dark bronze-backed and rose-sided male, terribly instinct with the ferocity and strength of self-preservation; black-spotted, big-finned, hook-nosed. I heard the heavy shuffle as he shook himself. Then he tumbled back.

ABOVE *Anglers cast to cruising browns on the shores of Lake Wakatipu near Queenstown on South Island.*

212

"Now!" yelled Captain Mitchell, right behind me.

I knew. I was ready. The rainbow turned. Off like an arrow!

"Zee! Zee! Zee!" he took a hundred yards of line.

"Oh Morton! Morton! … *Camera*!" I shouted hoarsely, with every nerve in my body at supreme strain. What would his next jump be? After that run! I was all aquiver. He was as big as my black Marlin. My tight line swept up to the surface as I have seen it sweep with so many fish. "He's coming out!" I yelled for Morton's benefit.

Then out he came magnificently. Straight up six feet, eight feet and over, a regular salmon leap he made, gleaming beautifully in the sun. What a picture! If only Morton got him with the camera I would not mind losing him, as surely I must lose him. Down he splashed. "*Zee!*" whizzed my line.

I heard Morton running over the boulders, and turned to see him making toward his camera. He had not been ready. What an incomparable opportunity lost! I always missed the greatest pictures! My impatience and disappointment vented themselves upon poor Morton, who looked as if he felt as badly as I. Then a hard jerk on my rod turned my gaze frantically back to the pool, just in time to see the great rainbow go down from another grand leap. With that he sheered round to the left, into the center of the wide swirl. I strode rapidly down the beach and into the water, winding my reel as fast as possible. How hard to hold that tip up and yet to recover line! My left arm ached, my right arm shook; for that matter, my legs shook also. I was hot and cold by turns. My throat seemed as tight as my line. Dry-mouthed, clogged in my lungs, with breast heaving, I strained every faculty to do what was right. Who ever said a trout could not stir an angler as greatly as a whale?

One sweep he made put my heart in my throat. It was toward the incline in the rapids. If he started down! But he ended with a leap, head upstream, and when he soused back he took another run, closer inshore toward me. Here I had to reel like a human windlass.

He was too fast; he got a slack line, and to my dismay and panic he jumped on that slack line. My mind whirled, and the climax of my emotions hung upon that moment. Suddenly, tight jerked my line again. The hook had held. He was fairly close at hand, in good position, head upriver, and tiring. I waded out on the beach; and though he chugged and tugged and bored he never again got the line out over fifty feet. Sooner or later – it seemed both only a few moments and a long while – I worked him in over the sand bar, where in the crystal water I saw every move of his rose-red body. How I reveled in his beauty! Many times he stuck out his open jaws, cruel beaks, and gaped and snapped and gasped.

At length I slid him out upon the sand, and that moment my vaunted championship of the Oregon steelhead suffered an eclipse. The great Oregon rainbow, transplanted to the snow waters of the Tongariro, was superior in every way to his Oregon cousin, the silver-pink steelhead that had access to the sea. I never looked down upon such a magnificent game fish. No artist could have caught with his brush the shining flecked bronze, the deep red flush from jaw to tail, the amber and pearl. Perforce he would have been content to catch the grand graceful contour of body, the wolf-jawed head, the lines of fins and tail.

He weighed eleven and one-half pounds. I tied him on a string, as I was wont to do with little fish when a boy, and watched him recover and swim about in the clear water.

As if by magic of nature the Dreadnaught Pool had been transformed. The something that was evermore about to happen to me in my fishing had happened there. There! The beautiful pool glimmered, shone, ran swiftly on, magnified in my sight. The sun was westering. It had lost its heat and glare. A shadow lay under the bluff. Only at the lower end did the sunlight make a light on the water, and it had changed. No longer hard to look upon!

I waded in up to my knees and began to cast with short line, gradually lengthening it, but now not leisurely, contentedly, dreamily! My nerves were as keen as the edge of a blade. Alert, quick, restrained, with all latent powers ready for instant demand, I watched my line sweep out and unroll, my leader straighten, and the big dark fly alight. What singularly pleasant sensations attended the whole procedure!

I knew I would raise another rainbow trout. That was the urge, wherefore the pool held more thrill and delight and stir for me. On the fifth cast, when the line in its sweep downstream had reached its limit, I had a strong vibrating strike. Like the first trout, this one hooked himself; and on his run he showed in a fine jump – a fish scarcely half as large as my first one. He ran out of the best fishing water, and eventually came over the sand bar, where I soon landed him, a white-and-rose fish, plump and solid, in the very best condition.

"Fresh-run trout," said Hoka. "They've just come up from the lake."

"By gad! then the run is on," returned Captain Mitchell with satisfaction.

RIGHT *A small spring creek winds its way down to meet the Eglinton River along the road to Milford Sound, South Island. This valley is probably one of the most beautiful in the world.*

This second fish weighed five and three-quarter pounds. He surely had all the strength of an eight-pound steelhead in his compact colorful body.

"Cap, make a few casts with my rod while I rest and hug the fire," I said. "That water has ice beaten a mile."

"Not on your life," replied the Captain warmly. "I've a hunch it's your day. Wade in; every moment now is precious."

So I found myself out again on the sand bar, casting and recasting, gradually wading out until I was over my hips and could go no farther. At that I drew my breath sharply when I looked down. How deceiving that water! Another step would have carried me over my head. If the bottom had not been sandy I would not have dared trust myself there, for the edge of the current just caught me and tried to move me off balance; but I was not to be caught unawares.

Sunlight still lay on the pool, yet cool and dark now, and waning. I fished the

ABOVE *A stealthy approach is critical in outwitting a feeding brown in the back eddy against a granite wall on this Southland stream.*

OPPOSITE ABOVE *Fish on! Well done, lads. A #14 Coch-Y-Bonddu strikes again on the Motueka River.*

part of the pool where I had raised the two trout. It brought no rise. Then I essayed to reach across the gentler current, across the narrow dark still aisle beyond, to the edge of the strong current, sweeping out from the bluff. It was a long cast for me, with a heavy fly, eighty feet or more. How the amber water, the pale-green shadowy depths, the changing lights under the surface seemed to call to me, to assure me, to haunt with magical portent!

Apparently without effort, I cast my fly exactly where I wanted to. The current hungrily seized it, and as it floated out of my sight I gave my rod a gentle motion. Halfway between the cast and where the line would have straightened out before me, a rainbow gave a heavy and irresistible lunge. It was a strike that outdid my first. It almost unbalanced me. It dragged hard on the line I clutched in my left hand. I was as quick as the fish and let go just as he hooked himself. Then followed a run the like of which I did not deem possible for any fish short of a salmon or a Marlin. He took all my line except a quarter of an inch left on the spool. That brought him to the shallow water way across where the right-hand channel went down. He did not want that. Luckily for me, he turned to the left and rounded the lower edge of the pool. Here I got line back. Next he rushed across toward the head of the rapid. I could do nothing but hold on and pray.

Twenty yards above the smooth glancing incline he sprang aloft in so prodigious a leap that my usual ready shout of delight froze in my throat. Like a deer, in long bounds he covered the water, how far I dared not believe. The last rays of the setting sun flashed on this fish, showing it to be heavy and round and deep, of a wonderful pearly white tinted with pink. It had a small head which resembled that of a salmon. I had hooked a big female rainbow, fresh run from old Taupo, and if I had not known before that I had a battle on my hands, I knew it on sight of the fish. Singularly indeed the females of these great rainbow trout are the hardest and fiercest fighters.

Fearing the swift water at the head of the rapid, I turned and plunged pellmell out to the beach and along it, holding my rod up as high as I could. I did not save any line, but I did not lose any, either. I ran clear to the end of the sandy beach where it verged on the boulders. A few paces farther on roared the river.

Then with a throbbing heart and indescribable feelings I faced the pool. There were one hundred and twenty-five yards of line out. The trout hung just above the rapid and there bored deep, to come up and thump on the surface. Inch by inch I lost line. She had her head upstream but the current was drawing her toward the incline. I became desperate. Once over that fall she would escape. The old situation presented itself – break the fish off or hold it. Inch by inch she tugged the line off my reel. With all that line off and most of it out of the water in plain sight, tight as a banjo string, I appeared to be at an overwhelming disadvantage. So I grasped the line in my left hand and held it. My six-ounce rod bowed and bent, then straightened and pointed. I felt its quivering vibration and I heard the slight singing of the tight line.

So there I held this stubborn female rainbow. Any part of my tackle or all of it might break, but not my spirit. How terribly hard it was not to weaken! Not to trust to luck! Not to release that tremendous strain!

The first few seconds were almost unendurable. They seemed an age. When would line or leader give way or the hook tear out? But nothing broke. I could hold the wonderful trout. Then as the moments passed I lost that tense agony of apprehension. I gained confidence. Unless the fish wheeled to race for the fall I would win. The chances were against such a move. Her head was up current, held by that rigid line. Soon the tremendous strain told. The rainbow came up, swirled and pounded and threshed on the surface. There was a time when all old fears returned and augmented;

218

BELOW *This angler is standing on a big rock – a few more feet and he would be up to his shoulders. The waters of New Zealand are incredibly clear and deceiving.*

but just as I was about to despair, the tension on rod and line relaxed. The trout swirled under and made upstream. This move I signaled with a shout, which was certainly echoed by my comrades, all lined up behind me, excited and gay and admonishing.

I walked down the beach, winding my reel fast, yet keeping the line taut. Thus I advanced fully a hundred yards. When I felt the enameled silk come to my fingers, to slip on the reel, I gave another shout. Then again I backed up the beach, pulling the trout, though not too hard. At last she got into the slack shallow water over the wide sand bar.

ABOVE *A Rat-faced MacDougall.*

ABOVE *New Zealand's streams are as colorful as an artist's palette. This is a back-country stream in the Springs Junction area of South Island.*

Here began another phase of the fight, surely an anxious and grim one for me, with every move of that gorgeous fish as plain as if she had been in the air. What a dogged stubborn almost unbeatable fish on such tackle! Yet that light tackle was just the splendid thing for such a fight. Fair to the fish and calling to all I possessed of skill and judgment! It required endurance, too, for I had begun to tire. My left arm had a cramp and my winding hand was numb.

The fish made short hard runs into the deeper water, yet each run I stopped eventually. Then they gave place to the thumping on the surface, the swirling breaks, the churning rolls, and the bulldog tug, tug, tug. The fight had long surpassed any I had ever had with a small fish. Even that of the ten-pound steelhead I hooked once in wild Deer Creek, Washington! So strong and unconquerable was this rainbow that I was fully a quarter of an hour working her into the shallower part of the bar. Every time the deep silvery side flashed, I almost had heart-failure. This fish would go heavier than the eleven-and-a-half-pound male. I had long felt that in the line, in the rod; and now I saw it. There was a remarkable zest in this part of the contest.

"Work that plugger in close where the water is shallower," advised Captain Mitchell.

Indeed, I had wanted and tried to do that, for the twisting rolling fish might any instant tear out the hook. I held harder now, pulled harder. Many times I led or drew or dragged the trout close to shore, and each time saw the gleaming silver-and-pink shape plunge back into deeper water.

The little rod wore tenaciously on the rainbow, growing stronger, bending less, drawing easier.

After what seemed an interminable period there in this foot-deep water the battle ended abruptly with the bend of the rod drawing the fish head on to the wet sand. Captain Mitchell had waded in back of my quarry, suddenly to lean down and slide her far up on the beach.

"What a bally fine trout!" burst out Morton. "Look at it! Deep, fat, thick. It'll weigh fourteen."

"Oh no," I gasped, working over my numb and aching arms and hands.

"By gad! that's a wonderful trout!" added the Captain, most enthusiastically. "Why, it's like a salmon!"

Certainly I had never seen anything so beautiful in color, so magnificent in contour. It was mother-of-pearl tinged with exquisite pink. The dots were scarcely discernible, and the fullness of swelling graceful curve seemed to outdo nature itself. How the small thoroughbred salmon-like head contrasted with the huge iron-jawed fierce-eyed head of the male I had caught first! It was strange to see the broader tail of the female, the thicker mass of muscled body, the larger fins. Nature had endowed this progenitor of the species, at least for the spawning season, with greater strength, speed, endurance, spirit and life.

"Eleven pounds, three-quarters!" presently sang out the Captain. "I missed it a couple of pounds. … Some rainbow, old man. Get in there and grab another."

"Won't you have a try with my rod?" I replied. "I'm darn near froze to death. Besides I want to put this one on a string with the others and watch them."

He was obdurate, so I went back into the water; and before I knew what was happening, almost, I had fastened to another trout. It did not have the great dragging weight of the other two, but it gave me a deep boring fight and deceived me utterly as to size. When landed, this, my fourth trout, weighed six and three-quarters, another female, fresh run from the lake, and a fine rainbow in hue.

"Make it five, Doc. This is your day. Anything can happen now. Get out your line," declared Mitchell, glowing of face.

The sun had set as I waded in again. A shimmering ethereal light moved over the pool. The reflection of the huge bluff resembled a battleship more than the bluff itself. Clear and black-purple rose the mountain range, and golden clouds grew more deeply gold. The river roared above and below, deep-toned and full of melody. A cool breeze drifted down from upstream.

I cast over all the water I had previously covered without raising a fish. Farther out and down I saw trout rising, curling dark tails out of the gold gleam on the water. I waded a foot farther than ever and made a cast, another, recovered line, then spent all the strength I had left in a cast that covered the current leading to the rising trout. I achieved it. The fly disappeared, my line glided on and on, suddenly to stretch like a whipcord and go zipping out of my left hand. Fast and hard!

What a wonderful thrill ran up and down my back, all over me!

"Ho! Ho! … Boys, I've hung another!" I bawled out, in stentorian voice. "Say, but he's taking line! … Oh, look at him jump! … Oh, two! … Oh, three! … Four, by gosh! … Oh, Morton, if we only had some sunlight! What a flying leapfrog this trout is! … *Five!*"

The last jump was splendid, with a high parabolic curve, and a slick cutting back into the water. This rainbow, too, was big, fast, strong and fierce. But the fish did everything that should not have been done and I did everything right. Fisherman's luck! Beached and weighed before my cheering companions: nine and one-half pounds; another silvery rosy female rainbow, thick and deep and wide!

ABOVE *My biggest brown to date … a little under 9 lb. I spotted him while eating lunch on a gravel bar next to a main highway.*

LEFT *A Czech Shrimp.*

Trout Among the Shadows

New Zealand

VERLYN KLINKENBORG

"Wilderness is not a state of being, but a principle of action. Clear water favors neither the angler nor the fish, though the angler thinks otherwise.

A big trout is wilder than a small trout, and more demoralizing when spooked. The angler was never a fish, though the trout is always a hunter. A trout expects trouble, though the angler wants sport. A trout in hand is the muscular instant that is always vanishing, taking your life away with it."

Tony Entwistle honks when he spots a harrier hawk. So infrequent are cars in this part of New Zealand that harrier hawks rise slowly from road kills, sluggish with possum flesh, fenders brushing their wing tips. Tony and I are driving toward trout-fishing through the top of the South Island. We may go up the Wairau River, a wavering boulevard of parched light that frays across a gravel bed two miles wide. We may ascend the Buller, which runs strong as sin down to the green Buller Gorge from Lake Rotoiti. We may wade in one of a dozen quieter valleys where dark beechen brush climbs from the granite flanks of a small river. We may end up catching fish on the cusp of a hill ripe with sheep.

Near Murchison, the land flattens into a short plain of houses and a street of level shop awnings that lend the town an Old West tang. (We are not far, in fact, from the site of an early New Zealand gold rush.) One buys one's sheep and stud needs at the Murchison Dairy Cooperative, down a dusty avenue, as well as the green slouch hat that Kiwi farmers wear in the rain and sun. (Jaws, necks, hands, and knees burned red, they stand in olive shorts with a pair of dogs at their boots, waving between the poplars as we pass, knowing Tony's car from half a mile away.) Paddocks with orange electric fences and shearing sheds yield instead to sparse yards. On an island in the Buller behind the agricultural arena, a herd of puritanical, nervous-lipped goats, thins blackberry and gorse. Along a side street is the house where Sharon, Tony's wife, was raised, across from a public building now crumbling into stucco rust. No one goes to Murchison to look at Murchison. It tails out soon in the late summer air, which already carries a fall breeze. The mountains steal the eyes away and lift the town apart.

BELOW *Sight fishing for big trout is the name of the New Zealand game. The trout are extremely wary here, so caution and stealth are paramount qualities when trying to catch them.*

Tony and I settle on a river not far distant. We hike on the edge of primal bush, birds ringing like triangles in the branches. We can hear the stream, and we can feel the influence of its freshness in the botanical mist. Darkness condenses around us until Tony, ten paces ahead of me, steps to the

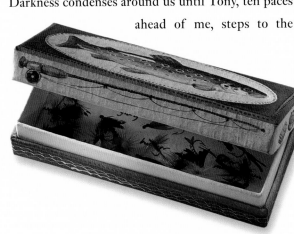

curtain of leaves and parts it, as he has been doing for some time now. This time he stops, and I look, too. A still pool in the river looks back, an eye with life on its surface, life in its depth. I am learning to see the trout Tony finds so cannily for me. What I see is a dark pulse kiting in water the color of twilight air. I backtrack and slither down the bank forty feet behind the pool. Now and again a lens of still water passes over the current, and through it I see a tail, a flash, the cotton mouth. Mostly I notice only shadow, a rock that snakes, a snaking stone with more longitude than latitude. So, like anyone, I cast to it. And it turns out to be a nine-pound brown trout. Tony watches from high on the bank.

We have our arrangements. A leaping nine-pound brown trout is the signal to bring a big net to the water's edge.

Apply your imagination to New Zealand. Think of it as it was in the mid-nineteenth century, when trout were not yet present, when Thomas Brunner and Kehu, his Maori sidekick, were still exploring the Buller Gorge. (They cut trail for 550 days.) The steelhead strain of rainbows would come in ships from California, the browns from England and Tasmania. But before the trout eggs packed on damp moss arrived, those hundreds of rivers, those ribbons of water so clear they look like air on the rocks, were (and still are) inhabited by eels, short-finned and long-finned, black eels the size of a dancer's leg but with teeth where the toes should be. Without the trout, this would be a story about the finest eel-spearing in the world.

If you had seen New Zealand with an angler's eye even then, you would have recognized its unbounded trout-carrying capacity. Imports take well to New Zealand, whether they are fish, timber (rows of furled plywood scroll evenly across the country), or rabbits, which by millions sap high-desert sheep stations, till foremen are forced to gather the shepherds for motorized night shoots week after week. The Kiwis could live without rabbits and thrive without Douglas fir. But the trout simply should have been native; it was an oversight in the Overall Plan.

Not until you get up in the sky does the magnitude of New Zealand's fishing potential really strike you. Streams flow down the knuckles of every wooded hill on the North Island. Like lions' spines, arid mountains ridge the South Island, and from them flow streams as well. Spring creeks, rocky burns, meadow rills, canyon chutes, glacial rivers that lace the desert – the country

RIGHT
A Greenwell's Parachute.

BELOW
A Grasshopper.

RIGHT *A Sawyer's Killer Bug.*

LEFT *A Pheasant-tail Bead Head Nymph.*

is veined and capillaried with water, almost all of it holding trout. Lakes are tentacled with inlets to which trout return to spawn so thickly, say the guides, that you could ford on their backs. Desire mingles with something else on these airborne excursions. You cross a wooded col (trees camouflaging an igneous outcrop) and take a thirty-foot body punch as wind slams the aircraft. The closer you get, the more the urge rises. Along the landscape lies the river, a bracelet of emeralds on a silver chain. "Screw the wind," you think. "Set this baby down so I can fish."

The pilot obliges. He chooses a crease in the hills, choppers groundward, grinning, through a slit in the trees, and on the stream's rubble, disgorges a party of wader-clad anglers (all as rattled as cattle in a cyclone). You feel like badly armed troops, like backyard astronauts in a Martian dust storm. Then the thunder and wind disappear, and the morning composes itself again. A sheath of cool air covers the water. You walk downstream to a pool showing every shade of green through which light can shine, where blowflies drowse on the sand, and foliage tumbles in a slow cascade to the canyon floor. The opaque oblongs in the pool are trout.

That is when you learn, if you have any sense at all, that fishing in New Zealand demands adaption. You realize that you have never seen clear water. Never seen trout this big or this wild. And so you listen carefully to your guide. What you learn by listening is how the game is played at its highest pitch. It is not the game most fly-fishermen know.

In America, insect life is so abundant that our few wild trout have learned to tolerate the presence of anglers by becoming finicky eaters. They push the casserole under their plates, feed the liver to the dog, and confine themselves to Tater Tots. The difficulty of the American game lies in choosing the right fly and making a natural presentation. The rest is peripheral. It can, some days, be golf on water.

But in New Zealand, trout commit suicide in the presence of anglers: they stop feeding. Better to shun calories, they conclude, than get snugged on the nose and lose faith in food. Or they ghost out of casting range, becoming visible to Americans only in the moment they flee. Such wildness adds depth to the game. It creates a Robinson Crusoe effect: if you find fresh footprints along a river, you go home and sulk (or seek another spot). Only rarely do you fish the water blindly.

LEFT *Morning mist rises from a pond on the South Island. New Zealand has few trout per mile of river, but the ones that are there are big. You need to spot them before they see you.*

ABOVE *This is Mitre Peak in Fjordland National Park, one of the wettest areas of New Zealand. I camped in my car overnight to catch first light on the peaks. It was cold and there were sand flies, but the absolute beauty of the morning made it all worthwhile.*

227

ABOVE *Local guides are invaluable as they know the country and the flies to use, but most importantly they can spot the fish which are perfectly camouflaged among the rocks on the river bottom.*

Instead, you stalk with great care in dim colors – pausing often to look for that long, pulsing rock on the bottom – or else you lose even the chance to cast. You eschew the vivid fly lines American makers favor (dye one dark olive instead), or in casting you lose the chance to touch the fish – the one going *pfffft!* in the corner of your eye. You learn a heron's stealth.

You also learn a heron's patience. Because New Zealand trout are bigger but more sparsely scattered than the American kind, you hike a long way through willows whose roots turn the shallows pink, through flax plants the size of hyper-trophied yucca, through tussock grass that looks from across the valley like flocks of long-fleeced goats being herded by the wind, through cutty grass that grows in knee-jolting hummocks and bites the hand that grabs it, through ankle-deep jungle moss (and always with a nine-foot fly rod in your fingers), just so you can part the vegetation, peer into the stream, and see a trout as big as any you have ever seen feinting like a boxer. What a miracle of concentration that sight imposes!

Having stalked the fish, you play the American game again. You choose the right fly and make a natural presentation, not so easy after all, because most of the time it means casting a weighted nymph directly upstream. Not far out of Murchison, a glassy little river

ABOVE *Susan Rockrise with a very nice brown trout in the net. Our friend and guide, Norman Marsh, looks happy too!*

LEFT *Sighting, casting, and hooking are the first challenges. Landing is another. The trout are very strong and head for their "hidy holes" right away.*

called the Owen flows down from limestone mountains to the north. Imagine me wet-wading it up to my keister. There is a light haze in the sky, and a kind of amber on the day. Tony, who gets to keep dry because of his good Kiwi eyes, is high on the bluff again, where it is easier to spot fish. I cast twice to a trout, then once to Tony, who catches the fly and changes it. (Tony says, "Trout count to three." The third time they see the same fly, they go *pfffft!*) We do this nine times, a different nymph each one. The keister gets cold. But then, as happens with New Zealand nymph-fishing, I am unconscious one moment, the next moment stumbling downstream after a seven-pound brown.

In American angling, the deception – making the sale and suckering the trout – is nearly all. But here it just opens debate: New Zealand trout must be captured, not played. On a North-Island river called the Rangitaiki, which curls through the man-made Kaingaroa Forest (a geometrical wilderness of pines and firs), a rainbow hopped before me, behind me, and forged a very large hook into an arrow, the curve bent out of it. On the Buller, a brown trout turned out of the slack, into the current, and peeled my reel. I started to sidestep downstream and looked to Tony for counsel, who shouted: "*Run!*" Run, that is, over a field of stone medicine balls. With 130 yards of line and backing out, the fish disappeared. On the Maruia, near Murchison, I turned the rod the wrong way for an instant as I sprinted beneath a low branch. When I looked back at my trout, away over there, it seemed as if he had fallen from a cloud.

RIGHT *Guide and angler work together as a team to spot trout and make the correct presentation. If the fish refuses to take a dry, try a nymph.*

ABOVE *Virtual solitude on a back country river in the fall, on the South Island.*

Sooner or later you land one, and everybody convenes on the river's edge, you, the guide, the trout coming head-up to the net in a final shower of spray. You free the teeth from the bag, the hook from the jaw. With wet hands holding the fish against the current, you look at what you've caught. In its details (you can almost never see it whole), you glimpse the final appeal of New Zealand angling. A brown trout with quarter-size black spots and pale green fire on the gill-plates and jaws, its tense back alligator-hued. A rainbow as sharp as stainless steel, whose black eyes, surveying the waterline, never catch yours. Fins and tails as broad as your handbreadth but which feather off into membranes of air. Jaws that could stitch the thick of your forearm. These fish are not just big; they are the healthiest, most beautiful trout you have ever touched. You release them, they flood their dive tanks, wriggle once, and are gone.

Some days, drizzle hangs in the trees all day long, and the sheep turn especially rank, their outlines blurred like the souls of rich tourists, rain-slicked turds left like tips in the grass. Some days the pumice dust in the wind tries to snatch at your eyes. But other days the autumn sun hammers down, and a gallery of cows watches you warm your legs in a valley that eats your heart up, a place set with pastures and willows and cabbage trees and a single red-tin-roofed cottage in a maze of corral. A gravel road and the river run in tandem to a vanishing point among low peaks. Hoof-wide sheep trails terrace the grassy slopes. In the bush above, there are bare-earth signs of wild pigs rooting. On the highest cliffs, a knot of feral goats rests too, descendants, some say, of Captain Cook's original crew. Despite the shadows and the season, the river will not let the sun fade. As your pants dry from wading, you draw conclusions:

Wilderness is not a state of being, but a principle of action. Clear water favors neither the angler nor the fish, though the angler thinks otherwise. A big trout is wilder than a small trout, and more demoralizing when spooked. The angler was never a fish, though the trout is always a hunter. A trout expects trouble, though the angler wants sport. A trout in hand is the muscular instant that is always vanishing, taking your life away with it.

Water that rises highest above the sea – the earthliest water – is freshest. Upstream, the river bottom is brighter, stones are sharper, and brush hangs tighter to the banks. Trout head upstream naturally, and anglers, pursuing them, do so too. In New Zealand the room for moving upstream seems nearly infinite. So few steps carry you into wildness, so many pools lie between you and a river's source. Wherever you pause, there is a bend farther upstream deepening to azure. It takes a lifetime of fatigue and some powerful nights to keep you from rounding that corner and the next and the next and the next. It occurs to you – just at the moment you turn back home – that New Zealand is upstream of the rest of the world.

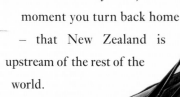

ABOVE *A Humpy.*

231

LEFT *A scene of jubilation between friends over a good fish in the net.*

NEW ZEALAND: FACTFILE

BACKGROUND

Zane Grey called New Zealand an "Angler's El Dorado". He was more enamoured of the big game fishing he found in Mercury Bay and the Bay of Islands, but his steelheading experiences back in the USA eventually led him to try the Tongariro River and Lake Taupo. The stories he wrote about them have fuelled the imagination of fishermen since.

If Taupo and the Tongariro are synonymous with giant lake-run rainbows, South Island is justly famous for its brown trout. The remote rivers of the south-west coast are ideally suited to the "stalking" method of fishing which for many epitomizes fishing in New Zealand. Armed with a handful of dry flies and nymphs and a pair of Polaroid sunglasses, fishermen walk upriver with a local guide, whose trained eyes help them spot the superbly camouflaged quarry. In such clear waters, careful fly presentation is as important as fly choice, and a "lined" fish (scared off by the line or its shadow) is a lost opportunity. Leaders need to be long to try to avoid this eventuality, but even so, many expert fishermen have been humbled by New Zealand trout.

A good day's fishing might consist of, say, 15 fish being spotted and five landed, typically between 4 and 8 lb, with a good possibility of double-figure fish being encountered. New Zealand looks set to remain the world's finest freshwater trout location.

WHEN TO GO

With the southern hemisphere summer, the season starts in October and goes on until April. Many New Zealanders take their summer holidays after Christmas, and January is perhaps the busiest time on the rivers. On North Island around Taupo, fishing is best in the winter months (April to August) when the rainbows leave the lake to spawn in the rivers that flow into it.

TACKLE

RODS: Single-handed 9–11 ft rods for 4, 5 and 7 wt lines.
REELS: Direct-drive reels, with good drag systems and capacity for 100 yards of backing.

LINES: Most fishing will be with floating lines, but sink-tips are useful.

LEADERS: Take plenty of spools between 3 lb and 6 lb as tippet changes may be frequent.

FLIES: Dry flies – Royal Wulff, Humpy, Adams, Irresistible and Caddis. Nymphs – Pheasant Tail and Hare's Ear.

FLIES 1 *Elk Hair Caddis*
2 *Rat-faced McDougall*
3 *Stonefly Nymph*
4 *Yellow Stimulator*
5 *Adams Irresistible*
6 *Gold Head Hare's Ear Nymph* 7 *Gold Head Pheasant Tail Nymph*
8 *Sawyer's Pheasant Tail Nymph* 9 *Hi-Float Beetle* 10 *Czech Shrimp*

The Start of the South

Chile

RODERICK HAIG-BROWN

"Most of the pools in this part of the Quepe are deep and dark, quite narrow

and quite short, with a heavy run of water through them. At the head of a pool

of this sort the green fly caught me a lovely four-and-a-half pound brown trout.

Soon after that I asked Fonfach to stop and let me work a pool where a narrow,

two-hundred-foot fall poured straight down past a solid bank of blooming

fuchsia. Another four-pound brown lay just past the foot of the fall and took the

fly in a swirl of bronze."

Jacko Edwards is a Santiago newspaperman, a keen trout fisherman and a former member of the Chilean international tuna team. He is a slender, volatile man, a charming and extremely civilized companion. He is a true Chilean, but was born in England while his father was in the diplomatic service there, and he was educated in Paris, returning to Chile when he was seventeen or eighteen. I spent the next month with Jacko, traveling the rivers and lakes of the south, from Temuco to Puerto Montt, and there wasn't a moment of him that I didn't enjoy.

Temuco is a town of some sixty thousand people, a clean and pretty place with some good stores and many things, including fishing tackle, camera film and Scotch whisky, which a tourist cannot always find readily in the south. I had all the tackle I needed; I am not a camera enthusiast and I had no intention of drinking whisky, Scotch or otherwise, in a country that produces a respectable gin, several good brandies, another admirable distillate of the grape called Pisco, and wines that are unequaled except in France. But I record the availability of these commodities out of respect for the good people of Temuco, and to counteract the arrogant assumption that, away from Santiago, shopping facilities in Chile are primitive. They are not. Osorno and Puerto Varas, and for all I know a dozen other places, are as much on the job as Temuco.

Temuco does, I think, still pride itself on being a frontier town – the name of its excellent modern hotel, Hotel de la Frontera, suggests that. It is the start of the south – the vegetation along the nearby rivers confirms that. And it is the heart of the Indian country, the land of the Araucanas, the proud race which never accepted conquest by the Spaniards. I say the heart of their country because Pedro Valdivia, the founder of Chile, is said to have been killed by the Indians on a rock bluff overlooking the Laja right by the Palacio, two hundred miles north of Temuco; because the last great war was fought around Villarica, fifty or sixty miles south; and because I saw more full-blooded Indians near Temuco than anywhere else. But in truth there has been in Chile such a magnificent freedom of intermarriage between the native Indians and the invading whites that it can be said the country is fairly apportioned between invaders and invaded, to the lasting benefit of both.

Jacko had already made arrangements to go fishing. After fourteen-hour days on the Laja and at Maule, they shocked me a little, but we were out of our comfortable beds by 4.30 the next morning and starting from the hotel entrance in a rackety truck by 5.00 am. The truck carried two fair-sized hardwood skiffs, ourselves, two boatmen, a driver and a swamper, whose sole business was to help unload the heavy boats.

We jolted along some fifteen or twenty miles of rough road to a bridge over the Cautin River, backed the truck down as near to the water as possible and slid the

RIGHT *Lago Yelcho is an ancient, deep, glacial lake in southern Chile famous among fishermen for the incoming and outgoing rivers Futaleufú and Yelcho.*

ABOVE *An eagerly awaited streamside* asado *(barbecue) is about to be served up by host John Jenkins of Patagonia Outfitters.*

boats in, not without difficulty. The driver, a keen fisherman himself, wished us good fishing, the truck pulled away and we started out into the stream.

My boatman, Gemán Fonfach, was a very dignified, respectable, middle-aged man, powerfully built and with the obvious confidence of experience. He was reputed to be the best boatman in the Temuco area, an enthusiast for the fly, and himself both a good fisherman and a good fly-tyer. He took me firmly in hand at once, which was reasonable enough, looked over my fly boxes and indicated very pronounced preference for large flies of an olive or yellowish-brown type; his favorite was the Norton, which seems to me a very large stonefly imitation, and after that a big green drake or else the San Pedro streamer, which is winged with long, barred cock's hackles dyed yellow. He would have none of Mac's Gray Ghost, which had done well for us on the Laja, or of a brown shrimp fly that had risen me some good fish. But he did let me use a fly of my own, dressed with green gantron chenille and a mixed polar-bear wing, in a somewhat smaller size than his favorites.

All this interested me very much indeed, because I knew I should be fishing with boatmen through much of Chile and I was at least as anxious to learn about the boatmen themselves as anything else. If one must have a guide, the manner of his guiding is all-important to the day's pleasure. Choice of fly usually does not worry me too much, especially when I am fishing wet, and I make it a rule to fish a boatman's preference rather than my own whenever I reasonably can – it gives him confidence and encourages him to make more important concessions; besides, he may have some special knowledge. Fonfach, as it turned out, had.

He understood at once that I wanted to wade and cast wherever possible, but the first reaches of the Cautin offered little opportunity for this and he handled the boat beautifully through them while I cast into the likely places. We caught one or two small rainbows of a pound or so, then I rolled a good fish at the head of a deep run. "*El flojo,*" Fonfach said. "The lazy one. Brown trout."

The river was easy and swift, over a gravelly bottom and through flat land; it is smaller than the Laja, it does not divide, as the Laja does, into many river-size branches, and the vegetation along its banks is generally richer and greener and stronger; yet the two rivers are somewhat similar and I could well believe in the Cautin's reputation as a great trout stream. But I could sense that Fonfach did not expect a big day. When I rolled a second big brown trout he was obviously surprised to see the fish, and just as obviously was not surprised when the fly came away.

He explained why almost at once: November and December were the river's good months; January and February were too warm; all the big fish were lying deep and disinclined to take, though they would be moving again in

ABOVE *Boca ("river-mouth") fishing on Lago Llanquihue in the shadow of the Osorno volcano frequently produces very large fish and causes the frantic fumbling known as "boca fever."*

March and April. I checked the river temperature and found it was 69°F (20°C).

As the stream opened up to shallower water Fonfach began to put me out at many favorable places, and I worked them comfortably and happily in the bright sunshine, finding an abundance of bright fourteen- and fifteen-inch rainbows, but nothing of any size. From time to time we passed and repassed Jacko and his boat-man, and it was plain that Jacko, using a light spinning outfit with an assortment of plugs and spinners, was faring much as we were – no better, no worse. So I came to the time and place of my first real fishing lunch in Chile.

I had heard of these magnificent meals, but I was by no means prepared for the formality or the efficiency of the affair. We stopped outside a wide, shallow reach of the river, where there were some fine trees and a heavy growth of bamboo. Almost immediately the two boatmen had a great fire of bamboo and hardwood burning strongly. Four bottles of wine were set in the river to cool. Jacko's boat-man was cleaning and filleting some of the trout we had caught; Fonfach was preparing a long bamboo stake on which he impaled several pounds of mutton, to be barbecued when the fire had died down. It was clear that there was nothing for Jacko and me to do except lie in the shade and take our ease, and that, Jacko assured me, was exactly what we were expected to do.

BELOW *A Zonker.*

239

"The boatmen will rest afterward," he said. "And for quite long enough. It is noon now. They will not start fishing again until three o'clock at the soonest."

"That's quite a while," I said. "What do they do?"

"Eat all the food and drink all the wine, then sleep. They say it is the bad hour for fish, from twelve till three, and nothing can be caught. But I don't see how they can know, because no one in Chile ever fishes at that time."

There were plates in front of us now, with fillets of trout swimming in black butter, another plate with an excellent salad of lettuce and tomatoes, hot green peppers and French dressing. The wine bottles were open. Fonfach had his meat browning over the fire, potatoes baking in the ashes, water boiling for coffee. I accepted the bad hour and was grateful for it.

Later, when the food was eaten and most of the wine was gone, I suppose I slept for a little. But I was awake at 1.30, listening to the chatter of parakeets in the trees above me. I could see them, none too clearly, against the sky, then suddenly the whole flock took off. They were brilliant green in the sunlight, slender bodies on narrow wings, like arrows, straight and swift in flight. I sat up and saw Jacko asleep on his back, the two boatmen asleep with their blanket ponchos thrown over them. I picked up my rod and stole away to the river.

It was an easy place to wade and I found a good run on the shady side of an island, within fifty yards of the boats. My pale green fly was taken solidly at the

LEFT The view from Isla Monita, a fishing lodge located on Lago Yelcho in a wildly spectacular setting of snowcapped mountains.

BELOW An angler tosses Wooly Buggers for rainbows off the boca of the Rio Paloma.

BELOW *Bamboo forests, monkey-puzzle trees, glaciers, waterfalls, and all sorts of unusual sights may thrill the senses on a float down the Rio Yelcho.*

first cast and the fish ran hard, well down into the backing. Then he jumped and I was surprised to see a silvery rainbow not much larger than those I had been catching in the morning. I netted him and quickly took two others from the run, both excellent fighters and exactly the same size as the first – sixteen inches and one and three-quarter pounds.

I had noticed some very pale green caterpillars on the bushes near where we had lunch and the quick success of my green-bodied fly made me curious, so I cleaned the fish at once. The caterpillars were in them, with a few apancora and another pale green, shield-shaped bug that Fonfach later called the sanfoin or copiala beetle. I understood why my green-bodied fly had taken his fancy.

It turned out that those three fish were the best of the day, though Jacko and I killed twenty-five or thirty between us, all of them over a pound. We ran through some fine-looking water during the afternoon, passed the boats over an irrigation dam a few miles above Temuco, and from there to the outskirts of the town itself saw a dozen places that must hold big trout. I was hopeful of the good hour between sunset and dark, but we came to the end of the run before that – among a multitude of the good citizens of Temuco swimming in their warm stream and with a welcome from the local fishing club, whose boats Fonfach had borrowed for us.

It was, I suppose, a disappointing day, because the Cautin has a considerable reputation for big fish. But Fonfach assured me the reputation is well deserved; in November and December one can expect an average weight of two and a quarter pounds on most days, with several fish of between four and six pounds. I have little doubt he is right because a random sample of our catch that day proved to be all fish in their second or third year, none had spawned and most were immature. A fourth-year fish would certainly be over two pounds and could be very much larger.

Our next day's fishing was in the Quepe, some twenty miles south of the Cautin and a very different stream. The Quepe is smaller than the Cautin, with brownish, rushing water, and it twists and turns its way between canyon-like clay banks that are often a hundred and fifty or two hundred feet high.

We started out cheerfully in the truck with the boats at some much too early hour, and pounded five or six miles over bad roads before discovering we had forgotten the lunch. Clearly the truck had to go back for it, and Jacko and I decided to walk until it caught up with us again. We were in rolling, rather dry country with a few primitive-looking thatched Indian huts scattered through it. Most of the huts had gardens, whose main crop seemed to be healthy-looking potatoes. We met many Indian women walking toward the town, some young, some old, all walking well and

ABOVE *A Bunny Leech.*

handsomely dressed in flowered dresses and dark blue capes of blanket-like material, often lined with red. They wore impressively heavy silver ornaments on their breasts, hinged and pieced, decorated with crosses and coins and sometimes beads. The workmanship was quite remarkable and the designs varied considerably; I felt they must have some significance, but our happy truck-driver insisted they were simply decoration. I asked Jacko why we saw only women. "Only the women work," he said. "They are going to market to sell the stuff we have seen in the carts."

Our truck caught up to us, we climbed aboard and went on again. The driver was regretful he could not fish with us. The Quepe was his favorite river and we would surely have great sport. As we launched the boats he gave me, with Fonfach's approval, two big dark streamer flies he had tied himself on No. 2 hooks, each with a smaller hook trailing behind it. They were, he assured me, the best possible medicine for the river, and as Fonfach seemed to agree I started out with the smaller one, a mixture of black and barred hackles.

The Quepe seemed to take us into herself almost immediately and we were lost between the high banks as though in a forest. The banks themselves were quite wonderful, dripping with fuchsia in full bloom, matted with bamboo, patterned with some lovely yellow flower almost like a pansy. Acacias and weeping willows and other handsome trees grew wherever there was root-hold. The enormous leaves of the giant gunnera, often five or six feet across, stood out as a perpetual reminder of strangeness. And the river itself butted against the base of its banks,

ABOVE *The Rio Simpson is one of the finest dry-fly rivers in Chile. You can spot the fish in the clear water when the sun is high, or fish to their rise forms in the evening.*

243

twisted round right-angled corners and broke white against log jams, in test after formidable test of Fonfach's skill with the boat. It was far from being the swiftest or fiercest of the boat rivers I saw in Chile, but in many ways it was the tightest and trickiest to work and I began to appreciate the skill and boldness that Chilean boatmen have.

It was a cloudy day and considerably cooler than any other day I had seen in Chile. The river temperature where we started in was only 60°F (15°C) and I began to believe we should have a good day. We did. By lunchtime I had five fish of over two and a half pounds, the biggest a rainbow of just under four pounds, all of them caught on the truck-driver's black streamer. There was a shower of rain at lunchtime, short and swift and violent, and when we began fishing again I noticed that fish were coming short to the streamer, so I changed again to my green fly – the only smallish fly I had that Fonfach would approve.

Most of the pools in this part of the Quepe are deep and dark, quite narrow and quite short, with a heavy run of water through them. At the head of a pool of this sort the green fly caught me a lovely four-and-a-half pound brown trout. Soon after that I asked Fonfach to stop and let me work a pool where a narrow, two-hundred-foot fall poured straight down past a solid bank of blooming fuchsia. Another four-pound brown lay just past the foot of the fall and took the fly in a swirl of bronze. Neither of these fish rated Fonfach's contemptuous nick-name, El Flojo, but later in the day, in a wider pool, I hooked a three-pound brown that walked clear across the current on his tail, for all the world like a marlin. I glanced at Fonfach and asked him, "El Flojo?" He laughed and shook his head. "Not always."

The truck met us at dusk by a bridge far down the river. I had returned over twenty fish, but Fonfach had kept smaller fish than I wanted and there were seventeen in the boat when we landed, eleven of them between two and a half and four and a half pounds. Jacko had a similar catch on spoon and flatfish though his best fish, to my surprise, was a three-pounder. As nearly as I could judge from the reactions of the boatmen and the truck-driver and his helpers, the catch was a good one for the river at any time. Scale readings confirmed this, as the big brown trout were five-year-olds that had spawned previously and the best rainbow, a fish of three and three-quarter pounds, had spawned at three years. I thought it a fine day, though I should have been content to fish only a quarter of the distance in the same length of time. We had passed dozens of wonderful places without fishing them, and it seemed to me we had come to the best water very late in the day.

No small part of the pleasure of a Chilean day like this is in the sharp contrast between the wildness of the river and its surroundings and the luxury of the evening at the hotel. By 10.30 we had changed our clothes, had a quiet drink in the bar and were sitting down to dinner in the big, graceful dining room of the Frontera. There was good food, well served, and good wine to go with it. A small orchestra played South American music at the far end of the room. Well-dressed men and handsome women sat at the other tables around the room; faded blue denims and Hawaiian sports shirts, weather-ravaged faces and casual manners simply were not to be seen. At 7.00 or 7.30 all this would have been an intolerable nuisance, to be avoided by any sensible fisherman. But at 10.30 or 11.00, the day is over, the last hour has been fished, daylight is exhausted. It is a perfect time to relax, to enjoy an appetite and feel thoroughly civilized.

BELOW *The Futaleufú, which flows into Lago Yelcho, is a large river, and glacial melt gives it a beautiful turquoise color.*

CHILE: FACTFILE

BACKGROUND

Chile is one of the world's most varied countries, covering 2,000 miles from north to south. It encompasses one of the driest deserts in the world, the beautiful Lake District, the western hemisphere's oldest vineyards, and the Patagonian region. In southern Chile the huge mountains, glaciers and fjords produce countless lakes and rivers, which harbour several species of trout and salmon.

Situated in the southern hemisphere, Chile is a great getaway location during the northern hemisphere's winter, and home to a hospitable people – under the code of the pilgrim, Patagonian *estancia* owners used to provide free meals and shelter for the wayfarer, a practice that has evolved into a cultural tradition.

Some of the best fly-fishing is found in Chilean Patagonia, a region with many similarities to the western USA and the North American Pacific coast. Innumerable lakes and rivers, some of them huge, are filled with predominantly brown trout, rainbows and a few brook trout.

Aquaculture is a rapidly growing industry, with many different species of fish being raised commercially. Unfortunately winter storms have caused flooding and many of these exotic species have escaped and spawned in the rivers, creating new runs of non-indigenous fish. It is still unclear if any of these runs will establish themselves into permanent spawning migrations.

Chile has had a strong fly-fishing heritage for the last 50–70 years. Roderick Haig-Brown wrote about his fishing experiences there in the 1950s in his classic *Fisherman's Winter*, an excellent choice of reading for anyone preparing a trip. The scenic beauty and the possibilities of adventure make the country an exciting option for the travelling angler.

WHEN TO GO

The season starts in November and finishes in April, although many of the rivers may be running high and coloured in the early weeks. At practically

LEFT A typical brown trout from the Rio Simpson. Note the purple patch on the gill plate.

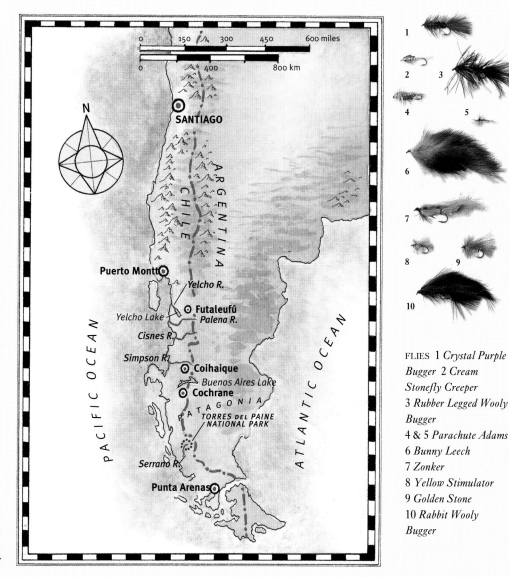

FLIES 1 *Crystal Purple Bugger* 2 *Cream Stonefly Creeper* 3 *Rubber Legged Wooly Bugger* 4 & 5 *Parachute Adams* 6 *Bunny Leech* 7 *Zonker* 8 *Yellow Stimulator* 9 *Golden Stone* 10 *Rabbit Wooly Bugger*

any other time in the season the fishing will be more consistent.

TACKLE

RODS: Single-handed 9 ft rods for 5–6 wt line and a 7–8 wt line.

REELS: Direct-drive reels with a good drag system.

LINES: A full complement is desirable: weight-forward floating, sink-tip and a couple of full sinking lines of different densities. The Teeny series and the Rio windcutters are popular choices.

LEADERS: Floating lines – leader of 5–8 lb test tippet. Sinking lines – 6–9 ft with 8–15 lb tippet.

FLIES: Classic dry-fly patterns: Adams, Wulff, Humpy, Elk Hair Caddis, Irresistibles, Hoppers and Beetles. For wet flies it is hard to beat the Olive or Black Wooly Bugger; also Hare's Ears and Pheasant Tail Nymphs. In the lakes, Dragonfly or Damselfly (wet and dry) where naturals are present.

La Fiebre de las Bocas

Argentina

ERNEST SCHWIEBERT

"It was a deep pool below a heavy chute of rapids, where the Chimehuin gathered its strength, sidestepping an outcropping of rhyolite, and churned into a wild spillway through the boulders. Its currents grew still in these ebony depths, and flowed quietly for fifty yards, welling up again into a smooth glide at the tail. There was a mile of rapids downstream – it looked like trophy-fish water. The light was falling as I caught a brown of eighteen inches – an average fish in such water; pumpkin-colored on its belly, and sprinkled with poppy-red spots."

The storm gathered on the broken escarpments of the Chapelco, and sheets of rain lashed across the truck. There were two riders above the Quilquihue bridge. The gauchos were hunched low on their ponies, their black, flat-brimmed hats and heavy woollen ponchos turned against the wind.

It was still raining, and the wind grew cold as we reached Junín de los Andes. The village stood dark and silent. Its adobe and brick-work houses were shuttered and huddled together in the storm, like the horsemen we had encountered in the road. There were lights at the Hosteria Chimehuin, flickering through the yellow poplars that sheltered it from such *puelche* weather.

Beyond the compound of the inn, the famous Chimehuin river works back across its almost treeless valley, past the cavalry post and the stock pens of the *carneceria*, and the poplar-lined Señoritas, a pool named for the camp followers who live in its bordello and offer company to the soldiers. Its channels split and merge again, changing from season to season, flowing past its smooth wind-sculpted foothills. These hills force the river south into the barren pampas, under a big cinder cone called the Cerro de los Pinos, toward the chalky bluffs where it finally joins the Collon Cura.

The lights were warm and inviting in the hosteria, and its windows were smoky with the chill. The storm lashed through the valley for hours, coming down the big mountain lakes from the Pacific. It had cut power lines from the north, and candles guttered and glowed on the tables. Fishermen were eating beef after a thick vegetable soup, and there were bottles of strong Argentine *tinto*. The candlelight flickered in the faces of the guests, until the room seemed like something transplanted from the stories of Dickens.

José Julian is the proprietor of the simple Hosteria Chimehuin, and his little fishing inn at Junín de los Andes has sheltered an impressive log of famous trout fishermen. Their mecca is the storied Chimehuin itself, which drops fifty miles between its birthplace at Lago Huechulaufquèn to its desert marriage with the Collon Cura, and it remains the most famous trout stream in South America.

The entire Chimehuin remains good, and a twelve-pound fish is possible anywhere in its mileage, although such trophies are probably fish that waxed fat in Huechulaufquèn, or migrated upriver from the desert pampas downstream. But a roster of famous anglers who journey each winter from both Europe and the

ABOVE *The hillside where I am standing is a great location to spot fish and enjoy the magnificent scenery of Lake Huechulaufquèn and the Boca Chimehuin beneath the volcano. The water is crystal-clear.*

United States are drawn to the famous Boca Chimehuin, where the river rises full-blown from the fifty-mile length of its immense Andean lake.

There were three familiar figures in the dining room.

I smiled when I saw their faces from the courtyard. They are there almost every summer, fishing the three-mile reach of river below its outlet. Sometimes they remain for the entire months of February and March. The triumvirate are old friends, among the handful of Argentine fly-fishing pioneers, and know the river in all its quixotic moods.

Prince Charles Radziwill is a Polish exile who lives in Buenos Aires, and has discovered a workable substitute for the shooting and fishing on his royal family estates in the Carpathian foothills – in the duck marshes and partridge fields near Buenos Aires, and in the tumbling rivers of Patagonia. His best trout at Junín de los Andes was a silvery fifteen-pound brown, taken with a big saltwater bucktail from the churning outlet currents of the Boca Chimehuin.

Jorge Donovan is a dairy farmer and stockman near Buenos Aires, and a burly athlete of extraordinary skill. His mastery of Argentine roll casting, which employs a second aerial loop to take advantage of the wind, is obvious on the Boca Chimehuin. He once owned a tackle shop in Buenos Aires called the Boliche de Pesca, the sole fly-fishing outfitter in Argentina during those years, and his fishing logs are filled with trophies between ten and fifteen pounds.

José de Anchorena (nicknamed Bébé) is the principal member of an Argentine clan, whose family seat lies at a magnificent livestock station called Estancia Azucena, in the coastal foothill country near Tandil. His attentions, most of the year, are focused on the sheep, blooded thoroughbreds and fine cattle that fill his township-sized pastures, but after Christmas at Azucena his thoughts turn restlessly to Patagonia and its fishing.

Anchorena held the world record for a fly-caught brown trout for many years, with a twenty-four pounder from the Boca Chimehuin, until it was finally displaced with a bigger fish caught at Correntoso.

These men spend almost every summer fishing the upper Chimehuin. "It's never boring," they explain. "We have seen what the river can produce, and its fish are migratory, dropping back from the lake – and we can see new fish almost every morning, particularly after a storm."

The storm blew itself out during the night, and it was clear in the morning. The sun was welcome and bright at breakfast. We turned west along the river at the cavalry post that guards the mountain passes into Chile. Beyond the treeless foothills, the cone of a solitary volcano rose into a cloudless sky, as symmetrical and perfect as Fujiyama.

"Lanín," Anchorena pointed. "It guards the Boca!"

"It's a bit too bright and clear today," Radziwill nodded. "But when the volcano wears its sombrero of ice clouds in bright weather, the fishing is usually good."

"But it's still good in this weather too?" I asked.

"Sometimes," they smiled.

Boca Chimehuin lies 12,000 feet below the summit of its great volcano. Centuries ago, a primordial earthquake opened a cooling fault in the lava fields, where the glacier that preceded the immense lake foundered on their serrated battlements. Its Pleistocene terminal moraines were shaped against the barriers of these igneous outcroppings. Great dams of ice gathered, collapsed explosively from time to time, and patiently grew again. The shards of ice raised the periglacial lake many times, until each successive ice dam collapsed in turn, releasing another spate of biblical proportions. Such torrents further exploited the seismic fault below the lake, sculpting a narrow box canyon called the Garganta del Diablo.

The Chimehuin still escapes through this narrow corridor in the broken rhyolite, after spilling across the drowned outcroppings at its boca, and begins its thousand-mile journey toward the sea. The winds gather strength to howl down the fifty-mile length of Huechulaufquèn, churning its ultramarine surface into great breakers that roll and crash into the mouth of the river. There is a sunken corridor in the lava outcroppings there, with depths that seem like a water-filled mine shaft, and I have seen a chest-high surf come rolling in. The river widens immediately downstream, where a huge glacial boulder lies in a whirlpool of conflicting currents. There is a deep, riffling reach of water before the currents shelve off into the famous Rincon Grande, gathering swiftly through drowned tablerock ledges, in twenty feet of crystalline water. It is posssible to walk the bluffs above the sweeping bend in the morning, taking a fresh census of trophy fish holding deep between these ledges, and marking down their holding lies. There is another shallow, weedy reach of water downstream, where the river slides toward the old timber trestle, and the throat of the Garganta.

Anchorena circled back along the ridge, and stopped on the narrow sawmill road, just under the monkeypuzzle trees. "Come on!" he grinned. "We'll show you some fish!"

ABOVE *The beautiful Malleo River, a favorite for visiting anglers, flows through the eastern Andes.*

We walked the bluffs above the Rincon, carrying a pair of fine German binoculars. The sun was getting high, and we could see deep into the pool, with every pebble visible on its bottom.

"Look!" Radziwill pointed. "Bébé, look there!"

There are several boulders between the big ledges, and a giant *coihue* log was wedged between the outcroppings. I looked intently where Radziwill was pointing, and finally saw the shadows before I actually saw the ghost-like fish themselves: six huge trout that seemed suspended in air. Anchorena was walking farther downstream. He gestured to us excitedly and pointed to a pocket between the rocks. "He's still there!" he hissed. "He's still there!"

"He's been watching a big brown," Radziwill explained.

"Some of them look like rainbows."

"They are," he nodded.

It was difficult to estimate their size, given the clarity and depth of the pool, and nothing to convey a sense of scale.

"How big?" I asked.

"Most of them are three to four kilos," Anchorena replied quietly, "but the one against the ledge will go five or six."

"And how big is your brown, Bébé?" I asked.

"He'll go seven kilos."

"Fifteen pounds?" I exhaled in disbelief.

"Let's get rigged and fish."

We turned back and crossed the trestle, where the river looped back into the throat of its little ledgerock canyon, and circled past the beach to stop under a sheltering moraine.

We put together our tackle carefully. Anchorena and Radziwill had talked so much about huge fish that I checked everything twice. My rod was a powerful nine-and-a-half-foot Parabolic 19, a saltwater weapon that had come from the collection of the late rodmaker Paul Young. I seated a big Hardy Saint Andrew salmon reel with great care, freshly oiled its spindle shaft and housing, and stripped line into the grass to rewind the pale backing in precise layers.

"You like dacron backing?"

"Yes." I layered the backing line carefully. "There's so much elasticity in nylon that it can deform a light alloy spool, and cause it to seize up."

The leader knot was reseated, tightened into the sinking line slowly, and tested with a series of steady pulls. I reworked each barrel knot too, wetting its intricate loops with saliva before teasing them slowly together. The leader was tapered to ten

ABOVE *Late-afternoon brings on the magic hour, when shadows lengthen and the river awakens.*

253

pounds. Everything seemed secure, and I knotted a big stonefly nymph to a fresh Maxima tippet. It was my baptism of fire.

I walked up the stony beach to the boca, and waded out into its rolling surf. Big waves surged up past my waist, and flowed past into the big whirlpool downstream. The wind was howling down the big lake, pounding its surf across the outlet ledges, and filling the air with blowing spray. The current came spilling through the deep chute of its drowned cooling fault, eddied into a big whirlpool of conflicting currents, and swirled back past the immense glacial boulder at midstream. Another huge wave rolled and broke, wetting my elbows as it passed, and its wild spume covered my shooting glasses.

"Surf casting," I thought wildly.

There were moments when it seemed like it was raining horizontally under a cloudless sky, as the wind ripped great gouts of spume from the breakers offshore, and I retreated to strip the tightly rolled rain jacket from my vest.

Five minutes later, I was nearly swamped when the surf surged to my armpits, and another great wave broke heavily across my back, sending an icy torrent of water down my neck. Anchorena had advised us to purchase Basque berets at the *almacen* in Junín, headgear favored by solitary sheepherders in the Argentine, as regular hats refuse to stay in place. It took a strong double-haul to compensate for the wind, punching directly across the current to drop our flies quartering downstream. The big flies whistled past our heads – I was grateful for the tempered shooting glasses protecting my eyes. I had been given the best place for my baptism: the churning currents just below the lake. I waded cautiously into position.

"They're a little like salmon," Anchorena explained. "They like to rest just after they leave the lake."

"They lie right in that heavy channel?" I asked.

"Sometimes," he nodded.

"How deep is it?"

"Four meters," he guessed. "Maybe five."

It seemed workable to sink our flies deep into the chute, but its surging currents were so strong that casting upstream was necessary, shooting line directly into the wind. It was difficult to fight the gusts, and a number of casts simply collapsed and came fluttering back.

"I'm not getting deep enough!" I thought.

Radziwill hooked a good fish in the sweeping bend downstream, and I stopped fishing to watch. His reel protested in a shrill soprano, as the big trout bolted and

ABOVE TOP *A Yellow Humpy.*

ABOVE BOTTOM *A Black Marabou Muddler.*

ran downstream. Twice it cartwheeled high into the sun, gleaming like an unsheathed sword, and tumbled back into the river.

"It's a brown!" Radziwill yelled.

"But it's silvery!" I shouted back above the howling wind.

"Yes," Anchorena nodded, "but it's a brown."

The trout was finally beached in the shallows, a sleek deep-bellied fish of about six pounds. It was covered with delicate cross-shaped markings. It looked almost like a salmon fresh from the salt, except for the configuration of its tail, and its dense little crosses of Saint Andrew.

"Doesn't look much like a brown," I persisted.

"No," they agreed, "it's like a sea trout."

"But it's from the lake?"

"Yes, but these lakes are volcanic, with hot springs in their beds, and quite fertile." Radziwill explained. "And they're rich in crustaceans."

"Shrimps or something?"

"Crayfish," they chorused together. "They look a little like dwarf saltwater crabs, but they're crayfish – about the size of a silver dollar."

"What're they called?"

"The Chileans call them *pancoras*," Anchorena nodded, "and the lake turns them silvery."

"I think I'll try them again," I said hopefully.

"*Buena suerte!*"

I worked back into the surf at the outlet, where the rolling surges came tumbling over the ledges into the big chute below the lake. The wind had dropped a little, until I was finally able to drive a long cast low and hard, and the big nymph actually dropped where I wanted it. The stonefly drifted deep into the heavy swells, until I tightened the drifting slack, and worked it through near the bottom. I gathered the line patiently as it bellied past, and suddenly the slow retrieve stopped dead, almost like I was snagged. It was a steady pull, strong and holding stubbornly against the straining rod. It still seemed like a snag, but it throbbed with obvious life, and then the fish moved slowly upstream. It stopped under the heaviest currents in the chute, shaking its head sullenly.

Suddenly it bolted and jumped. "It's huge!" I gasped.

It looked like ten or twelve pounds, lithe and silvery as it leapfrogged downstream. It gathered speed until the line sliced audibly through the current. The reel was a shrill keening that echoed the wind. The big fish jumped again and again, flashing silver in its writhing acrobatics.

ABOVE TOP *A Bead-head Gold Ribbed Hare's Ear.*

ABOVE BOTTOM *An Elwes Special.*

"Another brown?" I yelled.

"Not bloody likely!" Radziwill laughed. "With that trapeze act, it's got to be a big rainbow!"

Finally it surrendered, and I forced it across the heaviest currents. Its silvery sides and gunmetal back were clearly visible in the swift shallows. There were no spots, and no trace of the red-striped flanks and gillcovers typical of its breed. Its shining sides held only a faint wash of amethyst and rose. Filled with a sense of awe, I almost stopped fighting the fish.

"Looks like a fresh steelhead!"

"The lake can make them completely silver too," Radziwill nodded. "It's probably stuffed with *cangrejos*!"

"We call such rainbows *plateados*," Anchorena said.

"Silver ones," I thought.

But I had allowed the strong fish to get a second wind. I attempted to beach it with increased rod pressure, and it showered me with water. My shooting glasses were blinded, but I watched it jump twice more through the streaming beads of moisture. My arms were getting tired, and my heart was pounding. The fish finally turned, and had almost surrendered in the gravelly shallows, when it gasped and the fly came free.

"My God!" I shouted.

I plunged into the river in futile pursuit. The big fish was drifting weakly into deep water, righted itself after a few moments, and was gone. I waded unhappily ashore and my hands were shaking uncontrollably.

"Bébé!" Radziwill laughed. "He's got the disease!"

"Disease?" My fingers were shaking.

"*Fiebre de las bocas*," Anchorena smiled. "We all caught it years ago, and it's incurable."

"Boca fever," Radziwill explained wryly.

The big stonefly was well chewed, and its stout hook was slightly bent open. My fingers were still trembling so badly that I was unable to extract a replacement from my flybox. It took some time to collect another nymph from its Wheatley clip, and I had difficulty manipulating the knot.

"Look at him!" Radziwill grinned. "He's still shaking."

"Might be the worse case we've seen this year," Anchorena teased.

During the week that followed, we took a few good fish, but nothing like that trophy rainbow. I rolled a brown they estimated at fifteen pounds, but had broken the hook

with a low backcast, and it was quickly lost. They urged me to be patient.

"We'll still see the volcano wearing its sombrero of clouds," Anchorena insisted, "and the big fish will finally come!"

Two hours before daylight on the morning of my last day, the fierce *pampero* had gathered again, stirring in the dark mirror of the lake. It sent riffling patterns across the scimitar-shaped reaches of the Lago Paimun, moving in the rain forests of *coihue* and cypresses and bamboo, at the alpine threshold of Chile.

The wind rose and grew, stripping snow plumes from the shoulders of the great volcano. It gathered swiftly, forcing the surface of Huechulaufquèn into life, until great whitecaps came rolling across the lava outcroppings where the river leaves the lake. Wild gusts lashed downstream into the Garganta del Diablo, shrieking through the wooden trestles of the bridge, until the night sky was filled with spray.

Dust billowed high from the cavalry post road. There were silver *pesos* and a brass cartridge casing at the roadside shrine, but its votive candles had blown out in

ABOVE *The meadows of the upper Malleo with Lanín volcano behind, marking the border between Argentina and Chile. This section of the river resembles a western US spring creek, complete with intense hatches every evening. When the bugs really get going, every fish in the river comes alive.*

257

FLY	LINE		LENGTH	NAME	
BWB	ST	SEATROUT ♂	7.5	VALENTINE ATKINSON	1ST SEA-RUN BROWN EVE
VE N.B.	T200	SEATROUT ♀	2¾	JIM HOFFMAN	
PRAG.	T300	SEATROUT ♂	4,5	DOUG SATO	1ST SEA RUN BROWN C
RAINBOW	T200	SEA TROUT ♀	6 kg	JIM HOFFMAN	45th CAST - JUMPER! MALE
"	T200	SEA TROUT ♂	7 kg	JIM HOFFMAN	
	T200	SEA TROUT ♀	6 kg.		
WB	T200	SEA-TROUT	4.5	VAL ATKINSON	3 hooked - one Jau JUMPERS ALL
	T200	SEA-TROUT	4 kg	TOMAS STORIE	THE PRESSURE IS OFF
	T300	" ♀	2.5	DOUG LARSEN	GREAT TO BE BACK
	T200	" ♀	10.3 / 23 POUNDS	VAL ATKINSON	ON THE LAST CAST OF TH MEMORIES TO LAST A LI
TUBE	CORTLAND #9 FLOATING	SEATROUT ♀	2¼ kg	JOHN TRIM	A great eve...
"	"	♀	6½ kg	"	thanks to
"	"	♀	3½ kg	"	Federico
"	"	♀	4¼ kg	Randolph	Randolph's firs

ABOVE TOP *The log book at Kau Tapen Lodge in Tierra del Fuego records some very nice catches of big sea-run brown trout.*

ABOVE BOTTOM *The front door of the Kau Tapen Lodge reflects the promise of another great day's fishing. You can almost smell the coffee and bacon.*

the wind. The spent rifle shell was a curiosity, two young recruits from the military compound had lighted the candles, and the coins had been the property of a solitary Mapuche.

The wind dropped at daylight, and we reached the river early. There was still frost in the grass, and Anchorena started a small fire to warm our hands. The sun had still not reached the currents of the deep Rincon Grande below the lake, but it was bright on the monkeypuzzle trees.

"Feels right this morning," Anchorena said quietly.

Carola, Anchorena's wife, had come with us on my last morning, and after we got a big fire started to warm ourselves, she prepared a huge pot of coffee. We sat happily in the grass, sheltered from the cool breeze, talking about fishing tactics and workable remedies for boca fever. We agreed that the only remedy is more fishing.

There was still no sombrero of clouds on the volcano when we walked to the boca, and the sun was getting warmer. It was too bright and the river was still cold. We caught nothing of size all morning, although we scouted the bend from the monkeypuzzle bluffs, and its depths were filled with big trout. We withdrew to the sheltered meadow near the bridge, where there was a lamb *asado* with fresh tomatoes and bread, and some good *tinto*, and there was time for a leisurely nap in the warm grass. I found a sheltered place and fell asleep.

"Get up, Ernesto!" Carola was shaking me awake. "Lanín is wearing his sombrero!"

There was a saucer-shaped cloud of ice crystals over the big volcano. Shadows were lengthening across the river, and it was already twilight under the cliffs of the Garganta del Diablo. We each collected a sandwich, and shared a *mate*, before Anchorena led me downstream toward the canyon. We stopped above the boulder-filled pool where he had caught his record trout in 1966. I asked about the fish.

"It was quite a night," he smiled.

Anchorena pointed across the river, describing how he took the monster brown trout that held the world fly-record for several years. His effortless long casts had covered the pool as he worked downstream, covering the water with concentric fly-swings, dropping a big saltwater bucktail near the opposite bank. Reaching the deep holding water near the bottom of the beat, he climbed out on a boulder to fish farther down. He was working the big bucktail back across the primary currents when there was a sailfish-sized boil behind the fly. The strike was vicious, scattering spray on the wind. It was a heavy fish, and it sank back toward the bottom and sulked. The trout had hooked itself, and the rod was bent in a stubborn circle.

"I knew it was a good fish," he said.

He had no idea how big it really was, but it turned and lunged downstream, wrenching the rod tip into the water. The reel was overspinning wildly, fouling the loosely coiled line. Anchorena struggled among the sunk boulders to follow, trying to unscramble the reel, and fell hard. He had bruised his ribs, tearing his canvas waders, and gouging both knees. But finally the tangle worked free, as the great fish sulked, and he quickly cleared the slack into the reel. The big fish was still there, and Anchorena was grateful for its mistake.

"He just stayed there without moving," he remembered, "and it felt like I was fouled on the bottom."

His spirits sank, and his wounds were starting to ache. Anchorena worked farther down through the boulders, and tried pumping and reeling with almost no effect. He tried alternating strong pressure with slack. The fish still held motionless in the middle of the river, like a sunken snag.

"Just when I was sure he was gone," Anchorena continued, "the fish moved upstream and stopped again."

It was a minor victory, but hope was surging again, and it was the beginning of the end. He patiently pumped the fish from the bottom. The stalemate lasted another fifteen minutes, but as it finally wallowed in the surface, it rolled and attempted to bolt. The reel whimpered in protest, emitting a ratchety little rattle from time to time. There was a worrisome tangle of big deadfalls downstream, trees from the shoulders of the volcano, and carried down the lake in big storms.

It was getting dark quickly.

Anchorena kept pressuring the fish, forcing it off balance and nagging at its ebbing strength. The moon began to rise. Its light helped to illuminate the little canyon, and when the great fish floundered weakly, he saw its immense white belly as it shuddered and rolled. The big trout surrendered grudgingly, giving ground millimeter by millimeter, as Anchorena pressed it hard. It rolled in the rocky shallows, and he gasped when he saw its length, lying weakly at his feet. He reached anxiously with his gaff. The trout seemed to sense its peril, righted itself with great dignity, and tried to reach the current. Anchorena patiently forced it back.

"My arms were shaking," he confessed.

The great tail was fanning weakly in the faint moonlight, and he reached again with the gaff. It was finally the moment of truth. The hand gaff struck and held, but the fish thrashed wildly, showering him with water. It wrenched violently and twisted free, and Anchorena was close to panic. He floundered and almost went down in the river, but his quarry was exhausted too, and it surfaced near his feet.

"I just gaffed it again!" he said.

ABOVE *An alternative excursion across the Andes to Chile reveals some great sea-trout fishing in Torres del Paine National Park. Some think that these are the most spectacular peaks in the world.*

RIGHT *A five-pound brown, taken from a boca ("rivermouth") just at last light, is cause for jubilation.*

His pretty young daughters, Carolina and Paola, had come downstream in the darkness, worried that he had not returned. The girls were on the opposite bank, blurred silhouettes on the lava cornices. But they saw their father wrestle the great fish ashore, and shouted questions about its size.

"It might go twenty pounds!"

Both girls laughed derisively at such exaggeration. "Then it's not really a trout," they scoffed, "It's a crocodile!"

"They thought I was teasing," he said.

He pulled the small Chatillon from his fishing vest, struck a match, and was stunned to find the scale simply bottomed out at twenty pounds. Anchorena hooked the scale in the opposite gill cover, and struggled to raise the fish in the darkness. The Chatillon struck bottom again.

"It's heavier than my scale can weigh!" he yelled.

The girls stopped laughing and went running back along the rimrock, to tell the others and meet their father at the bridge. It was the largest trout anyone had ever caught at the Boca Chimehuin. They gathered around the cookfire, admiring its massive hookbilled kype, and its spotted length of more than a meter. It still weighed twenty-four pounds in Junín.

Radziwill was starting down the same reach of water now, working patiently along the opposite bank, and we stayed to watch him cover the water. The pool had surrendered a world record fish to Anchorena, and it had become something of a shrine. The light was starting to fail as Anchorena led me farther along the Garganta del Diablo.

He stopped to fish the next pool, explaining that its bottom was tricky to wade in the darkness, and directed me to an easier site downstream. There were shrubs armed with thorns like knitting needles, and I skirted them cautiously to protect my chest waders and thighs. I found the steep little trail he had described, and started down in the twilight.

"It looks good," I thought.

It was a deep pool below a heavy chute of rapids, where the Chimehuin gathered its strength, sidestepping an outcropping of rhyolite, and churned into a wild spillway through the boulders. Its currents grew still in these ebony depths, and flowed quietly for fifty yards, welling up again into a smooth glide at the tail. There was a mile of rapids downstream – it looked like trophy-fish water. The light was falling as I caught a brown of eighteen inches – an average fish in such water; pumpkin-colored on its belly, and sprinkled with poppy-red spots. It was obviously a river fish. I nursed it gently, until it bolted with better casting room. It was almost time to climb out from the canyon, before it was too dark to find the steep trail.

"It's just about over," I sighed.

There had been no trophies from the mecca of my dreams, and the week had passed swiftly. I had hooked and lost several large trout – my best was still a four-pound rainbow.

ABOVE *Anglers toss Wooly Buggers into the riverbank willows, on a float trip down the Collon Cura.*

"But four pounds isn't exactly bad," I thought.

Suddenly there was an immense swirl at midstream. The fish had engulfed the big streamer with a wild lunge, and the reel noisily surrendered huge staccato lengths of line. The trout bored deep into the heavy current at the throat of the pool. It was a mistake. I tightened to maintain a steady pressure on my tackle, without enough force to panic the fish. It was fighting both the river and the rod, and I wanted to stay there, steadily eroding its strength. The tactics worked surprisingly well, and it surrendered most of its explosive energy in those first critical minutes. It was nearly beaten when it finally drifted back, wallowing in the failing light.

"Careful," I thought wildly. "Careful!"

There was a moment that threatened to turn sour, when the fish floundered weakly on the surface, working toward the rapids downstream. I could not possibly follow at night. It seemed impossible to hold even a spent fish of such weight in the gathering currents downstream, unless I tricked it into helping me. There are times when a hooked fish will move away from the pressure of your tackle, so I stripped six or eight yards of line from the reel, without releasing it from my rod fingers. The fish seemed to stop momentarily. I lowered the rod tip to the current, and shook the loose slack quickly into its flow. It bellied tight past the trout, and hung there throbbing for several seconds. The struggling fish collected itself, and slowly started back upstream against its pull, slowly bulldogging past me in the darkness, and sulking in the depths of the pool.

There was a quiet little backwater in the shallows, and when I probed the bottom with my brogues, it seemed good. The fish rolled again, and surrendered a few grudging yards. I forced it closer, but it seemed to sense me in the darkness, and bolted back toward midstream. I coaxed it back patiently. It tried another half-hearted run, and this time I snubbed it short. It lay shuddering at my feet, until I seated my fingers across its gill covers, and carried it ashore.

My heart was pounding hard.

It was a big rainbow of fourteen pounds, and it proved difficult to climb out from the canyon with the fish, wrestling its thickly muscled bulk up the steep trail in the dark. I finally reached the top, and cut across the brushy little bench to the road. The river lay almost mute beyond the cornices of the little postpile gorge. I stopped to rest when I finally reached the road. The weather on the horizon was cloudless and clear in Chile. The seething constellations were very bright, and I stood there staring at the Southern Cross.

The mountains of the high cordillera were darkly purple in the dying light, and there was still a faint sombrero surrounding Lanín. The vast surface of

ABOVE TOP *A Giant Golden Stone.*

ABOVE BOTTOM *An Olive Green Wooly Bugger.*

ABOVE TOP *A Brown Wooly Bugger.*

ABOVE BOTTOM *A Black Zonker.*

Huechulaufquèn lay absolutely still, a mirror of vermilion and lavender and mauve. Two big herons flew past in the night. The rapids of the Garganta del Diablo were muted in the canyon, and I started toward the bridge. The other members of our party had already returned to the trucks. I could hear their laughter, and see the big cookfire near the trestle. I was suddenly surprised at the depth of my fatigue, and the tail of the great fish was dragging in the dust.

The night wind stirred in the monkeypuzzle trees, riffling restlessly across the still mirror of the lake. There was a tiny Mapuche woman resting with her children beside the shrine, and three candles flickered in the darkness.

BELOW A sweeping vista across the pampas and the Rio Grande in Tierra del Fuego – the magical home of the world's largest sea-run brown trout.

Casting off the Edge of the World

Argentina

Brian Clarke

"There were many memorable fish. There was the great fish that leapt clean

on to the distant bank to take its bearings when it was hooked, and that

then leapt immediately back into the water ready for the fight. There was

the fish that leapt above my head while I was wading chest-deep and

that trailed rubies behind it through the red, setting sun."

It must have been as a boy that the name first stuck. I do not know what the map was; or who the author was, if it was a book, but it seems as though the name has always been there, lodged in my imagination like a flaming arrow. Tierra del Fuego! Land of Fire! What images the name conjures up. Volcanoes, maybe, and red, spilling lava; or natives on a headland, silhouetted against flames. In my mind, in many minds, the name is synonymous with the remotest place the imagination can grasp. Tierra del Fuego, the very end of the world.

Nothing much can change in that extraordinary place, nothing much about it can alter. Jets, though, are bringing it nearer. Now flights carrying anglers arrive there most weeks in the Southern autumn before the hounds of Cape Horn slip their leash. The planes come down from Buenos Aires, partly over coast, partly over hazed deserts. They touch down at Rio Grande airport at the mouth of the Rio Grande river, the most famous sea-trout river in the world.

I once fished the Rio Grande for a week. It was a week that came flooding back to me, in tiny detail, long afterwards, thanks to a mishap in the post....

My young grandson was thrilled with his new car transporter. He was playing with it when he asked if Father Christmas had come to my house too. As it happens, Father Christmas did come. He popped a small package through my letter box. It contained what a film-processing laboratory had long since claimed it had never received: a set of transparencies shot in Tierra del Fuego.

The pictures cleared away the haze of distance and time. One brought back every detail of one of the most memorable hour's fishing that I have ever had. Another provided proof-positive of a sea trout beyond imagining.

It is a long time since I fished the Rio Grande. The river lies like a crack across the coccyx of South America's spine. It flows through desolately beautiful, limitlessly horizoned plains, more or less due east from the Andes. It empties into the South Atlantic, more or less midway between the Magellan Straits and Cape Horn.

I fished from Kau Tapen Lodge, twenty miles inland on a rolling dirt road. There were six of us there: three Argentinians, two Americans and me. We fished singly or in pairs, always with a professional guide armed with spare flies and a vast landing net that had a powerful spring balance built into the handle.

The fishing, in spite of the renowned size of the Rio Grande's sea trout, was all with single-handed trout rods. I used a seven-weight, nine-foot carbon rod equipped with a butt extension to take some strain off my wrist, a large-capacity disc-braked reel and, most of the time, a weight-forward, fast sinking line.

ABOVE *Tom McGuane casting for sea trout on the Villa Maria Water of the Rio Grande.*

RIGHT *A late-evening fly change on the Rio Grande. It is in these final moments before pitch black that the sea trout seem to throw caution to the wind as they aggressively attack the fly.*

RIGHT *An* asado, *or barbecue, with lamb and red wine after the evening fishing.*

The line had as much to do with the wind as the water. The Rio Grande is easily wadable on most reaches and most of the water is briskly paced, perfect for the fly. In calm weather, a floating line would have been a delight to use; but, when I was there, the wind blew almost without relent. It became a living, bullying thing. It whistled about my rod as through a ship's rigging, it flapped my waterproofs about my head like loose sails. The wind whipped tears from my eyes, impressed itself on my cheeks, moved the very ears on my head when it gusted from behind.

When the wind was up, the narrow, heavy sinking line was needed as much to help me cast as to sink close to the bottom. It was, though, part of the experience: the challenge was to work with the wind and not to struggle against it.

When the wind dropped, which it did from time to time, we shared the high, wide skies with spiralling condors and noisesome flights of Magellan geese. We shared the honey-coloured plains with honey-coloured guanacos, llama-like animals that studied us hair-triggered, edgily curious. We shared the water with the muskrats and the beavers and the fish.

My fear had been that I would arrive too soon; that coming in early January in a season that runs from January to the end of March would see me miss the main runs. Yet the river was already full of fish, now rolling and sploshing, now winking silver, now sullenly lying doggo in the long, wide pools.

There are rivers quite like the River Grande in Alaska: wide sweeps of rivers that are filled with salmon from bed to surface and bank to bank when the height of the season comes; but, in Alaska at these times, the fishing is easy. It can be a fish each cast and it is not so much the energy that needs to be paced, but the day.

Here, although there were fish in great numbers, they were more dispersed and had to be worked for. We each caught our share, but they were mostly hard-won.

And what fish! In most rivers in Great Britain that contain sea trout, the fish average around one pound, approaching maybe two. A three-pounder is a nice one, friends hear of four-pounders, five-pounders are noted on Christmas cards to old angling enemies.

In six full days and one evening on the Rio Grande, I caught twenty-three sea trout – by no means an exceptional score. The smallest weighed five pounds. The average was just a fraction under ten pounds. The largest was – well, very large.

The fish came at first in ones and twos, the daily score gradually creeping up as the week progressed, which is the proper way for any fishing week to unfold.

There were many memorable fish. There was the great fish that leapt clean on to the distant bank to take its bearings when it was hooked, and that then leapt immediately back into the water ready for the fight. There was the fish that

267

ABOVE *During a windy late afternoon a determined angler sets forth for the Rio Gallegos, a "hot" new sea-trout destination.*

leapt above my head while I was wading chest-deep and that trailed rubies behind it through the red, setting sun.

Above all there were the fish in the photographs: the one recalling a moment in the best day I had, the other freezing for ever that sea trout of my lifetime.

The best day began on a long pool with a high bank opposite. It was, my guide said, usually fished from the near bank at the upstream end. I said that for all the awkwardness of the high bank for casting, I favoured the side opposite, at the pool's lower end. To some head-shaking and what I like to think was mere tut-tutting in Spanish, I waded over. With the first cast, I hit a fish that shattered the surface at once and came off. Second cast, I had a solid pull but failed to connect. Third cast, I had a take so violent that it pulled my heart into my mouth.

I stumbled and splashed downstream behind an unseen force, tripped over a branch that lay white and bleached as an old bone and eventually landed the trout. We slipped out the barbless hook, my American companion took the photograph of the sea trout, my guide and me that I am looking at now – and then we returned the prize to the water, as we did with every catch that week. It had weighed thirteen pounds.

I made my way back to the same casting spot. Another cast, another thumping take, another rod-creaking, breathless fight. A ten-pounder. Next cast, a missed fish. The cast after that, a fish that took with such immense, sudden power that I found myself looking at a shattered line streaming head-high, downwind.

A new leader, a new fly, a new cast and a new fish, a cart-wheeling seven-pounder that was thirty yards downstream before I could gather up the loose line and follow. All of this, all of it, in less than an hour and still another

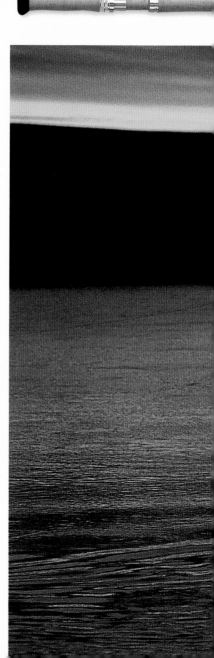

thirteen-pounder and another five-pounder to come.

The great fish came on my last day. It came from the neck of a deep, fast pool: a broad-shouldered, barrel-chested monster of a fish that was impossibly thick right down to the tail. It took for ever to land, time after time turning away from the net and bow-waving across the shallows towards the middle; but eventually he tired. I laid the fish gently on the grass, put my rod beside it to give some measure of scale, and took out my camera. Click. Seventeen pounds precisely.

That fish was as exhausted as I was. I can see myself now nursing it back to strength, holding it upright facing the current. I begin to feel it flex and shrug, see its pectoral fins gradually extend and splay; watch as it gulps oxygen steady and slow; and then the great tail sweeps aside my holding hands and the fish is gone, heading for its destiny in the foothills of the Andes.

So yes, I told my grandson, Father Christmas did come to my house this year. He came in a blue uniform, in broad daylight, on a bicycle; and he brought me a transporter, too.

BELOW In the gathering gloom of twilight Yvon Chouinard punches out another cast aimed at the far bank, where sea trout can be heard if not seen.

ARGENTINA: FACTFILE

BACKGROUND

With its high altitude, cold-flowing, clean rivers, little or no natural predation or pollution, and very low human density, Argentine Patagonia had always been a vast network of catchments waiting to become trout fisheries. Abundant varieties of oxygenating weed for cover, and large densities of freshwater crustaceans and insect life for food, ensured the perfect environment in which to nurture trout. Between the late 1920s and the early 1930s fertilized trout and salmon ova were shipped to Argentina from North America and Europe.

Original stocks of fish included Atlantic salmon, and rainbow, brook and brown trout. In the southern half of Patagonia the most successful strains of fish were the Loch Leven and Thames strain brown trout, brought from England. In addition to a non-migratory river-trout population, a sea-going race of these fish established themselves in the Rio Grande, Rio Gallegos and several smaller rivers by the mid-1950s. Joe Brooks, the legendary American angler, first publicized these fish in the late 1950s and early 1960s, and visiting anglers began to fish for them.

With the advent of catch-and-release fishing, an ever-increasing number of returning fish began to be noticed, with the result that the Rio Grande and Rio Gallegos are now recognized as the premium sea-trout fisheries in the world, with healthy runs of fish at a consistently large average size.

WHEN TO GO

The season starts in early November and finishes in mid-April. While there are usually good concentrations of fish in the rivers throughout this time, the most consistently good fishing, in terms of weather conditions and overall numbers of fish, is probably January to March. It should be remembered that some of the very largest fish seem to return in the earliest months of the season, and that by the end of the season the returning fish are more evenly spread

LEFT *Tom McGuane and guide Steve Estela land and release a 25-pounder on the Villa Maria beat of the Rio Grande. Caught on a bomber, this was the largest dry-fly-caught fish of the 1998 season.*

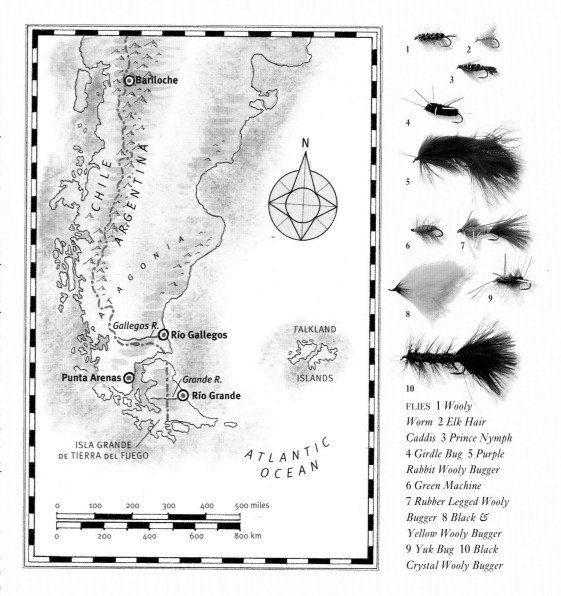

FLIES 1 *Wooly Worm* 2 *Elk Hair Caddis* 3 *Prince Nymph* 4 *Girdle Bug* 5 *Purple Rabbit Wooly Bugger* 6 *Green Machine* 7 *Rubber Legged Wooly Bugger* 8 *Black & Yellow Wooly Bugger* 9 *Yuk Bug* 10 *Black Crystal Wooly Bugger*

throughout the river, which can make for heavier daily bags. Not all fish caught will be fresh from the sea, but sport may be more constant.

TACKLE

RODS: Single-handed rods – 9 ft for 8 or 9 wt line. Double-handed rods – 12–14 ft for 8–11 wt lines.

REELS: Direct-drive reels with good drag systems capable of holding line and 150–200 yards of backing.

LINES: All fly lines from full floater to "Teeny 300" or "deepwater express" lines.

LEADERS: In general, leader weights should not fall below about 10 lb strength.

FLIES: A wide range of flies has proven effective against Argentine sea trout, from Bombers, large Wulff dry flies, and Muddlers fished in clear water conditions, to Zonkers, Wooly Buggers and other streamers fished wet in heavier, colder water. Several more traditional patterns have also proven effective.

Sterling Silver
Florida Keys

RUSSELL CHATHAM

"This is one of those spring mornings you always hope for; still, humid, and already warm, so that the guides at the Sea Center on Big Pine Key feel the air and call it a tarpon day. As you ease out of the cut, enormous clouds are stacked around the horizon, nacreous and pillowy. Later a breeze may rise out of the southwest, but now the water is slick as mercury, its pastel patina reflecting the tops of the tallest clouds."

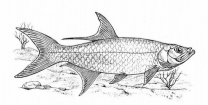

The elemental flatness of the Florida Keys is compelling and mysterious in its thin plane of reflective brilliance. Within their own horizontal galaxy, the flats are as inscrutable as the empyrean blue water of the Gulf Stream itself, far outside the shoals where you look down along sharp, beveled shafts of light that narrow into blackness thousands of feet above the ocean floor.

Inshore, and out of sight of the Atlantic's barrier reefs, among the very Keys themselves, the horizon is often lost somewhere behind refulgent bands of light and shimmering heat waves. On certain hot, humid days without wind, distant mangrove islands are seen only as extraneous tubes of gray-green, lying inexplicably in the silver atmosphere like alien spaceships.

Over in the backcountry, the Gulf side of the Keys, long plateaus of uneven coral stall the tide and agitate it so the waterscape vibrates and sparkles. The whole of this inside territory is an unfathomably complex tapestry of radical design.

Few people understand that this vast district is one of the great wildernesses of North America. Travelers, as they fly between Marathon Key or Key West and Miami, are temporarily enthralled by the complicated pattern of lime-green channels and basins, the ochre and light-sienna coral and sand flats, the islands. But almost no one ever goes there .

Most of those who do have occupational reasons: sponge, lobster and conch fishermen, shrimpers, and fishing guides. Groups of bird watchers sometimes visit certain special Keys. Skin divers occasionally go out and poke around old wrecks. And lastly, there are sportsmen.

Even within this last category is bracketed yet another minority within the minority: a fisherman who, in the opinion of some, carries it too far, bringing with him restyled nineteenth-century attitudes, seemingly inappropriate equipment and a full-on desire to proceed without secondary motives. Sometimes alone, sometimes with a close friend or

ABOVE *A collection of Fender Flies, Brook's Argentines, and Stu Apte's Flies. Hooks need to be extremely sharp to penetrate the tough, bony mouth of the tarpon.*

LEFT *Guinea-fowl feathers that have been dyed blue.*

274

perhaps a sympathetic hired guide, with benefit of only a small open skiff, a pole to push it, a fly rod and a perverse desire to be out of fashion, he goes out there to fish for tarpon.

It takes leisuretime and a nature disposed toward contemplation, and sometimes contradiction, to develop passion for pastimes with surface pointlessness. In the instance of fly-fishing for tarpon, a certain quantum of cash on hand is also required, although in no way is this an endeavor suited to the idle rich, or, for that matter, to anyone else slightly dotty. You need all your faculties.

Suppose you have the time, the money and the faculties. Assuming you want to expend them all on exotic fishing, why would you choose to go for tarpon rather than, say, marlin, a historically much more glamorous quarry? Enter your aforementioned

ABOVE *A pod of tarpon schooled up in shallow water. These are small, ten- to twenty-pounders. They go on growing to weigh up to 200 pounds or more.*

contemplative, sometimes contradictory character.

If you think about distilling fishing down to angling, then further, to angling's diamond center, you can scarcely come to any conclusion other than this: as the time immediately preceding that point at which the fish actually becomes hooked grows more difficult, intense and all-absorbing, the quality of the fishing improves.

After that, you want the take to be hard to manage – fascinating in and of itself – and the ensuing struggle to be, above all, noble. Now, these moments may follow so closely upon one another they seem as one, yet there remains a hierarchy, however blurred. Then, way down there at the bottom of the list, is the dead fish on your hands.

To catch a marlin you must troll. Say the word over and over again to yourself, drawing it out as if it were spelled with lots of o's and l's. There may be nothing on earth, except perhaps an unsuccessful bridge club luncheon, quite so boring as trolling. Trol-l-l-l-ing. Several hours of it should be enough to dull your senses so that when the captain or mate or speed of the boat, or whatever it is, finally hooks a fish and you are faced with the appalling prospect of an hour in the fighting chair, you simply would rather have a beer.

On quite another hand, nowhere else in the spectrum of available angling can there be found a more profoundly thrilling prelude to the hooking of a fish than in the stalking of tarpon in shallow water. The fly rod ups the ante considerably, too. In short, it's at least twice as much trouble as any other tackle you could use.

On the flats, where you must see everything, the search becomes an alarmingly patient and suspenseful intrigue. This game calls for a blend of refined skills, those of the hunter as well as the fisherman. It is a process, an experience, to which few, if any, ever really become fully initiated.

This is one of those spring mornings you always hope for; still, humid, and already warm, so that the guides at the Sea Center on Big Pine Key feel the air and call it a tarpon day. As you ease out of the cut, enormous clouds are stacked around the horizon, nacreous and pillowy. Later a breeze may rise out of the southwest, but now the water is slick as mercury, its pastel patina reflecting the tops of the tallest clouds.

You are two days into a series of spring tides. This means you will be able to fish places that have been neglected during the preceding weeks, when there was not enough of a flood to bring the tarpon in. The plan will be to stake certain corners, then later, pole out some other banks.

When you shut down at your first stop it is suddenly as still as an empty room. The pole is taken from its chocks and your companion begins moving you into a higher position. It is still early, the sun at too oblique an angle to give real visibility.

Already it is getting hot, the high humidity causing a haze to form. It is impossible to see anything of the bottom beyond a few yards and you wonder how your friend knows where to stake. He is looking for the corner, he says, but you can notice no variation whatsoever in the even carpet of turtle grass.

Shortly, he pushes the stake in and ties off. You get up on the casting deck. Fish will be coming up the bank on your right, then cutting across where you are staked.

LEFT *Billy Pate jumping a tarpon at Buchanon Bank off Islamorada in the Keys. I sat on a small wooden stepladder for two days waiting for this picture to happen. I was ready when the fish jumped once and threw the hook. I got one frame – this is it.*

RIGHT *A Stu Apte Tarpon Fly.*

ABOVE *To watch as a tarpon swims over and engulfs your fly, then feels the hook and goes screaming off deep into your backing, is guaranteed to get your heart pounding.*

You pull off enough line for a throw, make one, then coil the running line neatly at your feet. You hold the fly in your hand, leaving a loop of fly line in the water long enough for a false cast. Now you wait and look.

There is plenty of time to think about the short-comings of your fly-casting, the different ways you might blow the chance when it comes. Your feet start to ache and you shift them a little so that later when you look down to make sure the fly line is not tangled, you see you're standing on it. You cast and recoil it carefully.

"Rollers. Hundred yards."

You look with extra intensity at the indefinite sheen as if the harder you stare the more likely you are to see something. Then they glint in unison, closer, and are gone again. The first wave of fright settles into your abdomen.

They're coming just as we thought. This way. Up the bank. Where are they? Where are they! It's not too soon to false-cast. Get going. Oh no. No! They're right here. At the boat. Flushing.

The frightened fish are scooting away, back into the sheen. There are marl muds everywhere around the boat, and the boils the fish make as they depart seem to send a shiver beneath the skiff you can feel on the bottom of your feet. You wish you had your blanket and a bottle of Jergens Lotion.

Several other pods of tarpon work their way up the tide. Always, though, their trajectory takes them past the skiff out of range. In an hour the surge of fish seems to have passed, gone on to Loggerhead or wherever they were going. You decide to pull the stake and pole out the bank.

As your companion begins to pole, you wish the sun would climb higher, the haze dissipate. You offer to take the pole, and are turned down.

The drab grasses tilt in the slow current like a billion signposts gone wrong. Poling, you will be obliged to concern yourself with trigonometry; moving tide, moving boat, moving fish, degree of intercept.

Without notice, basins appear, deep and crisply emerald over their white sand bottoms. Sometimes there are barracuda arranged in them like dark lines of doom.

Small, tan sharks glide past the boat; rays, too, moving over the flat as the tide floods. The bank is 1,000 yards long. Somewhere on its easy slope there must be tarpon. You surge smoothly forward, transom first, that gentle sound being the only one you hear. 300, 400 yards. Nothing.

What a strange way to fish this is. You might be out here for eight hours, running the boat ten, maybe twenty miles, and you never lose sight of the bottom. A drastic change in depth, one that might mean fish instead of no fish, or an easy pass through a little green cut rather than a grounded skiff or sheared pin, is twelve inches. Coming down off a plane at thirty knots at the wrong moment can mean settling into the grass so you will have to get out and push the heavy skiff until the bottom slopes away enough to get back in and pole your way out of it. Down here they always tell you, if something goes wrong with the engine, just get out and walk home.

"Twelve o'clock. Way out." Quite far ahead, you see the chain of sparkles as tarpon roll, gulping air. Tarpon on the bank. 150 yards? A hundred? Can't let them get too close. Stay in front of the first fish. Are there two? Six? A dozen? Nothing. Sheen. Reflection. Haze. Useless glasses. Boat's closing. Fish coming on. Remember. Fly in hand. Ready. Loop of line trailing. Glance to see it's not back in the way of the pole. Fly line still coiled. Loose. Strain your eyes. Look. Wakes? They're colder gray. Light. And dark. Not warm, not tan like the bottom. Movement will tell. Long. They're long, cool gray. Temples pound. The glare, relentless. Sheen. No shapes. No gray. Another wake. Still farther out than you thought. Never mind. Roll the line. Think about it. Streamer gone, in the air. Back loop flat . . . not so tight! Slow down. There he is, within range, rolling, enormous scales catching the light. Your friend is urging, warning. Now! Wait out the back-cast. Don't dump it. Wait. Drift. Know the intercept. Correct. Don't change direction too much. Not too much drive. Ease the cast off. Strip hard. Get his eye. Strip. A wake. Water rushing, churning. A take! Stay balanced, feel the turn, the tension. Now strike. Again, to the side. Again. Don't look up. Watch the line clear itself. Tarpon's in the air. Eye level, upside down, twisting, rattling. Push slack.

ABOVE *Billy Pate catching a "rat," which he later releases. A "rat" is what he calls a tarpon under 100 pounds. Billy holds the world record at 188 pounds caught on 16-pound tippet. Anglers are now looking to break the 200-pound mark.*

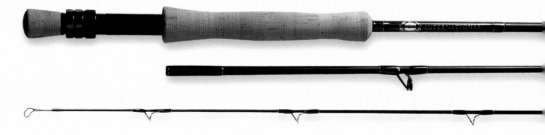

Running. Too fast. Another jump. Gone.

Tarpon are not used as food. You would think there must be some way they might be prepared, but they just aren't eaten. Nor are they taken for other commercial reasons. Once there was a scheme to convert them to pet food or fertilizer, a plan fortunately abandoned. In any case, there is no price per pound for tarpon, and no diners sit fidgeting with their utensils while their tarpon are being broiled.

On the other side of the ledger, this has come to mean a lack of sound information about the fish and its habits. Tarpon are thought to be migratory, moving from south to north and from salt to brackish or fresh water as part of their spawning cycle. They also travel from deep to shallow water to feed. However, a true species pattern is not clearly known.

To the fish's broadest advantage, this also means there is no wholly justifiable cause for anyone to kill one. Those slight reasons used to center entirely around man's own vanity. Fishermen may cart them to the dock, but the only one truly bringing them

home is the Southernmost Scavenger Service. The flimsy excuses, then, for killing tarpon rest in that zone somewhere between the charterman's ad only a tourist will buy, and the Kodak dealer.

It's possible to intrude upon the larger spirit of fishing in any number of ways besides pointlessly killing the animal. Not the least of these is to destroy privacy. For example, hardly anything can ruin the tranquility of a day's fishing like a good tournament. The reason keeps turning out to be greed in one form or another, with slices of unresolved ego gratification thrown in for good measure.

It's becoming practically un-American to disapprove of fishing tournaments these days. But if you take an affable, essentially non-competitive, harmless activity, the principal attribute of which lies in the quality of the time spent pursuing it rather than in the grossness of the last results, and you begin giving large cash prizes for the grossest last results, suddenly it's all gone.

Some negate the magic of angling by approaching it from a standpoint of overt, even bizarre practicality: equipment specifications, a humorless concern over questions that have only numbers as answers.

ABOVE *It takes great teamwork between guide and angler to fight a big fish. Especially when he decides to circle the boat.*

RIGHT *This is a giant tarpon weighing more than 150 pounds. A hundred years ago it was considered impossible to catch one this big.*

FAR RIGHT *Like the bonefish, tarpon are incredibly iridescent. Their scales shine like polished silver.*

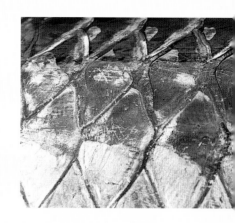

What hook size to use? What percentage of the point should be triangulated? What pound test should the shock tippet be? How long? What pound test should the weakest leader section be? What pound class world record do you want to qualify for? How long should the whole leader be? The butt section? What size line? What's its diameter in thousandths of an inch? How long are its tapers? The belly? How thin is the running line? How much of it is there? How long is the rod? How heavy? How many yards of backing on the reel? What pound test? How tight do you set the reel drag? How long is the boat? How much does it weigh? Its beam? How much water does it draw? How fast does it go? What horsepower is the engine? What's the capacity of the gas tank? How long is the push pole? How many knots can you tie? How far can you cast? How high is the tide? What time do you start fishing? What year is it? How many points do you get for a keeper in the Islamorada Invitational Fly Championship? How much do Minimum Qualifiers count per pound? How much do releases count? If you caught a 73-pounder, a 104½-pounder, three releases and a 90¼-pounder with cheese, what would you have? A large hamburger?

Everyone addresses a certain number of technical questions, but it seems this can be done cursorily, and as a matter of light concern. Attention to facts and figures as if they were really important often obscures the things of real importance, things that cannot be counted, recorded or even clearly explained. In the final analysis, those things will appear as states of mind, wordless, indescribable and of a dimension altogether intangible.

If you are going to replace the essential quietude of fishing with semi-industrial or businesslike considerations, it might be more sensible, simpler and certainly cheaper never to leave the office.

It is now early afternoon and you are being poled downlight over a brilliant, white sand bottom. Much of the earlier haze has cleared and visibility is extraordinary. Actually, you're just offshore from a low, tropical-looking key which shimmers in the heat, its long beaches curving nearly out of view.

Swells from the Atlantic roll the skiff so that it is important to remain keenly balanced. You are in about eight feet of water, somewhat on the deep side for fly-casting to cruising fish, particularly if they are near the bottom. As you shift your weight with the motion of the boat, the Cuban mix sandwich and the three Gatorades you so hastily challenged for lunch press heavily against your tee shirt.

You are in the middle of a long corridor of stark, bright bottom. On your right is the island; to your left, perhaps a hundred yards away, the sand abruptly ending against low coral; there is a thin, irregular line of green, breakers and then blue water. Once, you see an enormous hammerhead cruising the edge.

Visibility is so perfect there is no need to be on the alert for the surprise appearance of tarpon anywhere within a 200-foot radius of the skiff. If it came within fly-casting distance, a three-pound barracuda would look like a Greyhound Scenicruiser.

It is troublesome poling in the deep water, not only because of the depth itself, but because the bottom is quite hard, so the pole makes a clunking sound when it's put down. The foot of the pole doesn't grab well either, slipping off ineffectually behind the boat.

You and your companion see the dark spots at the same time. There is a moment of hesitation, then it suddenly becomes clear they are tarpon even though they are still very far off. You will have a full three minutes to try and get the upper hand on your mounting nervousness.

ABOVE *Poling a flats boat for six to eight hours is hard – it takes skill, which develops with practice and time. The elevated platform increases the guide's field of view so it easier to see incoming fish.*

BELOW *A Red and White Tarpon Fly.*

Were we wrong? No, they're tarpon all right. Eight, maybe ten of them. All big – seventy, eighty pounds and better. Still very far away. Funny how the school changes shape. They string out, bunch up. Fish must be very foreshortened at this distance. So clear. Almost like watching birds flying. Watch footing. Is the fly line tangled? School's turning. Traveling closer to the key. Boat's turning. Good. Must make the intercept. Must take them head on. Too deep for a side shot. They'd see the boat. It's going to work. Looking at them from in front.

"I'm down. Anytime." You look back and your friend has the push pole flat across his knees. "Go." He insists, never taking his eyes from the tarpon.

How far now? 150 feet. False-casting. Hold up all the line you can. Fish coming on, almost single-file. Watch. You want thirty feet on them. No slips. Loops open. Controlled. Cast. Wait. Fly settling. Two, three feet. Tarpon at six. Or eight. Closing. Is the lead fish close enough? Start bringing it back. He sees it. Accelerating. Elevating. Growing silver. Face disjointing. Dark. Has it. Turning back down. Tension. Hit hard. Again. Again. Again.

ABOVE *The Marquesas Islands off Key West are incredibly beautiful, and a great place to find permit as well as tarpon.*

He is already going another way and the strain disorients you so much the fly line is suddenly gone from your left hand. Whirling, it jams its way through the guides. You hear the sound of the power tilt as the engine goes down, starts. Slowly, you begin to follow.

FLORIDA – FACTFILE

BACKGROUND

If the Florida Keys have a fault, it seems to be that they have been over-loved. As far back as the early nineteenth century, people from the northern states were building homes in the Keys and spending the winter months there. The old sea captains quickly discovered places such as Key West, where they began to settle throughout the Victorian era. In modern times, the flood of immigrants from the Caribbean, coupled with the continued interest of northerners and Canadians, has rendered Florida the fourth most populous US state.

The Florida Keys are second in popularity only to the Rocky Mountains as a North American fishing destination. They are serviced by a single highway that often becomes a bottleneck of traffic. The intricate pattern of channels and banks is unique, covering some 4,000 square miles of shallows where tarpon, among other fish, can be sighted and caught on light tackle. The most popular locations are Islamorada, Marathon, and Key West. The town of Key West also provides access to the Marquesas Keys, an isolated group of islands that lies 28 miles to its west. All types of accommodation exist in the Keys, from basic fish camps, to motels, to first-class hotels.

WHEN TO GO

Located in the most southerly state, the Florida Keys have glorious weather for most of the year. The average annual temperature is usually around 77°F (25°C). If it gets too hot in the summer, you are never far from being able to jump in the water to cool off. Rainfall tends to be heaviest during the summer: Key West averages around 40 inches annually.

The peak tarpon fishing season is April through June, and, although in theory there are registered guides available everywhere, during this time it is often difficult to find one without giving prior notice. Many regular anglers book their favorite guides year after year.

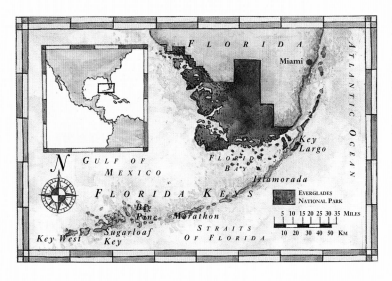

THE FISHING

There are, perhaps, more different species of fish to be caught in the Florida Keys than anywhere else in the world – but this is primarily tarpon territory. Bigger always seems to be better, and if the fish also jumps well, it quickly becomes the best. Fly-fishermen are now trying to break the 200 lb record on a fly rod. The tarpon is undoubtedly one of the most powerful of all gamefish, and exhibits spectacular, head-shaking, gill-rattling leaps when hooked, frequently shattering tackle and a fisherman's ego in the process.

A good many fishermen are serious about concentrating on one kind of fish, while others seem to enjoy catching as many different types as possible. Other than tarpon, the abundant species in the Florida Keys include bonefish, permit, snook, jacks, barracuda, snapper, and even several kinds of shark. Rods of 8 to 12 wt will suffice for many of these – the exception being large sharks. For the most part, it is necessary only to take floating, rather than sinking, lines.

FISHING FOR TARPON: Once cruising or rolling tarpon have been spotted, it is very important quickly and accurately to place the fly in front of the fish. Tarpon are not easily spooked and you can place the fly quite close to them. Allow the fly to sink to the level of the fish and begin to strip it back with a slow, steady retrieve. After he takes, wait until he

turns before setting the hook. This way the fly should slide into the corner of the fish's mouth (the softest part), which theoretically sets you up for the best possible hooking angle. Tarpon seem to have virtually concrete-lined mouths, so a super-sharp hook is an absolute necessity.

Point the rod tip at the fish and firmly set the hook with your stripping hand only. Then keep your rod tip close to the water (to eliminate slack) and pump the rod sideways with short, sharp tugs as you pull on the line and the rod simultaneously. This sounds almost simplistic, but if you haven't caught one of these giant primordial beasts before, the sight of one inhaling your fly is likely to give you a dangerously increased heart rate, which tends to scramble all rational thought processes.

TACKLE

RODS AND REELS: Use 9 to 10 ft graphite fly rods which can handle lines from 11 to 13 wt – the 12 wt is the most popular. These should be matched with a heavy-duty saltwater reel and a large disk-type drag system. The smoothness and reliability of the drag are absolutely essential for fighting tarpon. The reel must have the capacity to hold the fly line plus 250 yards of 30 lb test backing. Take extra rods in case of breakages.

LEADERS: For this kind of angling, leaders are designed for durability rather than invisibility, as tarpon are not shy. Tying these leaders is complex and rather involved for the novice. So the easiest thing to do is to buy pre-made big gamefishing leaders. However, if you would prefer to tie your own, a good reference-guide is *Practical Fishing Knots* by Lefty Kreh and Mark Sosin. A brief recipe for a standard tarpon leader is that it is tied in three sections, totaling about 6 to 8 ft. The butt section is made up of 3 to 4 ft of 30 lb test, joined to the fly line with a tail knot. A perfection loop should be tied at the other end. The class tippet is 2 to 3 ft of 8, 12, or 16 lb test. Join the butt section by

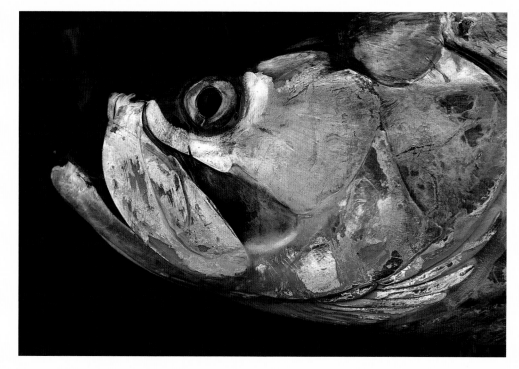

RIGHT *Tarpon are perhaps the ultimate challenge on a fly rod: they take a fly well, they jump high, and they grow huge. The all-time record tarpon on the Florida Keys is 283 lbs, and fish of 300 lbs have been spotted. Even a 10 lb tarpon is a bundle of energy on a fly rod.*

FLIES: TOP *A Red Grizzly Tarpon Fly.*
MIDDLE *A Red and White Tarpon Fly.*
BOTTOM RIGHT *A Cockroach.*

interlocking perfection loops. A Bimini Twist with a double surgeon's loop should be tied at the double end. The shock tippet should be 12 inches of 80 lb test connected to the class tippet with an Albright Special Knot. The fly is connected to the other end of the shock with a Homer Rhodes Loop Knot. This sounds complicated but with practice becomes second nature.

FLIES: When it comes to fly preference, tarpon can go from greedy to fickle in a matter of hours. Slight variations in the shape and color of a fly can make a huge difference in the number of takes an angler will achieve. A selection of the following flies should cover most conditions: the Cockroach, Chico's Shallow Water Tarpon, Stu Apte, Lefty's Deceiver, Whistlers, Seducers, and Tarpon Bunnies. All these come in a variety of colors.

ESSENTIAL TRAVEL EQUIPMENT

Temperatures can range from the low 70's up to mid-90's during prime tarpon time, when there is also high humidity. However, once you're out on the water there is often a breeze, so that the heat becomes more tolerable. It is most important, how-ever, to be especially aware of the intensity of the Florida sun – many a visiting angler has had a fishing experience ruined by getting sunburned on the first day out. A heavy-duty sunscreen or sunblock is absolutely critical, as are sunglasses, which should be polarized, so that you can see the fish (and have UV protection).

Remember that the intensity of the sun is amplified by its reflection off the water, and wearing a hat that simply protects the top of your head is not enough – it should have flaps for your ears and the back of your neck.

Dress is casual and you should wear what you feel comfortable in. If you feel able to brave the sun, wearing plenty of sunblock, shorts are the order of the day. Long-sleeved shirts for sun protection that are light in fabric and color are best. A good-quality, rubber-soled, non-slip boat shoe is advisable, with good arch support for those long hours spent standing on the casting platform. Take lightweight raingear for the occasional shower.

Sons

Mexico

TOM McGUANE

"We were actually fishing in the middle of the Sian Ka'an biosphere reserve

— over a million acres of the coast of Quintana Roo, savannas, lagoons,

seasonally flooded forest. Our camp, a simple comfortable place for fishermen

called Casa Blanca, meets the Mexican requirement of integrating human

use with preserving the complex and delicate local ecosystem whose

uniqueness derives not only from the phenomenon of a tropic sea inundating

a vast limestone shelf, but from long human history."

ABOVE *If you can tear yourself away from the fishing, there are many famous Mayan ruins to explore in the Yucatán, including Uxmal, shown here.*

My mother never accepted her move from Massachusetts and packed us children off every summer from our home in Michigan and took us "home." I do remember that my father seemed glad to watch us go. I still see him in our driveway with the parakeet in its cage, trying unsuccessfully to get my mother to take the bird too so that he wouldn't even have to be around to feed it. At the end of the summer, when we returned from Massachusetts, the bird would be there but it would never be the same bird. It was another $3.95 blue parakeet but without the gentleness of our old bird. When we reached into the cage to get our friend, we were usually bitten.

We traveled on one of the great lake boats that crossed Lake Erie to Buffalo and I remember the broad interior staircases and the brassbound window through which one viewed the terrific paddlewheels. I hoped intensely that a fish would be swept up from deep in the lake and brought to my view but it never happened. Then we took the train. I guess it must have been to Boston. I mostly remember my rapture as we swept through the eastern countryside over brooks and rivers that I knew were the watery world of the fish and turtles I cared so madly about. I also remember that one of these trips must have been made during hard times because my mother emphasized that there was enough money for us children to eat but not enough for her. We had wild highs and lows as my father tried to build a business.

Many wonderful things happened during my endless summers with my grandmother, aunts and uncles in Fall River; but for present purposes, I am only thinking of fishing. Those original images are still so burning that I cannot find a proper syntax for them. In the first, my father arrived and took me up to see some shirttail cousins in Townsend. A little brook passed through the backyard and, lying on my stomach, I could look into one of its pools and see the tiny brook trout swimming there. It was close to the rapture I felt when I held my ear against the slots of the toaster and heard a supernal music from heaven ringing the toaster springs. The brook trout were water angels and part of the first America, the one the Indians owned whose music I believed I heard from the springs of the toaster. I had seen the Indians' old trails, their burial mounds and the graves of settlers killed in the French and Indian wars. For some reason, I understood the brook trout had belonged to the paradise the Indians had struggled to keep.

It seemed to be part of a lost world like the world I was losing with my father as he became more absorbed in his work. It came to seem that we had good times together only when fish were present, and those brook trout are the first of those memories. It was casually easy for us to get along fishing; official father-and-sondom was a bomb. I think of the fathers and sons day at his athletic club with particular loathing, as it was an annual ordeal. Silver dollars were hurled into its swimming pool for the boys to struggle over. Each father stood by the pool, gazing at the writhing young divers, and waited for his silver-laden son to surface. I rarely came up with a coin. I was conscious of appearing to be less than an altogether hale boy and hardly worth bringing to this generational fête with its ventriloquists, Irish tenors, or more usually, the maniacal Eddie Peabody on the banjo. All of this was part of the background of the big dust we were meant to make in our mid-American boom town where sport of the most refined sort quickly sank into alcoholic mayhem. Steaks in the backyard, pill-popping housewives and golf were the order of the day and many youngsters sought to get their fathers away somewhere in search of a fish. Most of our fathers were just off the farm or out of small towns heading vertically upward into a new world. We didn't want them to go.

I thought that if I delivered a way to free my father from his rigorous job, we could fish more. I saw an ad for a Hart, Shaffner and Marx suit that said it was for the man who wanted to look like he would make $10,000 a year before he was thirty. Remember, this was many years ago. I told my father that he ought to make $10,000 a year, then $10,000 a year in eleven months, then $10,000 a year in ten months, and so on; and with this properly earned free time, he and I would go fishing together more often. My father said, "With an attitude like that, you'd never make $10,000 a year in the first place."

None of this mattered in Massachusetts. Across the street from my grandmother, across Brownell Street between Main and Almy, lived Jimmy McDermott, an elegant Irish bachelor who lived with his spinster sister, Alice, and they seemed very sophisticated and witty, especially compared to their immediate neighbors, the Sullivans, who were unreconstructed Irish, with a scowling mother in a black shawl and an impenetrable brogue. Jimmy McDermott took me fishing and bought me my first reel, a beautiful Penn Senator surf-casting reel, whose black density seemed to weigh coolly in my hands. Jimmy McDermott detected that I needed someone to take me fishing.

He thought it was crazy for a boy who loved to fish to be hanging around Brownell Street in Fall River in August; and so he packed a lunch and we went fishing for tautog along some small and lonely beach with its granite outcroppings and sunshot salty fog and tidal aromas. We caught several fish on the fierce green crabs we used for bait and I heard about several more because Jimmy was the sort of person who made sure at such a sacramental moment as angling that the full timbre of the thing must be appreciated in a recounting of holy incidents in time, of striped bass and flounders, of the gloomy conger eel who filled three skillets with grease,

ABOVE *A traditional thatched roof cottage at Boca Paila in the Yucatán. The locals particularly favor pastel shades for their homes.*

or the rich sports in the old days who baited their bass rigs with small lobsters. A Portuguese family picnicked on the nearby strand and in my somewhat more global view today, I think of us amusing ourselves on that *mare nostrum*, the Atlantic Ocean, casting our hopes on those ancestral waters toward Ireland, the Azores, toward the Old World. The sea heaved up around our rocks, pulling a white train of foam from mid-ocean and its mysteries of distance and language, drownings, caravels, thousand-foot unwitnessed thunderheads, phosphorous, and fish by the square mile.

It is a great triumph over something, biology maybe or that part of modern history which has prolonged adolescence to the threshold of senility, for a father to view his son without skepticism. I have not quite achieved this state but I have identified the problem. Therefore, when I stood at the airport in Cancún and watched my frequently carefree son emerge with several falling-apart carry-on bags and his shirt hanging out of his pants I did not take this altogether as a sign of complete disorganization. When we hugged, because he is so much stronger than I am, he rather knocked the wind out of me. And when we made our way to the small aircraft that would take us to Ascension Bay, I asked if he had practiced his casting. "Once," he said. "These aren't trout," I said, "a thirty-foot cast doesn't get it." "Don't worry about it," he smiled. "I don't expect to have any problem with bonefish." "How can you say that?" I asked. "You've never seen one before, you don't know how tough they can be." He just smiled. He knows how to drive me crazy.

We had a comfortable cottage, really wonderful, with cool concrete walls and a roof of thatched monkey palm. Birds were everywhere and the blue Caribbean breakers rose high enough that you could look right through them, then fell again. The coral garden seemed like a submerged quilt just past the line of breakers.

Thomas was slow getting ready to fish. He was bent over the sink, doing something and taking too long about it. I said we ought to hurry up and head for the boat. I said it twice. He straightened up from the sink holding a pale green scorpion he had just extracted from the drain. He said, "In case you were thinking of brushing your teeth." He grabbed his rod and we were out the door.

ABOVE (following heads of flies clockwise from top) A Braided Cuda Fly; a Gray Clouser Minnow; a Rabbit Candy; two Chartreuse Clouser Minnows; and a Gaitorbraid Anchovy.

ABOVE *A White Raghead Crab.*

Our guide was a Mayan Indian named Pedro, a solid fifty-year-old of easygoing authority. I thought of an Oak Bluffs voice of yesteryear, "We've been here for generations." Pedro's family had been on the shores of this bay since thousands of years before Christ. As Pedro was a mildly intolerant man, all business, one soon learned not to pester him with trifles. I did ask him if he had ever been to the United States.

ABOVE *A Chernobyl Crab.*

"I've never been to Mexico," he said coolly.

Walking to the boat, I was excited to see a lineated woodpecker who loves to eat Aztec ants from their home in the hollow pumpwood tree. A brave soul, he defends his nest against toucans. Ruddy ground doves scattered along our trail and we saw the splendid *chacalaca* on the edge of the jungle, noisy in flight as a chicken.

When we set out in the skiff, mangrove swallows scattered across the narrow channels. My son explained to me that some birds had taken to flying upside down over New York City because "there was nothing worth shitting on." Birds can tell us much.

Pedro ran the skiff through the shallow water wilderness with the air he seemed to bring to everything, an absence of ambiguity. There was no scanning the horizon, or search for signs. If a tremulous ridge of tidal movement betrayed a shoal in our path, Pedro adjusted his angle of travel without ever looking in the direction of the hazard.

When we emerged completely from the congestion of cays, the very similar bands of pale blue, of sky and sea, stretched before us at a sublime scale, white tropical clouds reaching upward to heavenly elevations. A scattering of small islands lay in the distance.

I was still thinking of Pedro's answer about never having been to Mexico. Quintana Roo was his country. In my minimal Spanish, I decided to pose a peculiar question to him. "Pedro, to us this is an extraordinary place, a beautiful place. But you have never been anywhere else. My question is this: Do you realize and appreciate that you live in one of the world's great places?"

Pedro pulled his head back and, pursing his lips to state the obvious, said in an impassioned growl, "*Si, Señor!*"

Thomas was in the bow of the boat, line stripped out, and Pedro was poling along a muddy bank near the mangroves. A squadron of bonefish had come out of the light, our blind side, and flushed in a starburst of wakes. It wasn't really a shot; so, Thomas remained in the bow, ready. After a while, I felt Pedro kick the stern of the bow out to position him and declare, "*macabi*" – bonefish – in his quiet but insistent way that made it clear he expected no screw-ups. We stared hard, testing Pedro's patience, then made out the fish about seventy feet away. He was feeding slowly, his back out of water at times, and his tail glittering when he swirled deliberately in the shallows to feed. The fish came almost to a stop, faced right, then moved forward steadily but imperceptibly. The bonefish seemed to be staring at the skiff. This seemed like a tough prospect: the water was much too thin, the fish insufficiently occupied; and since the bonefish was alone, its green and silver shape all too clear, I couldn't imagine it would tolerate the slightest imperfection of technique.

Thomas was false-casting hard. Faced with a good fish right in his face, his intensity was palpable throughout the boat. I told him that he was only going to get one shot at this fish, treading the parental thin-line of trying to remind him of the present cast. I watched his loop reach out straight, turn over, watched the fly fall about four inches in front of the bonefish.

ABOVE *A Rug Yarn Crab.*

ABOVE *A Nick's Casablanca Special.*

The fish didn't spook. The fly sank to the bottom. Thomas moved the fly very slightly. The bonefish moved forward over it. I looked up and the bend of the rod extended all the way into the cork handle. The fish burned off through the mangrove shoots which bowed and sprang up obediently. When the fish headed out across the flat, Thomas turned to look at me over his shoulder and give me what I took to be a slightly superior grin. A short time later, he boated the fish.

We were actually fishing in the middle of the Sian Ka'an biosphere reserve – over a million acres of the coast of Quintana Roo, savannas, lagoons, seasonally flooded forest. Our camp, a simple comfortable place for fishermen called Casa Blanca, meets the Mexican requirement of integrating human use with preserving the complex and delicate local ecosystem whose uniqueness derives not only from the phenomenon of a tropic sea inundating a vast limestone shelf, but from long human history. Every walk that Thomas and I took brought us past the earth mounds that covered Mayan structures. One superb small temple has been excavated and its inspired siting caused us, hunched under its low ceilings, gazing out on the blue sea, with bones and pottery at our feet, to fall silent for a good while.

Since I have been unsuccessful in bringing any formality to the job of parenting, I wondered about the matter of generations, and whether or not the concept added much to the sense of cherished companionship I had with my son. And I thought of the vast timescape implied by our immediate situation and the words of the leader of the French Huguenots when the terrible Menéndez led his band of followers into a hollow in the dunes to slaughter them. "In the eyes of God," said the Huguenot, "what difference is twenty years, more or less?"

We wandered through the barracks of an abandoned copra plantation. A carved canoe paddle leaned against a wall, the kind of ancient design used to propel dugouts but probably a backup for the Evinrude. Inside, the walls were decorated with really splendid graffiti, ankle-grabbing stick ladies subjected to rear entry and the prodigious members of grinning stick hooligans with rakish brimmed hats and cigarettes. And there you have it.

My anxiety about whether or not Thomas would be able to handle bonefish disappeared. He did just fine. He is not as obsessive about fishing as I am; so, it was always a matter of harassing him to organize his tackle, be at the skiff on time, and to keep fishing instead of crawling around the mangroves to see what was living in there. We began to catch plenty of bonefish in a variety of situations: schooling fish in deep water, generally small, easy fish; small bunches lined up along the edge of a flat waiting for the tide to come and help them over. The singles and small

ABOVE *Sunsets in the Yucatán are wonderfully colorful and offer an opportunity to reflect on the day's activities.*

RIGHT *Moonrise over a beachside bungalow. Anglers on the porch celebrate the day with a tall, cold one.*

bunches, tailing and feeding, on the inside flats. Several times I looked up and saw Thomas at a distance, his rod deeply bowed and his fly line shearing an arc toward deeper water.

We were happy workers on a big bonefish farm.

"Pedro, are there many permit, *unas palomettas?*"

"Yes, of course."

"Have you had many caught in your skiff?"

"No one catches many *palomettas.*"

"How many?"

"Maybe six this year."

295

Pedro stared in the direction he was poling, getting remarkable progress from the short hardwood crook he pushed us along with. Florida guides with their graphite eighteen-footers would refuse to leave the dock with an item like this one. He had a slightly superior look on his face, as though reading my thoughts. It was more likely that he felt the hopelessness of predictably catching a permit was his own secret. The look challenged you to try but declined to subdue skepticism.

After twenty-five years of pursuing permit, the intensity of the chase, the sense that the fish is an angler's Holy Grail, has never diminished. I feel, when searching for them, as a bird dog must when the unsearched country ahead turns into a binary universe of sign and absence of sign. Now I certainly couldn't expect my little son to feel the same way; here in the Sian Ka'an his attention was cast on all the wonders around us, the sea creatures scooting out in front of the skiff in response to Pedro's skillful poling, the spectacular flying squid that sailed across our bow, the cacophonous waterfowl that addressed our passage from the secrecy of the mangroves, the superb aerobatics of frigate birds trying to rob royal terns of their catch. Graciously, Thomas had offered me the first cast.

The little bay had a bottom too soft for wading. We were at a relatively low tide and the hermit crabs could be seen clinging to the exposed mangrove roots. A reddish egret made its way along the verge of thin water, head forward, legs back; then legs forward, head back until the sudden release, invisible in its speed, and the silver fish wriggles crossways in its bill.

Pedro said, "*Palometta*," and we looked back at him to see which way his phenomenal eyesight was directed. There was a school of permit coming onto the sandbar that edged the flat. Once noticed, the dark shape of the school seemed busy and its underwater presence was frequently enlarged by the piercing of the surface by the angular shapes of fins and tails. I checked to see if I was standing on my line. I tried to estimate again how much line I had stripped out. I held the crab fly by the hook between my left thumb and forefinger and checked the loop of line that would be my first false cast, now trailing alongside the boat. We were closing the distance fast and the permit were far clearer than they had been moments before. In fact, if they hadn't been so busy scouring around the bottom and competing with one another, they could have seen us right now.

The skiff ground to a halt in the sand. Pedro said that I was going to have to wade to these fish. Well, that was fine; but the only permit I have ever hooked

RIGHT *Over endless miles of poling and searching, the only sounds are the wind, and the occasional wave slapping on the hull of the boat. With talking kept to a minimum, sometimes the mind drifts, and it is then that the fish will usually come.*

wading spooled me while I stood and watched them go. Furthermore, I was using a Hardy freshwater reel, lots of backing but no drag. I picked it for the sporting enhancement it provided. This now seemed foolhardy.

I climbed out, eyes locked on the fish.

"Dad!" came Thomas' voice. "I've got to try for these fish too!"

"Thomas, God damn it, it's my shot!"

"Let me give it a try!"

"They're not going to take your bonefish fly anyway."

How could I concentrate? But now I was nearly in casting position. I heard something behind me. Thomas had bailed out of the boat. He was stripping line from his reel. He was defying his father! Our Mayan guide, Pedro, was celebrating his 3,000 years of family life on this bay by holding his sides and chuckling. For all I knew, he had suggested my son dive into the fray.

Once in casting range, I was able to make a decent presentation and the crab landed without disturbance in front of the school. They swam right over the top of it. They ignored it. Another cast, I moved the fly one good strip. They inspected it and refused. Another cast and a gingerly retrieve. One fish eased away from the school, tipped up on the fly and ate. I hooked him and he seared down the flat a short distance then shot back into the school. Now the whole school was running down the flat with my fish in the middle of it. Thomas waded to cut them off and began to false cast. I saw disaster staring at me as his loop turned over in front of the school and his fly dropped quietly.

RIGHT *A very happy angler with his first permit.*

298

"Got one!" he said amiably as his permit burned its way toward open water. Palming my whirling reel miserably, I realized why he had never been interested in a literary career. He wasn't sick enough to issue slim volumes from the interior dark. He was going to content himself with life itself. He seemed to enjoy the long runs his fish made; mine made me miserable.

Pedro netted Thomas' fish, his first permit, and waited with it, held underwater, until mine was landed. Thomas came over with the net. When the fish was close, I began to issue a stream of last-minute instructions about the correct landing of a permit. He just ignored them and scooped it up.

It was unbelievable, a doubleheader on fly-caught permit. I was stunned. We had to have a picture. I asked Pedro to look in my kit for the camera. Pedro admitted that he had only had this happen once before. He groped in my kit for the camera.

But I had forgotten the camera. Thomas saw my disappointment. He grabbed my shoulders. He was grinning at me. All my children grin at me as if I was crazy in a sort of amusing way. "Dad," he said, "it's a classic. Don't you get it?" He watched for it to sink in. "It's better without a picture." The permit swam away like they knew we weren't going to keep them anyway. Later, I stewed over his use of the word "classic." It was like when he buried a bonefish fly in the calf of my leg. He said that my expression was "timeless." I'd have to think about it.

LEFT *Early morning at Casa Blanca on Lighthouse Point. It's only a short walk from the cottage to the shore, so you can wander down with your morning coffee. Permit and coffee go together quite nicely – both set the blood racing!*

MEXICO – FACTFILE

ANCIENT SITES

STATE BOUNDARY

NATIONAL BOUNDARY

SIAN KA'AN BIOSPHERE RESERVE

BACKGROUND

The Caribbean coast of Mexico's Yucatán Peninsula may perhaps, for some, have unpleasant associations with the skyrise hotels of Cancún and Cozumel. However, over the last 10 years the Yucatán has become known as perhaps the world's most enjoyable of fly-tackle saltwater destinations. The diversity of the fishing and its healthy abundance has been nurtured by the United Nations which, in collaboration with the Mexican Government, created the Sian Ka'an biosphere. This biosphere has 1.3 million acres of tropical forest, savannah, mangrove swamps, flats, keys, springs, and a significant part of the second-largest barrier reef in the world. The biosphere's regulations restrict commercial angling and, combined with the catch and release policies of all the local lodges, ensure a fishing quality that should continue to improve for years to come.

WHEN TO GO

There is little doubt that the Yucatán Peninsula and its combined flats fisheries are more or less a year-round resource, but as is common with many other destinations, there are high and low points with regard to weather patterns. Most lodges close between July and October when hurricane risk is greatest. The most changeable weather in terms of rain and cloud is between November and January when the peninsula as a whole can be threatened by cold fronts moving down from the US. The peak fishing time is from February until July, when the sun warms the flats, ocean winds become seabreezes, and fish are on the flats in the highest concentrations. The numbers of large permit and tarpon are improved due to annual spawning migrations which make their way up the coast south to north during these months, making forays into the bays and flats along the coastline. Average temperatures are between 70°F (19°C) and 85°F (28°C), humidity levels can be high toward the end of summer, and light clothing is absolutely essential.

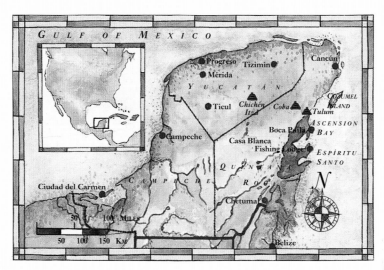

THE FISHING

Although the diversity of Mexico's Yucatán is well-known to all who've fished there, it is most often the numbers of bonefish and permit that have attracted anglers to its bay systems year after year. Resident fish abound on the flats, at times in great schools. In addition, tarpon and snook lurk under the shaded edges of mangrove lagoons. Mexico offers the best chance of the "Grand Slam" – a permit, a bonefish, and a tarpon all caught by one angler in a day. Whatever your preferred species may be, the geographical makeup of the lagoons and flats ensure an abundance of fly-fishing experiences.

If you decide to try for a permit, your guide will pole the endless flats, whether coral-bottomed or sandy, where the fish set up their feeding patrols.

Tarpon are usually found in the quieter, deeper, more sheltered mangrove lagoons, but occasionally giants on their migrational runs will be encountered in the shallow flats as they prospect into the bays. Nothing is guaranteed to make the heart beat faster in a fisherman than preparing himself and his tackle as the guide positions the skiff at an oncoming school of 100 lb tarpon.

It is the bonefish, though, that remains at the top of the quarry list of fish that are found on the flats. You may choose between being poled in a canoe or wading into the countless hard-bottomed flats, in search of individual bones or the huge schools of them that abound in these waters.

For anyone who has not experienced a bonefish searing off into the distance, after having stalked and successfully ambushed it on the flats, Mexico is a beginner's paradise. The large individual bonefish, which can weigh up to 10 lbs, provide excitement for the experienced angler, as do permit (notoriously fickle but powerful flats fish).

Although generally the tarpon here are not as large as those in Africa or the Florida Keys, they have been found weighing up to 150 lbs. Tarpon make up the last of the "big three" most commonly fished species in Mexico. Other species that can be caught on the fly include the aforementioned snook, barracuda (which are abundant, large, and under-rated), a multitude of snapper species, jacks, and small sharks.

TACKLE

RODS: Owing to the numbers of species likely to be encountered in a day, it is wise to have a cross-section of tackle, which will ensure that whatever fish you find, whether in a boat or wading, your rod is prepared and can be handed to you by your guide. Opportunities for a cast, especially at permit, may be fleeting, and an angler will not have time to change leaders and flies to suit a situation.

Nine feet is the ideal length to punch a line into the stiff breezes occasionally encountered, 10 to 12 wt for tarpon, 8 to 10 wt for permit, and 7 to 9 wt for bonefish. A useful fourth rod would be a 9 ft, 9 wt rod rigged with a wire tippet leader for barracuda and jacks.

REELS: Most fishermen opt for single-action reels with advanced adjustable drag systems that allow greater control of a runaway fish. All reels should hold the fly line plus a minimum of 150 yards of 30 lb braided Dacron backing.

LINES: Although there have been some experiments made with slow sinking lines and sinking-tips, nearly all fishermen use floating lines.

LEADERS: **Bonefish and permit** – 9 ft tapered leaders should be 8 to 15 lbs in strength, which will give you a little extra strength for bonefish in the more mangrove-filled flats. Don't think about using less than 12 lb for permit unless you've caught a few already or you're out to catch a specific IGFA line class record!
Tarpon and Snook – Buy or make tarpon leaders with a shock tippet of no less than 60 lbs and a class tippet strength of 16 lbs or more.
Barracuda – Use a 9 ft leader incorporating an 18 inch to 24 inch length of wire tippet with crimp system for easy changing of flies. The leader should be 15 lbs to 20 lbs strain with the wire tippet 25 to 40 lbs strength.

FLIES: Shrimps, small crustaceans, and baitfish make up the majority of food for all flats species. Practically all flats flies are imitations of these quarry species, though naturally there are favorites for different fish.
Tarpon – Sea-ducers, Cockroaches, Tarpon Bunnies, Whistlers, and Deceivers.
Permit – Rag-head Crab, McCrab, Isley Crab, Chernobyl Crab, Mother of Epoxy, and Clouser Minnow.
Bonefish – Crazy Charlie, Snapping Shrimp, Yucatán Special, Gotcha, Bonefish Bitters, and Gregs Flats Fly are all good examples, but there are also several other patterns.
Barracuda and Jacks – Poppers, Tarpon flies of all kinds, Needlefish patterns, and Oversize Clouser Minnows.

ESSENTIAL TRAVEL EQUIPMENT

Dress for Mexican flats fishing should consist of shorts and tee-shirts if you feel comfortable in the sun, with plenty of sunblock. In any situation, however, flats fishing exposes you to a lot of reflected sunlight, which can burn more than direct sunlight. There are several companies that manufacture long wading trousers and long-sleeved shirts made from quick-drying material. Bring a lightweight rain

jacket for passing showers. Total block sun cream for the face, neck, and hands is great, but check that it won't damage your fly line or leader as some of them do. Sun creams with a protection fact of 15 to 30 are good for legs and arms. A good hat that offers shade for your eyes, ears, and neck is vital and will assist in spotting fish. Good polarized glasses are invaluable. Pliers, Hemostats, or long-nose pliers, for unhooking toothy predators like barracuda, are vital. A small knife, or clippers, is useful in cutting some of the thicker nylon used, especially shock tippets. A small pair of binoculars for looking at the many species of bird and mammal life that inhabit the flats and mangrove lagoons are a good idea if you can tear yourself away from the fishing. If you can't, then a camera for the one that didn't get away is a must, though make sure you have a sealable waterproof bag in which to house it.

FLIES: LEFT-HAND THREE *Merkin Crabs.*
MIDDLE THREE, TOP TO BOTTOM *A Nick's Casablanca Special; a Chernobyl Crab; and an Olive Rag-head Crab.*
RIGHT-HAND TWO, TOP TO BOTTOM *A White Rag-head Crab and a Rug Yarn Crab.*

ABOVE *The permit is one of the most difficult fish to fool with the fly. Catching one is considered to be a milestone in one's fishing career, and the Yucatán Peninsula is probably the best place to try for them. Their sickle-shaped fins and their big black eyes make them a very sensuous-looking fish.*

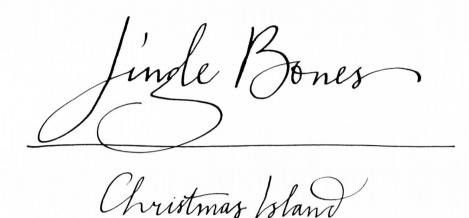

Jingle Bones
Christmas Island

PETER KAMINSKY

"We started to see the fish in the afternoon. The morning had been hard. We were into the wind on a falling tide. Then we shifted across the lagoons and hit it right. Five fish on five casts.

A cloud darkened the water. We lost sight of the fish. When the sun came out again I watched it light up the flat like a baby's smile. I counted six different colors to the water: white by the shore, then shadowy gray, then copper (from the coral), then light blue followed by green and ending in deep-water blue."

LEFT *A typical view of the one-lane road bordered by palm trees and ocean views. You rarely see any traffic other than trucks driven by fishing guides.*

RIGHT *Purple sea urchins, pushed together by the tides and dried by the sun, lie clustered together by the thousands on some Christmas Island beaches.*

Ship's Master William Bligh – later of the *Bounty* – spent Christmas Eve 1777 on board *HMS Resolution*, which rode at anchor at the mouth of a lagoon two degrees north of the equator and 160 degrees west of Greenwich, England. In honor of the day, his commanding officer, Captain James Cook, named the surrounding coral atoll Christmas Island.

Then, as now, the winter surf piled thirty-foot breakers against the protecting necklace of Cockrane's reef so that the low-lying island (average elevation: five feet) rarely felt the fury of waves that had traveled, unobstructed, across 5,000 miles of open ocean. Cook's journal of the visit betrays few of the rhapsodies that he lavished on Tahiti or the Sandwich Isles, but this is not surprising. Apart from some coconut palms and a scattering of salt bushes, the coral tableland of Christmas Island supports neither fruits nor vegetables, nor any of the game that lives on green things. Cook documented, "Should anyone be so unfortunate as to be accidentally driven upon the island or left there, it is hard to say that he could be able to prolong existence."

On January 1, Cook and Bligh observed the eclipse from their vantage point at the head of the lagoon. Twenty-four hours later the *Resolution* weighed anchor and made for Hawaii.

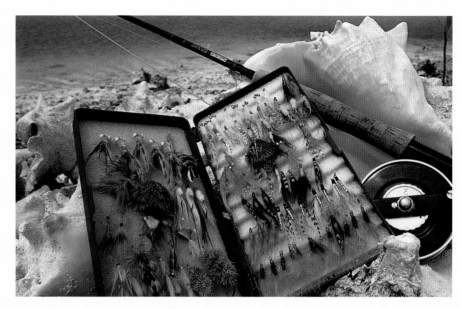

RIGHT *A fly box, with bonefish and permit flies, positioned among the conch shells, brings back fond memories of the trip.*

ABOVE (FAR LEFT TO RIGHT) *A Yellow Crazy Charlie; a Gray Greg's Flats Fly; a Pink Crazy Charlie; an Orange Snapping Shrimp; a Tan Greg's Flats Fly; a Brown Snapping Shrimp, a Gotcha; a Fuzzy Shrimp; a Spawning Shrimp; a Bonefish Special; a Brown Crazy Charlie; an Eric's Standing Shrimp; a Pink Flash; and a Cave's Shrimp Wobbler.*

I am dead sure that neither Cook nor Bligh was a bonefisherman.

Christmas Island, you see, is blessed with some of the finest, if not *the* finest, bonefishing in the world, which is how and why the following conversation took place in a rusting pickup exactly 207 years, 11 months, and 26 days after Captain Cook's arrival.

"I read that this is the only place in the whole Pacific where you can fish the flats for bonefish, Moana. Why is that?"

"You are wrong," Moana countered. "They have bonefish on Banaba, on Saipan, on many of the atolls. But there are no hotels and too many people who also fish for food. Here we don't eat the bonefish so much."

Moana is the premier fly-rod guide on Christmas Island even though, at the time of writing [1985], he has only been fly-fishing for a little over a year. His full name is Moanafua Tamaika Kofe, which is Gilbertese for "Only-Ocean-Small-Fish-Fishing Pole." Back on his native Tarawa, his father's people have always been fishermen; it is in their blood. His mother's family were warriors; hence his maternal uncle, "He-Who-Carries-His-Enemy's-Head-in-a-Basket."

RIGHT *A view of the sand flats extending as far as the eye can see. Every minute somthing new and unusual happens. The bonefish here are big, hungry, and strong, and will strip out all your backing. Strange fish scurry off the flats in front of you, and the birds are so tame that you can cradle them in your hands.*

On Day One with Moana I caught a fish. On Day Two, both my wife, Melinda, and I caught fish. On Day Three, came the big victory . . . we saw fish! Spotting bonefish is like wingshooting or hitting a baseball; it takes a day or two to get your eye back.

We started to see the fish in the afternoon. The morning had been hard. We were into the wind on a falling tide. Then we shifted across the lagoons and hit it right. Five fish on five casts.

A cloud darkened the water. We lost sight of the fish. When the sun came out again I watched it light up the flat like a baby's smile. I counted six different colors to the water: white by the shore, then shadowy gray, then copper (from the coral), then light blue followed by green and ending in deep-water blue.

Moana pointed to a big one. I tried, but three casts sent him back out to blue water. I moved on. Five minutes later Moana had the fish on. Five minutes after that he had him in, neat, clean, and quick. Twelve pounds.

"We catch bigger ones on the full moon. They return from spawning every month, and, best I can tell, nobody really knows their habits that well, but Moana operates under that assumption and he catches big bonefish.

"Fish across that flat," he said. "Take your time. Cross the islet and fish the lee. They are big."

The Trade Winds whipped the water and our ten-foot casts caught fish. We crossed the small island. Melinda connected with a school of four-pounders. I saw a larger shadow lurking on the edge of the shallows. I cast. He turned. I stripped. He followed. I paused. He lowered his head. I lifted my rod. It bent.

I palmed the reel and the fish slowed his run. When he stopped I pulled back on the rod just above the trademark. I felt him shake his head. He ran toward me and I recovered all my backing. He knifed left. I lowered my rod, Melinda raised hers, and we exchanged positions (she was still fighting one of the schoolies). Mine was nine pounds and change, the biggest bone I had ever caught. He took a while to revive. Finally, he shook his tail and his silver shape became a green shadow that melted off the reef.

Life was great. Moana was happy. I was happy. Melinda was happy, and the car wouldn't start. This is not a good thing anywhere, but especially on Christmas Island, where it is surprisingly easy to get lost and less easy to get found.

Moana covered the air intake. I hit the pedal. Melinda encouraged us. Moana covered the air intake again. I cranked again, and Melinda encouraged some more, *ad infinitum*, till we got it right. *Pachugga, pachugga.* Our semi-trusty car started.

We crossed Poland Channel, passing two bunkers where the British and Americans had observed their H-Bomb tests in the 1950's and '60's. The car didn't die for good until we were two miles from the hamlet of Banana. To my knowledge there are not, and never have been, any banana plants on the island, but it was named Banana by US soldiers in World War II and the name stuck.

We walked through town. All the houses were stamped out of the same cookie cutter: wooden slats, tin roofs, a catch basin for fresh water: all in all, no more exotic than a row of sharecropper's shacks. In the middle of the road, a young man lay on his back, playing his harmonica. A woman, bathing outdoors, picked up the harmony, her nudity taken as a matter of course by the neighbors.

A 300-pound man wearing the traditional lava-lava skirt *putt-putted* along on his long-suffering motor scooter. As he passed us, the reverse angle revealed his young son sitting behind him, looking no bigger than a postage stamp against his father's enormous back. There are very big men on the island – fearsome-looking with their long hair and gappy teeth, but very friendly, like the truck driver who, along with a buddy, invited us into the cab of his enormous rig.

"Where?" the driver asked.

"The hotel," I said.

"No. Where?" he said.

"What where?" I asked.

"You from where?" he said.

"New York," I said.

"Yes?" he said.

"Yes," I said.

"Me Tarawa," he said.

"Tarawa, yes," I said.

I tried to broaden the dialogue and remarked on the pretty sunset. The driver looked at me uncomprehendingly. My wife pointed to the sun and then made circular motions with her hands and said, "Good."

"Yes," he said.

When we slowed at the hotel, the buddy spoke his first words, "Hotel, yes?"

"Yes," I said.

"Thank you," Melinda said.

"Yes," he said, and waved goodbye.

LEFT *The "ole red Punt:" slow-moving but usually dependable. These are the local boats built to carry fly-fishermen to the outer flats on the island.*

ABOVE *It's hard to believe that the crystal-clear water on the flats could conceal anything, but the bonefish blend in so well that all you can make out, as they ghost across the sea-bed, are their shadows.*

Inside the hotel, the locals watched *The Spy Who Loved Me* on the video recorder, a ritual they repeated with fresh delight each night of our stay. And so civilization came to Christmas Island, and we went to sleep.

I haven't told you about the trevally yet, have I? A trevally is a large jack, not unlike the fish that we call a jack crevalle. However, the Gilbertese have no "c" in their alphabet so "trevally" is as close as they get to crevalle (or, as Captain Cook referred to it, "cavally").

If you want to catch a world record fish on a fly, I think two weeks of serious trevally hunting on Christmas Island may reward your quest. These predators often travel in pairs and they will swoop into the flats with breathtaking speed and disappear just as quickly. Be prepared with a nine- or ten-weight outfit, a gaudy streamer, and sixty-pound shock tippet. Once you spot them, you run along the shore as fast as you can, trying to get ahead of them. Lead them with your cast. Strip fast. Rip the water with your line. Make a commotion. They will charge your fly. When they do, let them take before you strike.

I am quite sure I had a shot at a record fish every day, and every one gave me buck fever. I did manage to hook one biggie, but I take no credit for it. I had a small bonefish on. Two trevally came over the reef straight for my fish. They were going

so fast that they overshot on the first pass. One of them swirled, took my bonefish, and headed for open water. The tug felt great. So did the bend in the rod, the zing of the reel, the length of the run. I palmed down on the drag and broke off before he spooled me.

I recall the return drive to camp, feeling about as whipped as a person can be – sun-baked, thirst-crazed, and dog-tired – thinking only of a cocktail, maybe a handful of peanuts, and 36 straight hours of sleep. No sooner had Moana screamed "*Trevally*!!" than I sprang out of the truck like an Israeli commando.

Trevally will sometimes pen up the baitfish and then stun them or cut them in half with a savage flick of their tail. It is a crisp sound: furious and exciting. Twice we cast to such fish: the first time I had to drill my loop through a swarm of man-of-war birds who mistook my lure for a fish. Actually I didn't feel that we were casting to fish. Shadows would be a better word, and everyone knows that you can't catch a shadow.

When the trevally departed, they left a mud swirl ten feet across. We held our breaths and looked for them to come in again. Moana walked into the water and began splashing, a tactic that can attract trevally, which take the splashing for a fish in distress. It made good scientific sense, but seeing him there at sunset, kicking and

311

ABOVE *The thatched-roof bungalows of the Captain Cook Hotel silhouetted against the morning sunrise. Ventilated for the constant trade winds, the rooms make sleeping easy and deep in the warm salt air, dreaming to the sound of the surf.*

watching and waiting. I thought for a minute that this was how his ancestors did it, some Micronesian sea magic that put a spell on the water and called the giant trevally to their deaths.

That was Christmas Eve. We made a pact to forego the festivities on Christmas Day. The fishing would be our Christmas. This did not go down well with our hotel mates, who were hoping to form a contingent to attend the singing contest down in the village of London.

"Fishing on Christmas? Are you out of your mind?"

"Where's your Christmas spirit? For God's sake, man!"

"Do you have any idea what kind of a once-in-a-lifetime event you'll miss?"

"Boy! What total jerks!"

Alas, there was nothing I could say. They were right.

Nonetheless, I wanted to fish. Truth to tell, I would rather fish than do anything. No doubt there are some of you out there who feel as I do, so you understand. As it turned out, we all got very drunk that night, which seemed to be the main activity up and down the length of the atoll. When we didn't roll out of bed until ten we decided, "What the heck? Let's go see Christmas on Christmas."

The entire population had camped out in London, the island's largest town. As befits its metropolitan status, it has a jail, a boatyard, a fire engine, a place where you can buy warm beer, and two tin-roofed open-air public meeting houses (each about the size of a basketball court). The dwellings are of the same minimalist design that we had observed in Banana.

Inside the Anglican Church (ladies on one side, men on the other, and please remove your shoes), the priest wore a white lava-lava, a white shirt, and a black tie. The ladies' bright dresses were of a cloth so sheer that you were surely meant to see that every woman on the island wore a brassière. Was this some extra show of propriety to prove that they had forsaken the pagan toplessness of yesteryear?

ABOVE *The local Kiribati people are friendly, and eager to share their culture with visitors. They love dancing and singing.*

We were invited to lunch following the service. We passed among the families camped within the perimeter of the meeting house. Their supplies of fish, meat, and coconut products filled the cupboards that are left there for the convenience of guests. Fathers slept. Babies cried. Teenagers flirted. A rectangle of pillars formed the inner support of the house, and a village elder sat against each pillar. As guests, and according to ancient custom, we were treated like elders.

Like modern vacationers, island people are used to traveling long distances. They think of the entire Pacific the way you think of your county. Still, they don't underestimate the rigors of travel. After all, they used to do it in canoes.

The village teenagers served us a great feast of pork, fish, curried octopus, and pandanus leaf chutney. The elders rolled cigarettes, using the paraphernalia they carried in their handbags. One after another they rose to deliver a benediction that touched on the miracle of Christmas and the importance of our arrival, treating each with equal weight.

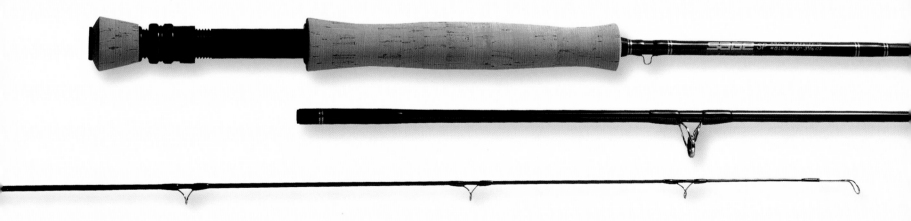

Then the singing began, the yearly contest between the villages of Banana, London, and Poland. Each village had its own uniform: intensely colored lava-lavas, beautiful bright shirts, and flower leis, wristlets, and hair ornaments. They sang Church of England hymns in Gilbertese. The four-part island harmony reverberated off the tin roof of the long house. I found myself on the brink of tears, neither of sadness nor of joy. I was just overwhelmed by the day, the place, the song, and the people.

Still, there were fish out there to be caught. I asked Moana how we could leave without looking ingrates. He told me to give the head elder a donation for the church. I did so in the understated (or is it embarrassed?) way that we "civilized" folk deal with money. Melinda and I rose to leave. The head elder rose with us. He began to speak in a loud voice as he waved our ten dollar bill. I was caught off guard. With great sweeping gestures and trumpeting declamation, he informed the multitude and rejoiced that we had journeyed 10,000 miles so that we might make

RIGHT *The Crazy Charlie is the most popular bonefish fly and is tied in many colors and sizes. No fly box would be complete without a wide selection.*

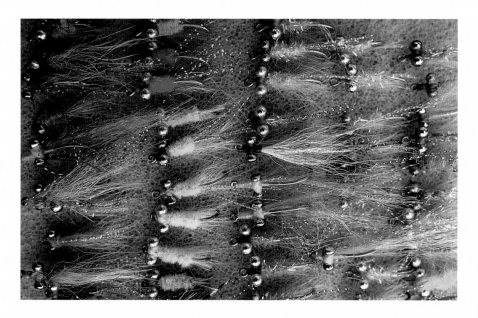

this donation to the well-being of their Church and that this was indeed one of History's Great Events. We blushed at the translation. When the old man finished, he waved the bill again, and in unison every man, woman, and child clapped their hands three times and shouted good wishes to us.

I know an exit line when I hear one.

Melinda and I blew them all a kiss and told them we would never forget them (which we won't). Moana put the pedal down and we rushed to catch the tide on Nine Mile Flat.

"There are five kinds of swimming bonefish," Moana said, apropos of nothing except wanting to make sure that he had told me all he could tell. I took it as his Christmas present.

"One type of swimming bonefish, he spooks at your cast but he doesn't run. Cast again and strip. He will follow. Another kind of swimming bonefish, he just swims along the coast for a mile. You follow him because he will stop. When he stops, he tails and when he tails, you catch him. The third kind is suspended in the current of the tide. He is easy. Cast four feet ahead of him and strip fast. He will strike from the side. The fourth kind he swims in a circle of five-feet diameter. This bonefish doesn't spook but you must use lighter tippet."

"And the fifth kind, Moana?"

"Tailing bonefish," he said. "They are the best of all."

The white flat stretched to the horizon. No action yet, so we walked. The water crept over our ankles. We began to see life. Little morays, small sharks, puffer fish.

CENTER *Anglers arrive by punt and prepare to fish the edge of a flat where it drops off into deeper water. That's where the big bones feed.*

LEFT *An outside flat by the reef is a good place to spot trevally (another gamefish which grows quite large), as they swoop along the edges of the flats, on the brink of the open ocean.*

They inched up the flat, following the water. The bones came last. First the small ones, then the big ones, unhurriedly, inexorably. The late afternoon sun caught their tails and fins – nine miles of tailing bonefish.

It isn't how many fish we caught; it was how we caught them that mattered. You pick one you want. You tiptoe into position. Take a half hour if you need it, but do it right. Work him like a rising trout. Cast as many times as necessary. Don't scare him. Strip when his fin disappears. Watch for the take.

Merry Christmas!

CHRISTMAS ISLAND – FACTFILE

BACKGROUND

This tropical destination in the middle of the Pacific ocean, some 1,300 miles south of Hawaii, is part of the Line Island group, in the Republic of Kiribati. Christmas Island has the largest land area of any coral atoll in the world (140 square miles) and is only 119 miles north of the equator. With its large colonies of seabirds, vast reefs, endless flats, lagoons, and surrounding ocean, it offers excellent opportunities to observe bird and marine life, as well as to enjoy outstanding fishing.

The island was discovered by Captain James T. Cook on Christmas Eve in 1777, hence the name. It remained part of Great Britain until 1979, when Kiribati regained its independence. Nowadays, there is a strong Australian influence throughout Christmas Island.

WHEN TO GO

The island enjoys equatorial calm, lying well east of Pacific storm development areas. Because of its proximity to the equator, it does not have seasons as such. The temperatures in January are virtually identical to those in July.

Easterly trade winds blow throughout the year at an average of 10 to 20 knots, and provide a cool breeze across the flat surfaces of the atoll. Out on the flats each day it is rarely humid or unpleasantly hot. The average daytime temperature is around 80°F (28°C), and the evenings cool down to a breezy 72°F (20°C).

Annual rainfall averages 30 inches and is normally in the form of afternoon or evening showers. It is best to be prepared with a light rain jacket in case you get caught in a downpour. There seems to be a 5-year drought cycle, which may be worth investigating.

Cloud cover is relatively sparse throughout the year compared with other tropical areas, and, in general, conditions are ideal for flats fishing. From June to September, the winds tend to be calmer and the sea less rough. Christmas Island certainly seems

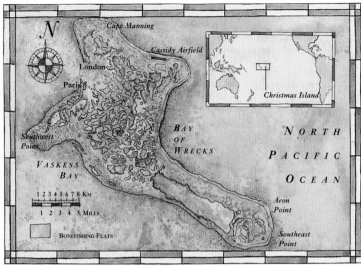

to have the most consistent and predictable sunny weather patterns of any bonefishing destination in the world.

THE FISHING

The island, with its long fishing season and sympathetic climate, is perhaps the single most popular year-round destination for bonefishing, boasting vast numbers of fish – some of them very big – on easily waded, clean, hard, white sand flats. Experienced flats anglers will sometimes average between 15 and 20 bones a day, with a 30-plus fish day possible at any time. While most of these fish may average about 3 to 4 lbs, several could be in the 6 to 9 lbs bracket. Trophy bones are always possible. There have been numerous reports of weighed and measured 10 to 13 lb fish, and even larger fish have been spotted, hooked, and lost – as, of course, is always the case.

Adding to the excitement daily are 3 different kinds of trevally (a type of jack) – giant (up to approximately 100 lbs), blue (up to 15 lbs), and striped (up to 20 lbs or more) – which are taken with fly, although, owing to their fierce fighting ability, they can also be caught on baitcasting or spinning tackle on the flats while you are out bonefishing, as well as along the lagoon edges and in the surf. Trevally are awesomely strong fish that strike savagely at or near the surface.

Virtually all of the bonefishing is by wading. Ninety per cent of the flats are white or yellowish sand, coral marl, or, in a few cases, coral shelves, which can be brownish in color. There is little or no "turtle" grass on any of the flats. Take some care, as there are some soft areas that generally should be avoided: be careful not to wade on the lightest (or whitest) areas, which sometimes have a puffy extruded appearance, or places where there are undulating depressions with burrow holes in the bottom, which will have been made by giant snapping shrimp.

Fishermen are transported to the flats either in light trucks or in lagoon "punts" – large flat-bottomed boats, which are also used for trevally fishing in the protected waters of the lagoon. Guides switch off the engines as they approach the fish, and will gently pole you into the perfect fishing position.

TACKLE

RODS: 9 to 9½ ft graphite rods in 7, 8, or 9 wt are ideal. Beginners and novices may be better off with an 8 wt: the extra backbone will facilitate casting, especially in windy conditions. It is advisable to take more than one rod in case of breakages.

REELS: Those with reliable, smooth, adjustable drags seem to work best. Few fish will stress a reel like a bonefish, so bring sturdy, high-quality models specifically designed for saltwater use. Reels must hold your line and at least 150 yards of 20 to 30 lb Dacron backing.

Although most Christmas Island anglers feel comfortable with direct-drive reels, some fishermen, especially novices, may prefer anti-reverse models. The handles on anti-reverse reels remain stationary when running bonefish pull line off the reel, as opposed to the handles on direct-drive reels, which spin rapidly when fish run – often resulting in bruised knuckles, and even lost fish. Take a spare reel and/or extra spools with you each day so that you can regroup on the flat if you lose a fly line.

LEADERS: Use 9 to 12 ft leaders in the 10 to 15 lb range, and don't forget extra spools of 8, 10, 12, and 15 lb clear tippet material. When fishing, check your leader frequently for wind knots and coral abrasion, and change tippets as often as necessary. The best results have been with stiff, abrasion-resistant leader and tippet material.

FLIES: There are several factors that dictate proper fly selection on Christmas Island. When choosing the color of the fly, it is best to try to match the bottom coloration as closely as possible. If you are fishing on a very light-colored flat, cream or white patterns work best. If the bottom is tan or off-color, then patterns in various shades of brown should be the most productive. The general guideline is to switch colors if you find that you are getting multiple refusals.

In most cases, Christmas Island bones tend to prefer patterns in size 4. If you are fishing in shallow water or where the fish are tailing, try smaller sizes as they can be presented more subtly. The Crazy Charlie is the most commonly used fly on Christmas Island. The guides can tie very acceptable flies and appreciate fishermen buying flies from them. They, of course, know which colors and patterns you are most likely to find successful.

Christmas Island custom encourages fishermen to pinch down the barbs on the hooks of their flies with pliers, as this makes it much easier to release the fish unharmed. Many people feel that the barbless fishing hook actually works better in penetrating the tough tissue of a bonefish's mouth, and, generally, you may catch more fish.

ESSENTIAL TRAVEL EQUIPMENT

Precautions against the sun should be a priority. It is a good idea to have long-sleeved shirts and long pants to tuck into your wading shoes or your socks. To be safe it is advisable to carry high-protection sun cream, which should be applied to all exposed skin, and reapplied every hour while you are outside. Even if you wear a wide-brimmed hat, the sun reflecting off the water will burn your lips and face unless you conscientiously apply sunblock.

As you will spend a lot of time on your feet, it is important to have comfortable wading shoes. Some

ABOVE Albula vulpes, *or the bonefish as he is more commonly known, is an amazing creature. First you need to see him as he ghosts along the flats. Then you need to catch him – he's as fast as the wind. Few other fish fight as hard, pound for pound. When you hold him, he is as bright as polished silver in the sun.*

people choose ankle-height canvas tennis shoes, one size larger than normal; others use conventional stream wading shoes. Flats booties, available at all large fishing stores, are especially designed for wading the flats.

Take a lightweight cotton fishing vest or shirt with plenty of pocket space. Polarized sunglasses with UV protection are essential. Clippers for cutting monofilament and a waterproof boat bag are also useful items.

FLIES: BOTTOM SIX, CLOCKWISE FROM CENTER *A Cave's Shrimp Wobbler; a Fuzzy Shrimp; a Yellow Crazy Charlie; a Gotcha; a Brown Snapping Shrimp.*
TOP FIVE, CLOCKWISE FROM TOP *A Pink Crazy Charlie; an Eric's Standing Shrimp; a Tan Greg's Flats Fly; an Orange Snapping Shrimp; and a Gray Greg's Flats Fly.*
RIGHT-HAND THREE, CLOCKWISE FROM FAR RIGHT *A Bonefish Special; a Brown Crazy Charlie; and a Pink Flash.*

About the Contributors

Russell Chatham *(Sterling Silver – Florida Keys)* is a world-renowned painter. He has published essays and articles in several books and many major magazines. His own books include *The Angler's Coast*. He lives in Montana.

Brian Clarke *(Casting off the Edge of the World – Argentina)* has an international reputation as an angling writer and innovator. He is fishing correspondent for *The Times* newspaper and author of *The Trout and the Fly*, *The Pursuit of Stillwater Trout* and *The Stream*, among other books.

Bill Currie *(Prolific Eastern Margins – Russia)* is a Scottish fisher for salmon, trout and sea trout, who has also travelled to Northern Europe, Iceland and Canada in pursuit of these fish. He has written more than a dozen books on salmon and trout fishing, including *The River Within* and *Scotland for Fishing*.

Clive Gammon *(I Know a Good Place – Alaska)* has worked for *Sports Illustrated* in the USA, during which time he went fishing from the Falklands to the North Pole (well, 200 miles short of it). Now, though, he rarely gets further than the Russian Far East. He lives in Wales.

John Gierach *(Headwaters – USA & Dances with Trout – Alaska)* is a self-described trout fanatic. He writes regularly for outdoor magazines, and has published numerous books, notably *Trout Bum* and *Sex, Death, and Fly-fishing*. He lives in Colorado on the St Vrain River.

Zane Grey *(The Dreadnaught Pool – New Zealand)* was born in 1871 and began his writing career in 1904. He is remembered today as a legendary writer of both fishing adventure books and Westerns. With more than sixty titles to his name, he died in California in 1939.

Roderick Haig-Brown *(The Start of the South – Chile)* was born in 1908 in Sussex but spent most of his life on the banks of the Campbell River in Vancouver. As well as the author of twelve books on fishing, he was a judge in the Provincial Court of British Columbia and Chancellor of the University of Victoria. He died in 1976.

J.W. Hills *(His Biggest Trout – England)* was born in 1867 and was brought up in Cumberland. An MP and Financial Secretary to the Treasury, he was never happier than when on the banks of his beloved river Test. He was a member of the Houghton Club and published some of the best-known works on chalkstream fishing. He died in 1938.

Peter Kaminsky *(Jingle Bones – Christmas Island)* writes the "Outdoors Column" for the *New York Times*, and his "Underground Gourmet" is a regular feature in *New York Magazine*. He is the author of *Fishing for Dummies*, published by IDG Press in New York.

Verlyn Klinkenborg *(Trout Among the Shadows – New Zealand)* has published numerous articles on fly-fishing for magazines such as *Esquire*. His novels include *The Last Fine Time*. He lives on a small farm in upstate New York.

Art Lee *(My Platform of Despair – Iceland)* writes articles for major outdoor magazines in the USA. He has published several books and is considered a leading authority on salmon and trout fishing. He lives in the Catskill Mountains of New York state.

Nick Lyons *(Mornings – The Rocky Mountains & Grimsa Journal – Iceland)* is a former professor of English at Hunter College, New York. He is a prolific author. Among his best-known books are *Bright Rivers* and *Confessions of a Fly-Fishing Addict*.

Tom McGuane *(On Wesley's River – Canada & Sons – Mexico)* is the author of several highly acclaimed novels, including *Keep the Change* and *Nothing but Blue Skies*. He has also written the screenplays to several feature films based on his own works. He lives in Montana.

Neil Patterson *(The Chalkstream Idyll – England)* writes regularly for fly-fishing magazines in the UK. His book *The Chalkstream Chronicle* has been acclaimed as a modern classic by critics on both sides of the Atlantic. He lives beside an English chalkstream.

David Profumo *(Never on Sundays – Scotland & Fly-fishing in the Middle Ages – Russia)* is an award-winning novelist whose books include *Sea Music* and *The Weather in Iceland*. He is also co-editor (with Graham Swift) of *The Magic Wheel*, a classic anthology of fishing in literature. He lives in London and Perthshire.

Ernest Schwiebert *(Raspberries in the Rain – Norway & La Fiebre de Las Bocas – Argentina)* is regarded as one of the world's most distinguished fisherman-writers. He is a prolific author.

David Street *(Mighty Mask – Ireland)* was born in 1924 and educated at St Edmund Hall, Oxford. He resigned from a Lieutenant's commission in the Royal Marines and was ordained in 1955. He wrote for a host of publications until his death in 1998.

Leonard M. Wright, Jr. *(The Miramichi River – Canada)* has published numerous articles and books on fly-fishing, including *Trout Maverick* and *Fishing the Dry Fly as a Living Insect*.

About the Photographer

R. Valentine Atkinson is an internationally acclaimed and much-published photographer specializing in fly-fishing lifestyle and nature worldwide. His assignments have taken him to twenty-seven different countries. He divides his work between advertising, corporate and editorial and is published regularly in most major fishing magazines. He runs his own stock library with 75,000 images on file and in 2003 he received the honour of being inducted into the Federation of Fly Fishers' Fishing Hall of Fame. Please visit him on his web site at: **www.valatkinson.com**

Acknowledgments

The publishers would like to thank the following authors, copyright holders and publishing houses/magazines for their kind permission to reproduce pieces in this book.

"Headwaters" by John Gierach (pp.8–19), previously published in *Trout Bum* (Pruett Publishing, 1986).
Copyright © John Gierach, 1986.
Reprinted by permission of Pruett Publishing Company, Boulder, Colorado.

"Mornings" by Nick Lyons (pp.22–35), previously published in *Spring Creek* (Atlantic Monthly Press, New York, 1992).
Text copyright © Nick Lyons, 1992.

"The Miramichi River" by Leonard M. Wright, Jr (pp.38–49).
Text copyright © Leonard M. Wright, Jr.

"On Wesley's River" by Thomas McGuane (pp.50–59), an extract from his book *Live Water* (Meadow Run Press, New Jersey, 1996).
Text copyright © Thomas McGuane, 1996.

"Dances With Trout" by John Gierach (pp.62–75), an extract previously published in *Dances With Trout* (Simon and Schuster, New York, 1994).
Text copyright © John Gierach, 1994.

"I Know a Good Place" by Clive Gammon (pp.76–89), an extract from his book *Welcome to the Chocolate Factory* (Swan Hill Press, Shrewsbury, 1990).
Copyright © Clive Gammon, 1990.

"My Platform of Despair" by Art Lee (pp.92–105), previously published in *Wild Steelhead and Salmon*.
Text copyright © Art Lee, 1997.

"Grimsa Journal" by Nick Lyons (pp.106–119), which first appeared in *Flyfisherman* (1975).
Text copyright © Nick Lyons.

"Never on Sundays" by David Profumo (pp.122–133).
Text copyright © David Profumo, 1998.

"Mighty Mask" by David Street (pp.136–145), an extract from his book *Fishing in Wild Places* (Penguin Books, London, 1989).
Copyright © Penguin Books Ltd, and by permission of Mrs Margaret Street.

"His Biggest Trout" by J.W. Hills (pp.148–155), an extract from his book *A Summer on the Test* (André Deutsch, London, 1984).
Text copyright © André Deutsch Ltd, and Mrs S.M. May.

"The Chalkstream Idyll" by Neil Patterson (156–169), previously published in *The Chalkstream Chronicle: Living out the Flyfisher's Fantasy* (Merlin Unwin Books, London, 1995; Lyons and Burford, New York, 1995).
Text copyright © Neil Patterson, 1995.

"Raspberries in the Rain" by Ernest Schwiebert (pp.172–179), adapted from his book *Remembrances of Rivers Past* (The Macmillan Company, New York, 1972; Collier-Macmillan Ltd, London, 1972).
Text copyright © Ernest Schwiebert, 1972 and 1998.

"Fly-fishing in the Middle Ages" by David Profumo (pp.182–193).
Text copyright © David Profumo, 1997.

"Prolific Eastern Margins" by Bill Currie (pp.194–205).
Text copyright © Dr William Currie, 1998.

"The Dreadnaught Pool" by Zane Grey (pp.208–221), an extract from his book *Tales of the Angler's Eldorado*.
Copyright © Dr Loren Grey.

"Trout Among the Shadows" by Verlyn Klinkenborg (pp.222–231), previously published as "Trout Among the Kiwis" in *Esquire* (October 1988).
Text copyright © Verlyn Klinkenborg, 1988.

continues

"The Start of the South" by Roderick Haig-Brown (pp.234–245), an excerpt from his book *Fisherman's Winter* (Douglas & McIntyre, Vancouver, 1954).
Copyright © Roderick Haig-Brown, 1959.
Reproduced with permission of Douglas & McIntyre, Harold Ober Associates Inc. and Nick Lyons.

"La Fiebre de las Bocas" by Ernest Schwiebert (pp.248–263), previously published in *Remembrances of Rivers Past* (The Macmillan Company, New York, 1972; Collier-Macmillan Limited, London, 1972).
Text copyright © Ernest Schwiebert, 1972.

"Casting Off the Edge of the World" by Brian Clarke (pp.264–269), an extract from his book *Trout Etcetera* (A&C Black Ltd, London, 1996).
Text copyright © Brian Clarke, 1996.

"Sterling Silver" by Russell Chatham (pp.272–283), previously published in *Silent Seasons: 21 Fishing Adventures by 7 American Experts* (E. P. Dutton, New York, 1978).
Text copyright © Russell Chatham, 1978.

"Sons" by Tom McGuane (pp.286–299), previously published in *Live Water* (Meadow Run Press, New Jersey, 1996).
Text copyright © Thomas McGuane, 1996.

"Jingle Bones" by Peter Kaminsky (pp.302–315), previously published in *Field & Stream* (December 1985).
Text copyright © Peter Kaminsky, 1985.

ILLUSTRATION CREDITS
Fish illustrations on part and chapter openers are by James Prosek: those on pp.9, 51, 107, 123, 137, 149, 173, 195, 209, 235 and 265 are copyright © James Prosek, 1996, and are from his book *Trout: An Illustrated History* (Alfred A. Knopf, Inc., New York); the one on p.77 is copyright © James Prosek, 1998, and is from *Trout and Salmon* (Duncan Baird Publishers, London).

PHOTOGRAPHER'S THANKS
The photographer would like to thank the following friends for their continued support: Alex Mitchell, Nick Zoll, Duncan Baird, the design and editorial teams at Duncan Baird Publishers, Frontiers International Travel, Susan Rockrise, Louise Grimsley, Nick Lyons, and all my friends who have been models along the way – thank you, you're a part of all this. Here's to truth, adventure, and passion in fly-fishing, travel, and life!

FURTHER THANKS
In addition, the publishers and photographer owe thanks to the following organizations and individuals for their invaluable assistance in the completion of this book:

Lord Stratford and the Piscatorial Society; Dru Montagu; the Laverstoke estate; Janice Mitchell; Brian Fratel, Nick Armstead and Robin Elwes at Farlow's of Pall Mall; Robert Rattray at Finlayson Hughes; Henry Mountain and Tarquin Millington-Drake at Frontiers; William Daniel at Famous Fishing; Anthony Edwards; Commander Bruce Trentham; Les Kirby; Bo Ivanovic; Barry Oldham; George Ross and all at the Oykel Bridge Hotel; Captain J.R. Wilson; Duncan Watt; the Balmoral Estate Office; Peter Voy and Fraser Campbell of Assynt Estates; Peter Fowler and John Gordon of Glencalvie Estate; Stuart and Fiona Mcteare; Dennis O'Keefe; and Brian Joyce.